IT'S NOT ABOUT THE POM-POMS

BALLANTINE BOOKS  NEW YORK

IT'S NOT ABOUT THE POM-POMS

How a 40-Year-Old Mom
Became the NFL's Oldest
Cheerleader—and Found
Hope, Joy, and Inspiration
Along the Way

LAURA VIKMANIS

...HN

Published in the United States by Ballantine Books,
an imprint of The Random House Publishing Group,
a division of Random House, Inc., New York.

BALLANTINE and colophon are registered trademarks
of Random House, Inc.

ISBN 978-0-345-53290-9
eISBN 978-0-345-53291-6

Printed in the United States of America on acid-free paper

www.ballantinebooks.com

9 8 7 6 5 4 3 2 1

First Edition

Book design by Elizabeth A. D. Eno

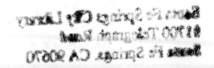

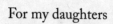For my daughters

And with every passing hour
I'm so glad I left my tower
Like all you lovely folks
I've got a dream.

—Rapunzel in *Tangled*, lyrics by Glenn Slater

We're like movie stars without movies.

—Washington Redskinette Syndi
Stewart, *Cosmopolitan*, 1982

CONTENTS

AUTHOR'S NOTE

This is a work of nonfiction. Some names and identifying characteristics have been changed, and I have altered certain details of chronology. *It's Not About the Pom-Poms* is otherwise an account of my expericences as I remember them.

IT'S NOT
ABOUT THE
POM-POMS

THE TUNNEL

WE BURST OUT OF THE LOCKER ROOM AND HEAD DOWN THE narrow white hallway in pairs, talking and giggling. I am so nervous, my palms are wet and I have to blot them against my thighs so I won't stain my miniskirt. We're going over moves and checking one another's faces. "Don't let me forget that head flip!" "Remind me to move out of the way on our second formation change." "Which arm goes up first on the intro dance?" "Do I have lipstick on my teeth?" "Does my bra show?" "Does my second bra show?" "Is my eyelash falling off?"

The narrow hallway leads to the wide underbelly of Paul Brown Stadium. This part of a football stadium is not glamorous—it's gray and dingy, with exposed pipes and cinder block walls—but on Game Day it's kinetic, so packed with people that it's like the backstage of a Broadway musical. Our black, orange, and gold pom-poms swaying as we walk, we pass the security guys, the referees, coaches, reporters, cameramen, and the pyrotechnicians who are readying the fireworks equipment. I look at the other girls in their halter tops and low-slung skirts and realize, *I'm one of them. I look like that, too.*

The girls and I have known one another just a few months but it feels like we've been through combat training. In some ways we have. We have made it through three rounds of competitive try-outs, a summer of exhausting practices, constant dieting, twice-a-week weigh-ins, and brutal athletic conditioning. Now it's all about to pay off, as we cheer the first home game of the preseason. It's August 27, 2009, and the Cincinnati Bengals are playing the St. Louis Rams. But if you had asked me right then, in the passage of the stadium, who our opponents were, I would have had to think twice before answering. For us the games are not about the opponents or the score, though cheering is always more fun when we're winning. They are about performance. The games are our shows and the field is our stage.

Like all modern cheerleading teams, we are a physically diverse group of women. Some of us are lithe, others petite and muscular. Some are curvy, some thin as a rail, some have legs that go on forever. Some are brunette, some blonde, some redheaded. Most are white, but our group includes an Asian American girl, two African American girls, and a pretty blonde who is part Cherokee.

I am different from all of these girls in one significant way: I am forty years old.

As we near the tunnel, people grin or ogle or give us the thumbs-up. Everyone smiles around cheerleaders, it's Pavlovian. We're iconic, beautiful, and fit, but we're also over the top. We know it, we don't mind, it's why we're here.

A group of fans is taking a tour of the stadium, led by an official. They can't stop staring. We don't stop to chat; we don't have time. I'm going over my moves in my head. Each one of us is nervous about something different. *I think I'm going to throw up. Why didn't I pee before we left? What do I do on the second eight-count of* *"Welcome to the Jungle"?*

Thirty-two of us have shown up to the stadium today but only twenty-four of us are on our way to the field. The others are upstairs working the private suites. I have been selected to cheer because I'm a good dancer, I'm consistently on time, and I always make my weight limit, one hundred twenty-three pounds for my five-foot-four-inch frame.

Our Game Day uniform, which we take home after every game and must return when we retire from the team, is a micro miniskirt in orange and black, and a white-and-orange halter top with a rhinestone B between the breasts. We wear calf-high, low-heeled white leather boots, shipped to us from a small shop in Los Angeles. (They are the only thing I will get to keep at the end of the season.) Beneath our skirts, which have a built-in panty, our legs are encased in suntan color L'eggs Sheer Energy panty hose with the waistband removed so we don't have muffin tops, and the toes cut off so we have circulation.

We are all wearing tan, heavy foundation, fake eyelashes, and French-manicured or clear-polished nails, as required by our rulebook. Some of us have foundation or powder on our stomachs to give us great abs, whether we really have them or not. If you took all the silicone bra inserts, which we call chicken cutlets, that girls have stuffed inside their halters and put them in a pile, it would be about the size of a linebacker. I myself need no chicken cutlets; I got breast implants almost a year before, as part of the same midlife crisis that led me to believe I could get on the Ben-Gals in perimenopause. Real or fake, each set of boobs is pressed together and up.

On our mouths we wear a hideous bright orange lipstick—

Orange Flip by Revlon. It makes you look like someone's pushy grandmother who leaves kiss marks on your cheeks after she greets you. The Ben-Gals have been wearing it for decades.

We pass the players' locker room, which always feels forbidden. Cheerleaders are not allowed to enter the room at any point. I have memorized the white sign on the door: NOTICE! NO PERSON EXCEPT AUTHORIZED CLUB AND LEAGUE PERSONNEL AND AC-CREDITED MEMBERS OF THE MEDIA SHALL BE PERMITTED TO ENTER THE LOCKER ROOM OF ANY PARTICIPATING CLUB ON THE DAY OF THE GAME. The locker-room door is connected to the tunnel by a "yellow brick road." It's not really yellow but a gray, black, and orange pattern that leads the boys to the field before a game and from the field after a nail-biting victory or humiliating loss. We are not allowed to step on the road lest we get in their way.

The boys are streaming in on their way back to the locker room after their warm-up exercises. Chad Ochocinco (who changed his last name from Johnson to Ochocinco to match his jersey number, eighty-five) and Dhani Jones are coming toward us. We avert our eyes, not wanting to distract them, but we peek at their faces to gauge their pregame state of mind. It's almost seven-thirty at night but we have been at the stadium over four hours— practicing, eating an early dinner, and getting ready. We have been here longer than some of the players.

We form small groups, touching our toes and doing lunges, warming up our muscles. We arrange ourselves into a circle to the side of the Bengal brick road and say a quick prayer, led by Tara, our captain, a leggy brunette with deep, dark-brown eyes, a straight little nose, and wavy hair so long it touches her elbows. We stand shoulder to shoulder, cross our arms in front of our chests, and link pinkies, because our poms (cheerleaderspeak for "pom-poms") prevent us from holding hands. Tara lowers her head and says, "Lord, thank you for allowing us to be here today and for keeping us safe. Make sure the fans are safe, the players are safe, and we are safe. Make sure everyone gets home all right after the game. Thank you for making sure that we have no injuries, and for allowing us to cheer."

"Amen," we say in unison.

We all stand, hands on hips, and bend our right knees. This is Ben-Gal Pose. We will do it a hundred more times over the course of the game, at the end of our short dances, the "fillers." We shake our poms just below our breasts and say "Yay!" quietly, so as not to disturb the officials around us.

Then we go into the tunnel. I get chills. It's short, maybe forty feet or so, just a passage with air vents, decorated with Bengals banners, but it feels holy to me. Through the opening I can see fifty-two thousand Bengal fans in the seats, drinking beer, cheering, thrilled to be back for another season, praying that the team can do better than the four-eleven-and-one record it had in 2008. Electric energy radiates from the stands because hopes are always highest at the beginning, and not in the middle, of a Bengals season. My sister, brother-in-law, boyfriend, mom, and two daughters are here. I can hear the public address announcer Bob Kinder in the background, talking about the game. The neon yellow-green goalpost is bright against the sky. A Bud Light ad is to the left, a Pepsi ad to the right.

We stand in two lines. All around me, hair is flying, poms are shaking. Orange Flip flashes over artificially whitened teeth. Fans are leaning their heads over the tunnel wall, screaming and clapping. I start tearing up. *Remember this. This is real.*

Bob Kinder is saying, "Here are your 2009 Cincinnati

Ben-Gals!" The crowd goes crazy, cheering. We walk onto the field, chins high, smiling, past the officials, the photographers, and the video cameras, to the middle—right on the Bengal tiger.

Our intro dance is a revue that includes an "Eye of the Tiger" remix, Cobra Starship's "Good Girls Go Bad," and LL Cool J's "Move Somethin'." The synthesizer chords are booming through the $1.7 million video and sound system. "Back, back, back/Risin' up." We start to move. The fans' favorite part is the kick line, when we arrange ourselves like the Rockettes on the hash marks. My chin is raised to the sky, so even the fans in the top tiers, thousands of feet away, feel like I'm performing for them. "Snotty, snotty," Tara always tells us. "You're smiling but be a little snotty."

From the other end of the line, Tara's yelling, "Back up, Brandy! Laura, half-step forward!" We can yell at each other during dances, but we always smile so no one can tell. I'm kicking in sync with the other girls. For these four minutes everyone's attention is on us— unlike during the game, when many fans will glance over our heads in annoyance to the action on the field, seeing us as a distraction.

We ripple. We do high kicks. As my leg shoots out in front of me, I think about what it took for me to get here. Seconds pass and the music and crowd begin to fade out, until my head is silent. I am no longer on the field of Paul Brown Stadium. I'm an hour away and seventeen years younger, inside the ugly yellow house. I am a twenty-three-year-old newlywed, locked inside a bedroom, desperate to escape, and the only way out is to kick.

Brian and I fight often. It is the first year of our marriage, and we are living in a newly renovated yellow-brick house in Centerville, an up-and-coming suburb of Dayton. Usually we fight after we've been out together. His jealousy comes out whenever I'm around other men. He glares at me, becomes uncomfortable, and is short with me on the drive home. He always thinks I'm flirting with guys. Though only a few years older than me, he acts like an angry father. When we are out, he keeps his arm around me, glancing around protectively, as though gunning for a fight, preventing me from socializing with anyone, male or female. If a man says anything to me, no matter how innocuous, Brian becomes curt with me. When I dance, he watches angrily but rarely joins in. He rarely interacts with other people when we go out and doesn't like to dance. We are opposites and somehow we have married.

Double dates with my girlfriend Renee and her boyfriend, Ted, are a disaster. Brian and I often have to leave in the middle of the evening because we get into a fight. In the morning I call and make apologies to our friends. But Brian doesn't like me going out without him, even if it's just with Renee.

Earlier that night, Brian and I had gone out to a bar near the University of Dayton. It was old and musty-smelling, and the upper level had a dance floor. The patrons were twentysomething college students, young and attractive. Smoke and alcohol wafted through the air. Brian and I danced together and then, according to Brian, I moved too provocatively or answered a man who said something to me. Whatever it was, I infuriated him. It didn't take much.

In the kitchen now at home, Brian says, "I saw the way you were dancing. You were dancing dirty and men were looking at you. You're such a fucking bitch."

"I was just having fun," I say.

"You can't act that way. You look like a slut. Women who dance like that are sluts. You're a married woman."

His repertoire of names for me is limited and nondescript, like those of a fifteen-year-old boy: "stupid bitch," "dumb bitch," "slut." These names stun and anger me. I call him names, too: "asshole," "idiot." Later I will give up, realizing that I don't want to be a name caller. Now I still have some fight in me.

The words are taking a toll, though. I go to my dietitian internship at Miami Valley Hospital in Dayton, and when I make an incorrect calculation on a chart, I hear, "Stupid bitch, you don't know anything." I am in traffic and when another driver swears at me, I shudder. I wonder how my husband can hate me so much. He needs to own me but doesn't seem to like me. Some fights begin because he has a problem at work and comes home angry. I try to keep things calm and easy, make a nice dinner for him, but some nights it doesn't matter what I do. I am the target for his rage.

"I wasn't doing anything," I tell him in the kitchen. "You're making this up."

"Why do you always have to be the center of attention?"

"I wasn't trying to be the center of attention. I just liked the music!" I don't want to sleep with other men but I do want to enjoy myself, relax, dance with friends, and meet new people. I want to be a normal twenty-three-year-old who can go out with her husband and not have every weekend night end in a rip-roaring fight.

"Why don't you admit you're a slut?" he says.

"You know what?" I say. "I don't have to take this. I'm going out." I often threaten to leave the house but never leave. We are playing chicken. This is my way of trying to frighten him into backing down from the accusations he is hurling at me.

I go upstairs to the bedroom to freshen up, part of the charade of preparing to leave. He follows. In front of my vanity I put on my lipstick. He is in the mirror behind me. "Get out of this room," I tell him. "I don't want to be around you right now."

His face reddens, he clenches his fists. He is not a physically imposing man but he scares me. He paces back and forth. "You're not going anywhere," he says.

Our house is big, four bedrooms and three bathrooms. When I first set foot in it, it impressed me. But there is something eerie about it. Later I will learn that he bought the house in foreclosure from an ex-girlfriend's mother. The mother had been an alcoholic who hit the girl. I saw photos of holes in the walls and doors. The house has decades of abuse inside of it but I have no idea.

It's generic, like a spec house, devoid of personality. We have a king-sized bed with no headboard. Some of our furniture is from Brian's parents' house. Our dresser is the one he grew up with, that of a small boy. There is a walk-in closet with beige wall-to-wall carpeting and pale-yellow walls with no pictures. We are playing house—married, young, and attractive—but miserable.

I blot my lipstick and go for the bedroom door. He blocks it. "Get out of my way!" I shout.

"I'm not moving. You're staying here." I try to dart past him but he shoves me to the floor and kicks me in the chest and stomach. In the past, he has pushed me, but it seemed designed to scare me. Now he is really hurting me, jamming his foot into my ribs and neck and arms. I cover my body to protect myself, silent, feeling the shock more than the rage.

Then something snaps in me and I realize that I don't have to take it. I scream at him to stop. I kick in defense, as hard as I can. He is stronger. He jabs me in the stomach and shins, yelling, "I hate you! I hate your guts!" He kicks again and again.

Somehow I scramble to my feet and rush to the door but he is faster and slips outside of the room. I grab the doorknob but it won't budge. Brian is holding it shut from the other side. "Open this door!" I cry.

"You're staying here! You're not going anywhere!"

I pull the knob as hard as I can but he is pulling from outside. How can this be happening? The trapping infuriates me even more than the kicking. Who does he think he is to shut me in a room? How am I going to get out? I let go and start pacing, angry, confused, humiliated.

I wonder what Renee, my mom, and my older sister Lisa would think if they could see this. What kind of husband does this? Though Renee has seen Brian's temper, no one knows how often we fight, or the names he calls me. Lisa and my mother think I am happy, besotted, a newlywed.

I have never been so lonely. I am in prison, locked in an awful ugly bedroom with no love inside it. I feel shame for having married this man, just a year after we met, and getting engaged to him after knowing him only three months. We met in Dayton but our courtship took place primarily over the phone, while I was finishing college in Los Angeles, and he sweet-talked me, complimented me, and went on and on about his adoration. When we moved in together, he began to show this cruel side. I feel young and dumb.

I go back to the door and struggle with the knob. I shake it so hard that the force begins to knock off the door trim. But he is pulling harder. So I do the only thing I can do: kick a hole in it. My foot makes its way halfway through. It must scare him because when I turn the knob again, the door opens. He's in the hallway, looking chastened. I rush past him, saying, "I can't believe you did that." I run downstairs to the kitchen, trying to find my keys.

"Don't leave," he says, following. "I'm sorry, I'm sorry."

I turn and hold up my finger. "You do not touch me ever again. If you lay one hand on me again, I swear to God I will leave you."

"I'm sorry. I won't, I won't." He begs me to stay. I get in the car and drive, not thinking about where I'm going, just driving. But I know I will go back. I'm a newlywed. Newlyweds don't split up. I have to forgive Brian. I *will* forgive Brian. I will do it again and again for a decade and a half, through two children and across three states. I will begin to believe the cruel things he says about me, the words he hurls in my face. I will lose my verve, my laughter. I will lose my spirit until one day, I won't even remember that I had one.

BELLES & THE BEAU

TO UNDERSTAND WHY I MARRIED A MAN WHO LOCKED ME IN A room, you need to understand a little about the family I grew up in, and the strange combination of personalities that made me who I am. My parents, Linda Horn and Juris Vikmanis, met in Kettering, Ohio, a suburb of Dayton that was named for the famous engineer and inventor Charles F. Kettering. It was 1955 and they attended Kettering Fairmont High School—the same high school from which I would one day graduate. Although they were aware of each other, my mother was heavy, so boys weren't really interested in her. They preferred her sister, Max, who was a beauty—tall and slim with long legs.

After graduation, my mom went to Bowling Green State University, and at the advice of her parents, she was put on a strict diet by a doctor. She lost over fifty pounds, and in the spring of 1960, right after she had lost the weight, she went out to Kramer's Tavern in Dayton with some friends. Dad was in the engineering program at University of Cincinnati but he had come back for a cooperative education session with the manufacturing and engineering giant, Sheffield Corporation. He spotted Mom in a crowd of friends, and flirted with her as though seeing her for the first time. He thought she was beautiful and more sophisticated-looking than her peers. She was entranced by his charisma and Latvian accent; born in Latvia, he had immigrated to Berlin with his family during World War II, and came to Ohio at age fourteen after the war.

When my mom saw my dad, she saw her future. She had grown up wanting what her parents had: a beautiful house, a nice car, lots of friends, vacations, and parties. Her father, Burchell Horn, had been a home builder after the war and had made a good living. My mother wanted to marry a good provider, a man as successful as her own father. To do that, women of her generation had to pay a price—chores, childbearing, child-rearing, and loss of autonomy. She believed it was worth it.

He had excelled at school and worked hard at becoming American. He told people to call him Vic because it sounded more American, instead of the foreign-sounding Juris, with its silent "J." He began school a year delayed because he spoke no English but he was smart and driven enough to go on to be admitted to UC for engineering. His personality was more that of a businessman than of an engineer—confident, charming, and suave. He was handsome, too, with full lips, a winning smile, and a good hairline. In his love letters to her he always signed off "Juris" even though she called him Vic. It was as though he could be himself with her.

My parents got serious within weeks. My dad returned to UC to complete his studies. Knowing she would soon be a wife, my mother transferred to Western College for Women, a daughter school of Mount Holyoke, to study home economics. There she learned all the skills of a perfect hostess: sewing, wardrobe planning, shopping, baby care, and housekeeping.

When they married in October 1961, my mom left school and moved in with my father. He took a job at Sheffield, making

$10,000 a year, which is about $75,000 in today's economy—a huge salary for someone just starting out. My mother worked as a bookkeeper for an optician.

My father soon began to reveal a harsh, cruel side my mom hadn't seen before. He had spotted her at Kramer's because she was so attractive, but there must have been an element of conquering to his interest. He constantly accused Mom of having affairs, even though she was faithful and completely in love with him. Nothing she said could reassure him.

Since they had only one car—my dad's beloved 1961 Austin Healey convertible, his graduation present to himself—after work she had to take the bus home or wait for a ride from him. One day he was driving her home in the Healey. It was so low to the ground that people stared when they saw it. They got into a traffic jam, my father slowed down to let another car go in front, and my mother nodded at the driver. Noticing this exchange, my dad screamed, "Why did you smile at him? How dare you do that to me?" She couldn't convince him it had meant nothing. When he believed

With my idol, my big sister Lisa

something, no one could tell him that he was wrong, especially not a woman.

In response to the stress of constant accusations, my mother began to gain back the weight. His jealousy subsided. He no longer thought she was cheating. Instead he made derogatory comments about her appearance. She decided that his insults were more tolerable than his jealousy, so she remained heavy.

In 1964 they bought a house in the Kettering neighborhood of Oak Creek. Their neighbors were young married professionals with children. It was like *Leave It to Beaver*, suburban middle-class America. The men were engineers at GM or the National Cash Register Company, and the women were housewives.

My father soon started an affair with his secretary, Jean. After a while, Jean's husband contacted my mother to tell her. My parents invited them over to discuss it, which I guess was how people dealt with these things back in the early 1960s. My dad promised that the affair was over, and after the couple left, my parents resolved to strengthen their marriage.

The detente didn't last long and my father continued to cheat. As many wives did back then, when divorce was virtually unheard of and women had no economic independence, my mother looked the other way. He called her fat, stupid, and incompetent. She began to believe what he said and blamed herself—and her weight—for his affairs.

After my sister Lisa was born in September 1966, my mother quit work. She didn't want to but my father believed that a woman's job was to cook, clean, and take care of the children. He was in charge of all financial decisions and he made her account for every penny she spent. (Society clearly supported my father's attitude; until the mid-1970s in most states, a married woman could not even open her own checking account.)

I was born two years after Lisa, on September 10, 1968. Five days after my birth, an American Football League expansion team called the Cincinnati Bengals would play its first regular season home game in the University of Cincinnati's Nippert Stadium.

It was an idyllic time for Cincinnati and its suburbs—prosperous and optimistic. Our street, Berrycreek Drive, was wide and quiet and every house had a huge front lawn. Women organized card parties, and for the Fourth of July, kids decorated their bikes with crepe paper and drove up and down the street. My dad's favorite pastime was to work on his Healey. On hot days we put the top down, drove to the neighborhood Baskin-Robbins, and ate our ice cream outside at the picnic tables. It was one of the most peaceful and happy times that I can remember.

Starting as early as age three I loved to perform in front of a crowd.

As a little girl I began taking ballet, after tagging along with Lisa to her classes and falling in love with dance. Every year my class would put on a recital, and I got dressed up in my tutu and performed under the hot lights, all those grown ups staring at me.

My mom came to all our recitals but I don't recall my father ever attending one; he was traveling, working late, or with his tennis group.

Foursomes tend to break up into pairs and our family was no different. The pairs were clear, and in my memory they existed from the moment of my birth: Lisa and Daddy, Laura and Mommy. Dad and Lisa were the big personalities, while my mother and I were quieter. Lisa loved everything my dad loved— the Healey, driving fast, being outside. A tomboy through and through, she was like his first son, and he seemed to have unlimited time for her.

Since she had been a little girl, Lisa had been obsessed with horses. She loved horseback riding, went to ranch camp, drew horses, and loved to talk about them. Though I liked horses I didn't share her level of excitement. One Christmas there was a lot of talk about a gift my father had bought for Lisa and me. We saw a big box under the tree. Every day, as Christmas got closer, he would say, "I bet you wonder what's in that box. Well, you'll both have to wait until Christmas Day."

"Is it new dolls?"

"No."

"Is it a new game for us?"

"No." I couldn't wait to open it and find out what was in there. What wonderful present had he dreamed up for both of us? When Christmas Day finally came, he made us open all our other presents first. I was thrilled with my dresses and tea sets but kept staring over at the one big box. Finally it was time. With wrapping paper strewn all over the floor, the big present was the only box left. Lisa and I opened it as slowly as we could, untying the ribbon, running our fingers under the tape, and lifting the lid off. Inside the box was an expensive pony saddle. It was obvious to me that he had picked this present with no regard for what I might want and with no consideration as to my interests and passions. And he had passed it off as a gift to both of us when clearly it was for Lisa. I felt like my name had been put on the box as an afterthought. I felt like I didn't completely exist.

If my father made his favoritism of Lisa clear, my mother did not do the same with me. She nurtured both Lisa and me equally. She was my booster, my cheerleader. In the morning I came down the stairs and she looked up from her tea and sang, "Here she comes, Miss America!" I would sit down with her and she would say, "You look so pretty today, honey."

Though I enjoyed her positive attention, I felt that her love for me didn't match Daddy's love for Lisa. As wounded as I was, I understood why he loved Lisa more. They were two peas in a pod. How could I compete with someone who was like my father in every way?

Many Sunday nights we visited my mother's parents, Grandma Colleen and Grandpa Burch. Their house was in Oakwood, a posh neighboring city to Dayton that was (and still is) home to the most successful families in the city. Orville Wright had lived there, and John H. Patterson, who founded the National Cash Register Company. To get to Grandma and Grandpa's house, we would drive slowly down a brick road, singing, "Over the river and through the woods/To grandmother's house we go."

At the end of their street, Sweetwood Lane, was the Dayton Country Club. During summer nights Lisa and I would lay on the grass, looking up at the stars. We had a Siberian Husky named Nikki, with one brown eye and one blue eye, and we would let her off the leash to run across the golf course.

Grandpa and Grandma's house had wide steps in front and I

loved to dance on them, practicing what we had learned in ballet class. The steps were my stage, and I imagined an audience in front of me. Everyone else would be inside, getting dinner ready, and I would twirl around, envisioning thousands of people watching me in a theater.

Grandma and Grandpa were a couple for the ages, respectful and kind. Their roles were very defined—she was the cook and homemaker, and he worked—but I never saw them speak an unkind word to each other. Later on, when I got married, my grandparents would be my model for how a man and a woman should treat each other. They watched *The Lawrence Welk Show* on TV, and every Sunday in the fall that they weren't at the stadium watching the Bengals live, they had a football game on.

Cleveland Browns coach Paul Brown had been forced off the Browns in 1963 by then-majority owner Art Modell, and after five years away from football, he had founded the Cincinnati Bengals, choosing the name of a football team that had been in Cincinnati from 1937 to 1941 to link the past with the present. A love affair between the city of Cincinnati and the Bengals was born. Like all Cincinnatians, my grandparents had been Browns fans before there was a football team in Cincinnati, but like all Cincinnatians, they soon converted to be Bengals fans. They had season tickets to the Bengals from the 1968–1969 season on.

When Paul Brown founded the team in 1968, he hired George Bird, who had been his entertainment director at the Browns, to perform duties for the Cincinnati Bengals. At Browns games, Bird had led a band called the Musical Majorettes, a group of pretty girls in skirts who marched and played instruments. The Cleveland Browns had been such a successful team during the late forties and early fifties—they had a twenty-nine-game undefeated streak—that it got to the point where fans would leave at halftime, knowing that the Browns would win. To keep them in the stands, Bird came up with the idea that the Majorettes should perform a halftime show. The fans stayed. One year he decided that the Majorettes' skirts should be cut shorter because it would get them more attention. It did.

When Bird was hired to be entertainment director for the Bengals, he brought along his daughter Shirley, a music teacher who became the assistant entertainment director. He named his new band Bird's Bengal Band, and both he and Shirley directed it. During the first two seasons, when the Bengals played at the University of Cincinnati, their cheerleaders were the UC Bear Kittens, the UC football cheerleading squad. The Bear Kittens did flips and pyramids and sideline cheers. After the Bengals moved to Riverfront Stadium in 1970, George Bird came up with "Ben-Gals" for the cheerleaders, and the team decided to hire its own girls. The dance style changed from the university-style flips to a dance line. Shirley Bird's daughter Christy Allen Varrato, who

The woman who birthed the Ben-Gals, Shirley Bird

cheered on the Ben-Gals during the eighties, said her mother had told her that the switch to the new dance style had to do with insurance: Once the NFL (after the 1970 NFL-AFL merger) was responsible for what happened on the field, they didn't want to pay the high premiums required if the girls did stunting. So the cheering got safer, which led to the dance lines we see today. No one disagrees that today's cheerleaders are sexualized, but who knew that it was all to save money?

Shirley Bird was ahead of her time. Even at the dawn of the Ben-Gals in 1970, every Ben-Gal was required to have a full-time job or be a full-time student. Bird herself had worked all her life and thought that women should work. She also opposed fraternization between players and cheerleaders long before this became the norm for the NFL as it is today. Any girls that did date football players kept it hidden from her. During the early eighties when one Ben-Gal fell in love with offensive guard Glenn Bujnoch, Bird told her, "You can have him or you can have the Ben-Gals." She chose Bujnoch.

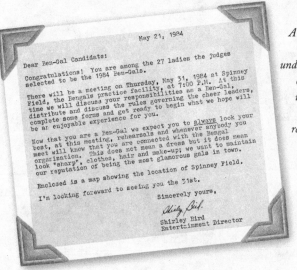

May 21, 1984

Dear Ben-Gal Candidate:

Congratulations! You are among the 27 ladies the judges selected to be the 1984 Ben-Gals.

There will be a meeting on Thursday, May 31, 1984 at Spinney Field, the Bengals practice facility, at 7:00 P.M. At this time we will discuss your responsibilities as a Ben-Gal, distribute and discuss the rules governing the cheer leaders, complete some forms and get ready to begin what we hope will be an enjoyable experience for you.

Now that you are a Ben-Gal we expect you to <u>always</u> look your best, at this meeting, rehearsals and whenever anybody you meet will know that you are connected with the Bengal organization. This does not mean a dress but it does mean look "sharp", clothes, hair and make-up; we want to maintain our reputation of being the most glamorous gals in town.

Enclosed is a map showing the location of Spinney Field.

I'm looking forward to seeing you the 31st.

Sincerely yours,

Shirley Bird
Entertainment Director

A 1984 acceptance letter from Ms. Bird, who understood the importance of projecting a positive image—something our director Charlotte still reminds us about today.

By the late sixties, professional cheerleading was sweeping the nation. College cheerleading had been around since 1898, when a male cheerleader at the University of Minnesota got in front of the crowd at a football game and directed them in a cheer, but now professional sports franchises were bringing on cheerleaders, too. In the sixties, new football teams had been popping up due to NFL expansion and the 1960 formation of the AFL and they needed instant fans. Cheerleaders helped because they were fun to watch, fostered loyalty, and kept people interested during long games. By 1968, twelve NFL teams had cheerleaders, including the Cincinnati Bengals and the Dallas Cowboys, whose first cheerleaders, from 1961 to 1971, were a coed squad of high school students called CowBelles & Beaux that did traditional-style cheers. Soon traditional cheerleading would prove unpopular, paving the way for a new and more provocative style of cheering.

When I was five, my father, whose company had been acquired by the Bendix Corporation, was promoted to Bendix's director of en-

Dressing up for a dance recital also meant getting to try out makeup. This explains why I had no trouble with applying all that cheerleader foundation decades later.

gineering. We moved to West Bloomfield, Michigan for his new job. It was wealthier than Oak Creek and everyone there was from other cities.

In Bloomfield, Lisa and I enrolled in the Michigan Ballet company. One day some of the teachers asked if any of us wanted to be extras in *The Nutcracker*. I was one of the children in the first act party scene. I remember being backstage, getting makeup, wearing a petticoat and a ruffly blue party dress, pink ballet slippers, and a ribbon in my hair. In the second act I watched from the wings as the different sweets from around the world danced for Clara and the Prince. The Arabian Dance was different from all the other dances, with its slow, seductive music, performed by a beautiful, scantily clad woman who gyrated slowly. During the Arabian Dance the audience was silent. No one coughed or adjusted their programs. This was amazing to me: that a woman could have so much power over all these people. I was only six or seven and too young to understand sexual attraction but I knew that what I was seeing was important. Women had power over men that could be dangerous.

My father's affairs were continuing, and though he was making no moves to end the marriage, he treated my mother with a lack of respect. At my parents' parties he always had a drink in his hand and talked to other men's wives. (The only drinks I ever saw him with during my childhood were beer and water—never soda or anything else. My mother had to always have the bottom two shelves of the refrigerator stocked with beer in tall-neck bottles for him.)

On a bright summer afternoon in Michigan, I was in the back-seat of my parents' car, a white 1969 GTO with green vinyl seats that made my legs sweat when it was hot outside. We were going about forty miles an hour and I realized that my parents were having an argument. It went from a heated talk to a shouting match within seconds. My mother opened the car door and said, "That's it! I'm getting out!" I was terrified that she was going to jump out of the car and get hurt.

My dad slowed down, shouted, "Don't get out of the car!" and reached over to shut the door. I understood then that there was darkness in their marriage. If their other arguments had indicated hostility between them, this pointed to something even worse. We weren't a perfect family, and though I didn't yet know what that meant, it unsettled me.

One afternoon in September 1975, my father called my mother at home and said, "I need numbers off of some life insurance policies in my desk drawer. Would you read them out loud to me?" She thought it was odd that he would have a work policy at home but went in and found the files. When she took them out, she noticed an unsealed envelope sitting on top. She set it down, opened the files, and read him the numbers. Then they hung up. She put the files back and started to put the envelope in the drawer, and then she got curious. She opened the flap and found photos inside of different women posed in the nude, taken in hotel rooms. My mother didn't know if he had set her up to humiliate her or had done it because he didn't have the courage to end the marriage himself. The next day she went to a lawyer and filed for divorce. It was her fourteenth wedding anniversary.

The day my parents told us that they were divorcing, they led us into the family room. The TV was off and it was very quiet. I knew something big was going to happen. I was on my mom's lap and Lisa sat on his lap, on a cushioned turquoise couch. "We made a decision to separate," my mom said, patting my arm. I twisted my face around and saw a look on her face that I had never seen before: terror.

Soon afterward, my mom, Lisa, and I moved to a condo near the house. Dad would visit us there and pick us up on the weekends. I didn't understand what had happened, and wondered if it had something to do with the way they had fought in the GTO. I worried about my mom. It seemed like she still loved him. Had this been her decision or his? What could make my parents split up after all those years and two great kids? What made love run out?

EXCEPT YOUR LEGS

SOON AFTER THE DIVORCE MY MOTHER MOVED US BACK TO OHIO, so she could be closer to her parents and the support they could provide. We moved back to Kettering, which had a good school district but wasn't as pricey as neighboring Centerville, to a street called Millwood Road. I understood that we didn't have as much money as we had when Dad was around.

Despite the lack of money, the years following the divorce were fun, fast, and wild—just us three girls. My mom worked full-time as a bookkeeper, so Lisa and I were on our own every afternoon. We often ate dinner at McDonald's if Mom didn't have time to cook. I kept taking dance lessons, which I loved—ballet, tap, and jazz. Dance class was the only place where I felt really good about myself, where I was Laura, not Lisa's little sister.

Lisa had a big personality and a loud, attractive style. Even at ten she was legendary. She wasn't just pretty, but funny, too. She was friends with boys and girls and everyone wanted to be with her. I idolized her, so I understood why everyone loved her, but at the same time I was confused about who I should be.

I tried to get some ideas about who I should be from TV. With Mom gone at work, Lisa and I got to watch it at home in the afternoons. My favorite show was *I Dream of Jeannie*. I loved Jeannie's cute bandeau bra and balloon pants, her lashes, her makeup, and her belly. I understood that she was sexy but appealing. I wanted to have that intoxicating effect on men, who could never stay angry with her for long. Whenever she got in trouble, Tony would put her in the bottle, but it was so cozy and sparkly in there, with the velvet and bright colors, that it didn't seem like such a bad place to be.

My best friend during this time was Janice, a funny, confident girl who was in my grade, took dance classes with me, and was keeper of all my secrets. Janice spent a lot of afternoons hanging out on our lawn, playing with Barbies, or suntanning and talking about boys. Like my mom, Janice's mom was divorced, but it was clear that she was much poorer than we were. Janice, her sister, and mom lived in the bottom apartment of an eight-unit building near a strip mall, close to a busy road. You had to go down a few steps to get to the apartment and they had a smelly carpet and worn-out furniture. One day I was visiting her and I went over to her sink to put my cup in it. There were dirty dishes in the sink and when I set my cup down, it jostled them and roaches scrambled out everywhere. I was horrified. From then on I never spent the night there because I was too afraid.

While I tried to steer clear of Janice's house, I didn't worry that my mom would end up like Janice's mom because I understood that Grandma Colleen and Grandpa Burch could help her if she really needed it. One Christmas soon after the divorce we went to visit them in Oakwood. As we were all opening presents, Grandpa handed envelopes to my mom, her sister, Max, and her brother Larry. My mother opened her envelope and started to cry. I went over and saw that it was a check made out for $10,000. They knew she needed it.

For entertainment, my mother would take Lisa and me to the Kentucky Horse Park in Lexington or to Kings Island amusement park just north of Cincinnati. When I was ten, a new roller coaster opened at Kings Island called The Beast. It was the largest, tallest, and fastest wooden roller coaster in the world at the time. Hard rock would play on the stereo system when you went through, and the teenagers were crazy about it.

I was deathly afraid of The Beast. The very first time I saw it, I was relieved to find that I was too short to ride. I sat with my mom and we waited for Lisa to come out. By the time I was a teenager Lisa convinced me to go on The Beast—but only once. Though the ride was only a few minutes long, I hated every second. The downhills were misery. My stomach lurched. I never rode The Beast again.

Once we settled in Kettering, my father chose not to move back to Ohio but to stay in Michigan, three and a half hours away. Lisa and I saw him only a few times a year, for weeklong stays on holidays or during summer vacation. I was hurt that he had chosen to live far away. He must not have loved me enough because if he had, he would have wanted to see us more often. He soon became a distant figure, more like an uncle than a father. When I was ten, he remarried a secretary at Bendix named Chris and they had a baby boy named Eric. It was as though he had started over without his daughters and never looked back. If we had been truly important to him, I felt, he wouldn't have wanted to make a new family in another state. He didn't seem to want to remain a part of our day-to-day lives. Although it would be thirty years before I would put a name to my feeling, I understood that my father had abandoned us.

After the split, my mother created a new life for herself, centered around family and friends. She went to Bengals games with her parents, her fandom refusing to wane, even with no man in the house. Soon after the divorce, a friend called up my mom. Hearing the television in the background, the friend said, "What are you doing?"

"Watching football," my mother said.

"You mean you're watching football and you don't have to watch football?" her friend asked.

Within six months of my parents' separation in 1975, there had been seven other divorces in their circle of friends in West Bloomfield. There was a tidal shift in the country due to feminism, increasingly liberal values, and new ideas about sex roles. Between 1965 and 1975 the number of divorces in the United States went up 116 percent. Women were beginning to feel that they didn't want to be married any longer to men who tried to dominate them. In 1970 a pamphlet called *The Myth of the Vaginal Orgasm* was published and quickly began to circulate among women; they were realizing that a penis didn't necessarily lead to sexual satisfaction. Consciousness raising was growing in popularity. In 1971, Gloria Steinem and others launched an insert to *New York* magazine called *Ms.* that later became an independent publication, and in 1973 the Supreme Court decided *Roe v. Wade*, which overturned, on constitutional grounds, state laws limiting a woman's access to abortion during the first trimester of pregnancy. Colleges were beginning to offer women's studies courses, and shelters for battered women were opening in major cities.

While feminism was on the rise, professional cheerleading was, too. Cheerleaders were everything that American women were beginning to say they weren't—simple, cheerful, and put on the earth to make men happy. They were a stark contrast to feminists, whose power was rising but who were vilified by men afraid of independent women. And let's face it, cheerleaders were also smoking hot.

America's craze for cheerleaders began in 1972 with the invention of a new cheerleading team called—you guessed it—the Dallas Cowboys Cheerleaders. Cowboys general manager Tex Schramm hadn't much cared for the coed squad, the CowBelles & Beaux, that had cheered for the Cowboys until 1971 and in preparation for the 1972 season, he decided that it was time for the cheerleaders to have more pizzazz. As the DCCs detail in their website history, "With his extensive background in television, [Schramm] recognized that professional football had become more than sports—it was sports entertainment. He knew that the public liked pretty girls." The CowBelles & Beaux director Dee Brock and Schramm decided "to expand the established football tradition of sideline cheerleaders into a glamorous, choreographed squad of accomplished dancers that would serve as a counterpoint to the game itself." Brock hired Texie Waterman, a Broadway actress and dancer, to put together the squad.

Waterman chose seven women to become her new dance team, teaching them the Broadway-style moves she knew well. The Dallas Cowboys Cheerleaders, in their iconic, blue-and-white, midriff-baring uniforms, were introduced to America in 1972. NFL cheerleading as we know it—with its skimpy costumes, provocative routines, and gorgeous women—was born.

Four years later, on January 18, 1976, at Super Bowl X in Miami, came a pivotal moment in cheerleader history. The Dallas Cowboys were playing the Pittsburgh Steelers and, like about half of the NFL teams at the time, the Steelers did not have cheerleaders, so the DCCs were left to do the entertaining on their own. Fifty-seven million Americans were glued to their television sets. To understand the weight of this number, one must keep in mind that the population of the United States at that time was about 220 million. A quarter of the U.S. population was watching the

Super Bowl. This was before the Internet, before TiVo, before television on demand, before Netflix. This was at a time when there weren't a thousand channels you could watch—and you couldn't DVR the game to watch it later. Football was American entertainment.

During a lull in the game action, a cameraman went over to a row of Dallas Cowboys Cheerleaders and one cheerleader, a for-

The Ben-Gals in the early 1980s, influenced by the Dallas Cowboys Cheerleaders and sporting modified mullets

The skirts today are just as short but our halter tops make these bodices look Puritan. (Current Ben-Gals director Charlotte is fourth from right; Christy, Shirley Bird's daughter, is second from right.)

If only our current Santa suits were this warm.

PHOTOS: Christy Allan Varrato

mer beauty pageant contestant named Gwenda Swearingen, noticed him filming and gave him a big wink. In 1976 this was akin
to a bump and grind. Back then there was no MTV, no VH1, no
Jennifer Lopez, Lady Gaga, or Madonna, no iPods, no iTunes, no
cell phones, no Victoria's Secret. Thongs were something you
wore on your feet, not your behind. *Flashdance* was another seven
years away.

This type of camera angle, a human interest shot of an attractive woman, had been seen on local sports broadcasts but not on
national ones. It was known as a "honey shot" and as Mary Ellen
Hanson has detailed in her history of cheerleading *Go! Fight!
Win!: Cheerleading in American Culture*, its progenitor was Andy
Sidaris, an ABC television sports director and, for twenty-five
years, the director of ABC's *Wide World of Sports*.

Sidaris was convinced that honey shots were the way to keep
people watching at home and in the stands. "Once you've seen one
huddle you've seen 'em all," he told *Los Angeles* magazine. "So you
either look at the popcorn, the guys, or the ladies. The choice is
clear to me." After that shot of Gwenda Swearingen, the DCCs
were famous overnight. Everyone wanted a piece of them. Within
days, Tex Schramm's secretary, Suzanne Mitchell, who had been
moonlighting as the DCCs director, had to direct the team
full-time. She was so overwhelmed with her new responsibilities
that poor Tex had to find a new secretary.

The DCCs squad poster eventually outsold the iconic 1976 Far-
rah Fawcett poster in her nipple-revealing semisheer red bathing
suit. The cheerleaders guest-starred on *The Love Boat*—the ultimate
seventies claim to fame. They did a Fabergé shampoo commercial,
they went on *Family Feud,* and they traveled all over the world making appearances. In 1978 a pornographic movie called *Debbie Does
Dallas* was released. In it a group of cheerleaders try to find a way to

go to Dallas to audition for a team that has blue-and-white uniforms bearing a striking resemblance to the DCC uniforms. The DCCs sued on trademark grounds and their victory—an injunction against further distribution and advertising of the movie—was a sign of their increasing prominence and brand power.

In a 1978 *Sports Illustrated* article on cheerleaders, even John Madden, then coach of the Oakland Raiders, weighed in on the phenomenon of cheerleader popularity. "I can see what this game is coming to," he said. "Choreographers instead of coaches. It will be a contest to judge which set of girls gets more TV time. After the gun sounds, the losing choreographer will tell the press, 'We lost our momentum. We couldn't maintain intensity. That's the name of the game—intensity. We'll have to regroup, go back to fundamentals. Put it in the paper, we'll be back.'"

As sexual mores were opening up, not only on the football field but in American bedrooms, pop culture was beginning to push the envelope in terms of sexual content. In June 1978, a feature film based on the hit Broadway musical *Grease* was released. It starred John Travolta as Danny Zuko and Olivia Newton-John as the innocent Sandy Olsson. Lisa and I were visiting Dad when the movie came out. I made him take us to see it, and then went back fifteen more times with friends. I had a girlfriend in Michigan whose parents drove a bright yellow Corvette. We would sit in the Corvette in the garage, smoke candy cigarettes, and pretend to be the Pink Ladies.

Like every other young girl at that time, I fell in love with Olivia Newton-John. I loved all of her outfits in the film, her dancing, and her voice, but I was particularly fascinated by the ending of the movie, when Sandy shows up at the carnival dressed in a tight black outfit, leather jacket, and red Candies slide heels. One of Danny's friends has a match in his mouth and when he sees Sandy in her new getup, he pulls out the match in shock. That image of his awed expression was stamped upon my brain.

When Danny sees her, he says, "Sandy" in an awestruck voice. Sandy says, "Tell me about it, stud." I didn't know what a stud was but I knew it was something dirty. They sang "You're the One That I Want." The choreography for the song has Danny lusting after her body. At one point he drops to his knees before her. If *The Nutcracker*'s Arabian Dance had been my intro to gender relations, *Grease* was advanced studies.

I desperately wanted to be that sexy to a man someday, but I was afraid I never would because of my flat chest. Lisa, on the other hand, had developed early and by age fourteen already had double-D boobs. She was such a head turner, even as a teenager, that when my mother drove us to McDonald's for dinner, men would ogle Lisa and wolf whistle. If you can picture a five-foot-six-inch tomboy with huge boobs, a husky voice, and a love of all-terrain vehicles, that's Lisa. The women on the Horn side of the family, my mother's, were buxom, but most of the ones on the Vikmanis side were flat-chested. It seemed that Lisa had inherited Horns and I'd gotten stuck with Vikmanises.

When I was about twelve, something happened that altered my views about my body and men forever. It was summertime and Lisa and I had gone to visit my dad, his wife, Chris, and their baby son, Eric, in Detroit during summer vacation. I was in the bathroom and the toilet paper had run out. I opened the cabinet under the sink to get a new roll, and discovered a stack of *Playboy* magazines.

Nervous but curious, I opened one of the *Playboy*s and found a picture of a woman with huge breasts, squatting on a beach with her knees shoulder-width apart, wearing a bathing suit that was just two strings running down her nipples and pushed to the side at the crotch so you could see everything. I was shocked. The woman in the magazine didn't look anything like my mom or even Chris, who was athletic and small-breasted. Was this what my dad truly found sexy? If it was, why had he married two women who didn't look anything like this? My mother had told us that she had divorced him because he had been unfaithful, and now I had another part of the story. I viewed his cheating as linked to his *Playboy*s. He looked at these magazines because he was a cheater and he cheated because he read these magazines.

Although I was angry at my dad, I also felt as though I was getting a true look at what men wanted in a woman. This was perfection in their minds: a skinny body with enormous boobs. I wanted to look like that someday. I hoped puberty would hit me like a ton of bricks.

Shortly after that, two things happened, and I connected them to the *Playboy* incident, like pieces of a jigsaw puzzle. It all began with my decision, in seventh grade, to join the cheerleading team. Student cheerleaders at my junior high just did sideline cheers for the boys, nothing very exciting, but I liked the outfit, a pleated royal-blue skirt and a yellow sweater with a K for John F. Kennedy Junior High, and the pom-poms, of course. After school, I was always busy with dance class and cheer, while the cool crowd was running around socializing and having fun. This was the age when a lot of us got mopeds and we had independence for the first time in our lives. I felt like I was missing out.

At the beginning of eighth grade I joined the cool crowd and decided not to sign up for cheerleading. I stopped all my dance classes, too. My social life had become more important to me than my cheerleading and dance. That year my grades plummeted—I kept up with my schoolwork but was no longer as motivated to get As. Lisa had gotten her driver's license and was often out of the

*I made it on to my
first cheerleading team
in seventh grade.*

house in her huge Chevy pickup truck. On rides with Lisa we drank Mountain Dew from glass bottles, cranked the windows, and listened to AC/DC, Led Zeppelin, Ozzy Osbourne, and Def Leppard.

Many days after school, now that I didn't have dance class or cheering, I went to Burger King to drink milk shakes with my new friends. I soon put on about fifteen pounds. On weekends my crowd and I went to parks or doughnut shops or parking lots, buying beer and chips at a drive-through convenience store. We'd listen to a boom box and lean against cars, or go to bonfires in the woods. I got drunk for the first time, on beer. We raided parents' liquor cabinets and drank Jack Daniel's or Jim Beam mixed with cola. I tried black beauties (amphetamines) and Sopors (quaaludes).

Some afternoons we would end up at a kid's house when the parents were gone, and we would couple off and make out to Lynyrd Skynyrd's "Free Bird" or Led Zeppelin's "Stairway to

Heaven." Making out meant second base, because there was always someone sitting next to you and you didn't want to go further with all those people around.

Through this crowd I met a boy named Paul. He was short and blond and because his family lived in an apartment and not a house, I thought he was tough. His parents weren't around and I liked that. He was a bad boy, just like Danny Zuko. (Thank you, John Travolta, for making millions of teenage girls fall for guys who had nothing better going for them than great hair and a swagger.) Paul asked me out and I said yes. This meant that I would go to his apartment after school to make out. I knew that if we kept making out, eventually he would want to have sex. Though I was frightened by it, I was also curious about it. Sex was the way Danny looked at Sandy, sex was the Arabian Dance, sex was my father's stack of *Playboy*s. It was seeing new colors of the rainbow, like a scene out of a Beatles movie or *Hair*. Staring at myself in a bikini in the mirror one summer afternoon, when I was twelve, I had discovered how to pleasure myself and I enjoyed it. Sex, I thought, would be a million times better than that.

Paul and I had been dating for a few months when one afternoon we went further. I realized we were about to do it. I thought that if I stopped him, he wouldn't like me anymore and he would dump me.

Once he was inside me, let's just say it was no *Magical Mystery Tour*. I didn't see fireworks or new colors of the rainbow. I definitely didn't have an orgasm, and it actually hurt. I hated it. I looked up at Paul, panting away, and it wasn't like the way Danny looked at Sandy. It was all about him, not me. I was a hole and there was no love and I could see that he would like me even less once it was over.

On my walk home I felt dirty and ashamed, wishing I had

stopped him. I hadn't been ready for this, but now it was too late and I'd already done it. When I got home, I showered and scrubbed myself all over, but I couldn't wash away the dirty feeling.

After that day, I gave up on sex and pretended it had never happened. I never spoke to Paul again. How could I? Every time I saw him it reminded me of how awful he had made me feel. The news soon got out that we had had sex. Girls whispered about me when I passed. I was a slut, a tramp. I hated the gossip. I wanted to forget about what had happened, forget about the wild ways that had led me astray. In my mind you could be good or bad and I had been bad. I stopped hanging out with the fast crowd. I went back to my old friends, good girls. I never did Sopors or black beauties again.

It didn't take long to change my friends, but my body was going through puberty. That, combined with the milk shakes and the lack of exercise, meant that I had curves—hips and thighs that I'd never had before—though I still wore an A cup.

The second thing that changed my views of men was a conversation I had with my father. It was the summer after my rebellious eighth-grade year and he had just picked Lisa and me up for a visit to Michigan. I got into the backseat of his car; Lisa always sat in the front. He looked at me in the rearview with a frown and said, "What have you been doing? You've gained weight since the last time I saw you." It hurt me so deeply, I can still feel the hot shame on my cheeks.

I was aware that I had put on weight, but no one had said anything; it wasn't my mother's style to insult Lisa or me. Not only was I flat-chested, but he was right. I was fat.

That fall, as soon as ninth grade started, I enrolled in my dance classes again. I focused on my schoolwork and began reading women's magazines for fitness tips. I was hungry for information and became fascinated by how the body worked. If I could learn to control my body, then people couldn't say hurtful things about it anymore. Exercise was the way to do it.

I began tagging along with Mom to her Jazzercise classes. I was always the youngest student. My mom went Mondays, Wednesdays, and Fridays, and I made a couple of calls to find out where to take Tuesday and Thursday classes, too. Exercise was hard and sweaty and not always fun, but it gave me focus and it helped me lose weight. The only time I felt really good about myself was when I was exercising. On days when I didn't, I vowed to work extra hard at Jazzercise or dance class to make up for it. I couldn't recognize it then, but my relationship to exercise was beginning to have an addictive quality. It wasn't as dangerous as drug or alcohol addiction—but it was just as all-consuming. Exercise was all I thought about and it became the most important thing in my life.

I was not alone in my enthusiasm for jazzy aerobics dancing, one of the reasons I was excited to keep pursuing it. At this time, the early eighties, America was in the midst of an aerobics dance craze, all because of *Flashdance*. The movie starred Jennifer Beals and it was about a welder who dreams of being a ballet dancer but instead dances at Mawby's, a kind of bar that doesn't exist anymore where women dance provocatively but don't take off their clothes. The movie was shot like a music video with long, extended dance sequences over popular songs of the time like "Flashdance . . . What a Feeling," "Maniac," and "Gloria."

My favorite part of the movie was when one of the Mawby's girls, Tina Tech, danced to "Manhunt" on the stage of the bar. She wore a bondage outfit and gloves, and her moves were sharp, angry, and sexy. At one point she crawled down the stage like a tiger. She was fit and firm and not superskinny. I wanted to be that confident. I wanted to have my sexuality be a positive, empowering force, the way it seemed to be for Tina Tech and for Lisa, not the negative force it had been when I lost my virginity at fourteen.

Though *Flashdance* got many women into dance (and artfully ripped sweatshirts) it also painted a realistic portrait of how hard it was to go from amateur to professional. Jeanie, Alex's friend and an aspiring figure skater, trips during an audition and instead of landing the role of pro skater, winds up stripping at a nude club. Alex has to go and rescue her. I feared that Jeanie's fate might be mine if I tried to pursue a professional dance career and failed. It was impractical to think I could make money as a dancer. I was only five-four, with short legs, big calves, and thick thighs. My classmates were tall and slender with long necks and gazellelike legs.

But even if I knew it wasn't dance, I wasn't sure what career was right for me. I was a good student but I wasn't in the advanced classes like the really smart kids, and for a long time I had been feeling that I wasn't bright. When my mom and I talked about the future, she would say, "Do whatever you want to do, honey!" but she didn't steer me toward elite colleges. It seemed that my career choice would be entirely up to me.

In tenth grade we were given an interest inventory test at school. We had to answer questions about our personalities and a day later our teacher told us which careers were suitable for us. I put stock in the idea that this test would tell me my future. It was like a professional Magic 8 Ball. I spent a lot of time deliberating over my answers and when I finished, I ran my finger down to find my future. . . .

The military. The test said I was suited for the military. I felt exactly the way I did when my father said I had gained weight. In my unsophisticated teenage mind, the military was where you went when you didn't have any special talents. After class, we shared our results. All my classmates had gotten professional careers as their answers—doctor, lawyer, nurse, or architect. I was the only one in my class to get the military. I was not going to join the military, and the test didn't say I was meant to be a dancer, so what was my future? Who was I meant to be?

In ninth grade I fell in love. His name was Joel and he worked at a garden center. He was tall, muscled, and cute, but he was also very smart, a straight-A student. Joel was in a band called Cousin It, which played New Wave music like "One Thing Leads to Another" by The Fixx. New Wave was cutting-edge, and I would go to his gigs in basements and dance to his music, proud that my boyfriend was in the band.

Joel and I waited to do it. We cared about each other and thought it should be special. After consulting with my mother, I went on birth control so Joel and I could be responsible about it. I still didn't have orgasms but I cared about him and understood that sex could be an expression of love. One summer at our community pool, Joel and I were lying on lounge chairs. I felt as cute as Phoebe Cates in *Fast Times at Ridgemont High*. Joel looked over at my body, his eyes traveling from my face down to my toes. He leaned in. "You have such a perfect body," he said. "Except your legs."

I couldn't believe he had said this but I felt the shame of knowing he was right. I was already self-conscious about my short thighs, and now my own boyfriend had noticed them. My father had been onto me and now Joel was, too. I wasn't perfect and I never would be.

That summer a new TV show came on the air, weekday mornings at six, called *20 Minute Workout*. My mom would wake up early to do the exercises—and one early morning I did them with her. The show was taped in a completely white studio and two or three women would do the exercises on a circular white platform that rotated slowly so you could see them from the front and the back. They wore aerobics chic: high-cut leotards with matching leg warmers and headbands, suspenders, belts, tights, all in outrageous colors. I videotaped the show religiously and played the tapes in the afternoon, sometimes two back to back. One day I would go out for pizza with my friends, the next day I would do two hours in front of the VCR to burn off the calories. I liked the adrenaline, the rush, and the results. I could see my thighs become thinner, my arms become stronger and leaner. I didn't see the ridiculousness of a fourteen-year-old girl standing in the living room doing exercises designed for adult women. I loved it, the routines that incorporated dance but also made you sweat, the sexy outfits, the pounding music. Lisa made fun of me but it didn't stop me.

Right around the time that I was developing into an exercise addict, a young Cal State Northridge student named Paula Abdul was doing the same thing two thousand miles away. Even shorter than I was, five-two to my five-four, the budding dancer ate salads and drank diet soda to keep her weight down, and exercised up to four hours a day. By the time she went public with her bulimia-and-exercise battle in 1995, after having become a Laker Girl, successful music video choreographer, and pop star, the person she was describing felt familiar to me. I understood what it was like to hate your body, to feel shorter and fatter than all the other girls. I understood what it was like to feel so much pressure to be skinny that you were willing to sweat for hours at a time to burn calories.

But no matter how hard I worked to control my body, it wasn't enough to keep Joel's interest. One day, after we had been dating about a year and a half, I drove over to his house in my little red Honda and he came out and sat in the passenger seat. "We really need to talk," he said. "I like you a lot but I don't have enough time for you because of my school work, my family, and my band." I was crushed. I was convinced that if I were really special, he would have made time for me. I connected the breakup to what he had said about my legs. My thighs weren't skinny enough, and if they had been, he would have stayed my boyfriend. The irony was that he was telling the truth when he said he was busy. He was serious about his schoolwork and wound up getting into MIT—but back then all I could hear was that I wasn't good enough. Henry Kissinger could have said he didn't have time for me and I would have traced it back to my thighs.

In my senior year of high school I auditioned for a company called Dance Theater Dayton and was accepted. Our director, Debbie, was a serious woman with a bob, tall and lithe, who gave compliments only when a girl really deserved it. She was like Debbie Allen's character in *Fame,* no-nonsense, but inspiring.

Every time I went to the dance company I had to be weighed in. This was the norm then. There was no acceptance of different body types, not in the narrow dance world I was in. To be a good dancer you had to stay slim. The constant weigh-ins were not the greatest thing for a girl already obsessed with her body. Each of us would get on the scale and I noticed that some girls would frown when they saw their weight, go to the bathroom, come back, and hop on the scale again. I suspected that they were vomiting. I didn't want to do that to myself, but my obsession with weight had become a pathology. I soon developed a condition that had no name then but that is now called Eating Disorder Not Otherwise Specified (EDNOS).

I began deleting entire food groups, like meat. I didn't educate myself about the healthy ways to be a vegetarian. Instead of brown rice and beans I ate nothing but yogurt, fruit, and granola bars, not nearly enough protein for a growing girl. With my low calorie intake and the intense dance schedule, I began losing weight quickly. I developed a diet soda habit, and a taste for NutraSweet. These bad habits, combined with constant dance and aerobics, made me get too thin. I didn't feel too thin. I loved the way I looked, my slim, strong figure, even though my breasts had never arrived.

As my weight loss became more extreme, my mom got worried and took me to our family doctor. Karen Carpenter had died a few years before and there was a new awareness of anorexia. The doctor ran tests and said that based on the results, I wasn't anorexic. I took this as license to continue with my extreme exercise and limited diet.

On top of all the dancing I had also made my high school drill team, which provided the entertainment at our school football games. As Hanson described in *Go! Fight! Win!*, drill teams involved more dance than the sideline cheering teams. They were more competitive, larger, and all female. (The drill team had been invented in 1940 by a high school teacher named Gussie Nell Davis. She had been hired by the president of Kilgore College in Texas, a Baptist who wanted to encourage temperance during games; fans frequently left their seats to drink from flasks under the stands. The president asked her to produce a halftime show that would keep them in their seats. Her first show had a "drill-and-dance group" of short-skirted girls. The fans stayed seated. A connection had been made between fan attention and pretty women.)

The Fairmont Firebird drill team senior year turned out to be much more exciting than my junior-high cheerleading team. We

I never forgot the white boots on drill team. Little did I know I would be wearing them again a quarter of a century later. I'm second from left.

did dancing and kick lines before the game and during halftime. We did marches, snaps, and transitions and we got a lot of attention within the school. Our uniforms were zip-up military-style jackets with puffy sleeves, white gloves, and short A-line white skirts. We wore knee-high white boots, just like the ones I would one day wear on the Ben-Gals, and carried enormous pom-poms that looked like the head of Animal on *The Muppet Show*. That year I cut my hair to chin length to feel more edgy. I wore it short and curly, with headbands like Madonna in *Desperately Seeking Susan*.

Senior year I had a boyfriend named Hal, a tall, thin class clown. He wanted to move to Los Angeles after graduation because he had an uncle out there. Without a viable career plan, I decided to move to California with Hal and go to college there. I found out that there was a dietetics program at California State University–Long Beach. When I read about the major, I perked up. Already fascinated by nutrition, I liked the idea of teaching other people healthy ways to eat. My mother had told me to "Do what you love" and dietetics, I now realized, was what I loved. This was a way to take my pastime and turn it into a career.

Because the out-of-state tuition was expensive, I came up with a plan: I would attend a junior college for a year, get state residency, and then go to CSULB on an in-state tuition. The whole thing would take me five years, not four, but I could go to the school of my choice. My mom and I asked Grandma Colleen for money and she agreed to pay the first year's tuition. My father would pay for the rest.

I was excited to get out of the Midwest. Maybe I would become a little surfer girl like in the Beach Boys song. Grandma had given Lisa some money that she said she could use for college or for buying a house, and Lisa had bought her own house at eighteen. I didn't want to stay in Ohio like Lisa and my classmates. I was going to the West Coast, even if it was with a boyfriend. In July 1986, at seventeen, while my mother waved goodbye and cried, I drove away with Hal in his gray Honda Civic hatchback, looking like Madonna and running off with a clown.

MANHATTAN CLUB FOR WOMEN

HAL AND I MOVED IN TOGETHER IN REDONDO BEACH BUT BY THE time school started a few months later, our relationship had petered out. We were always better off as friends and broke up amicably. I entered El Camino College in Torrance, moved to Hermosa Beach, and got a female roommate. At the end of my street was a blue-and-white Cape Cod–style house that was later used for exterior shots of Jennie Garth and Tori Spelling's beach house on *Beverly Hills, 90210*.

I got a job in a yogurt store in Redondo called Heidi's Frogen Yozurt. The chain owner, Heidi Miller, was a body builder, and on the walls of the store there were photos of her in competitions. I was fascinated by her. I had never seen a woman be muscular and pretty at the same time. Heidi was part of a trend in women's fitness; the Ms. Olympia contest had started in 1980 and the movie *Pumping Iron II: The Women* had come out in 1985. The muscle scene at Gold's Gym in Venice Beach was exploding and *Pumping Iron* star Arnold Schwarzenegger had become an action star, winning over audiences in *Conan the Barbarian* and *The Terminator*.

Despite my body consciousness, my job at a yogurt store turned out to be a liability. Because of all that "frogen yozurt," over the course of a year I gained fifteen pounds again, going up to 135, which in my skewed dance-company eyes, was fat. I wanted to do something to get back in shape. After I transferred to CSULB, a female classmate told me there was a women's sports club down the street from my apartment called Manhattan Club for Women. I went over to check it out. It was clean and well-lit with Nautilus machines and dance studios, and there was not a man in sight. This was my nirvana.

Who knew frozen yogurt could make you fat?

The membership fee was high but the first month was free, so I signed up and took aerobics classes. One of my teachers was named Christy Curtis. She was a gorgeous, busty blonde with wide eyes, and she was a model, the choreographer for *Days of Our Lives*, and choreographer/cheerleader for the L.A. Clippers Spirit. We became friendly. She told me I was really good at aerobics and asked if I wanted to be an instructor. I knew this would let me take classes for free, so I said yes. I got my certification and every morning I taught aerobics or supervised weight training. Afterward I

An aspiring Jane Fonda

would drive to school and then I would go back to the club at night to teach again or work out. My exercise focus was becoming an addiction. But the addiction wasn't all bad; when I worked out, I felt more confident in the company of sophisticated women like Christy. The endorphins also gave me a respite from the occasional panic I felt about school; I wanted to get good grades and show my family that I could graduate with honors, which I eventually did.

The fitness-conscious fashions of the time now look ridiculous, but back then we Manhattan Club girls were on the cutting edge of cool. In class we wore Brazilian-cut or thong leotards with tights that went to mid-thigh or just below the knee, scrunchies, and high ponytails. The scrunchy color always matched the leotard. Everything on our bodies was spandex. You couldn't tell where the sweat began and the spandex ended.

Because of Christy, several of my aerobics students, all of them older than me, were cheerleaders for the L.A. Clippers or L.A.

Lakers. Christy was dating Johnny Buss, son of legendary Los Angeles Lakers owner and real estate magnate Jerry Buss. Jerry Buss had created the first NBA cheerleader squad with the Laker Girls in 1979, and by the mid-eighties they had become internationally famous—the Dallas Cowboys Cheerleaders of basketball. Their former choreographer Paula Abdul introduced more provocative, sophisticated moves, putting her stamp on professional cheerleading—and music videos—for the next thirty years and counting. Johnny Buss was very close to Paula Abdul and had dated her, and I kept hoping that one day she would stop by the club.

My cheerleader aerobics students loved to gossip about the players they were dating; this was before the days of no-fraternization policies. I was intrigued by these women's exciting, glamorous love lives, but while I admired the girls, I felt much younger than them and didn't consider myself one of them. I was focused on work and my studies. During my five years in California I didn't go on one date, make out with, or sleep with a man. I didn't see myself as a single woman; I saw myself as a college student. I was afraid of the big, urban dating world and the dangers that casual sex could bring: pregnancy and STDs.

That didn't mean I didn't have fun. I roller-skated up and down the Strand in my bright neon pink bikini and tan leather roller skates with hot pink wheels, listening to my Walkman. I laid out and sunbathed, watching the guys on the Association of Volleyball Professionals tour, which had just started. I was more comfortable watching men than interacting with them. Sometimes I watched the way they watched other girls on the beach. I saw the way they turned into panting dogs when an attractive woman passed by.

When men smiled at me or tried to engage in conversation, I kept it short or skated away. And I am not being overly modest when I say that compared to the other women on the Strand, this bony college student was no great shakes in the looks department. They were in their twenties and thirties, with tight, tan skin, fake boobs, and thong bathing suits with rock-solid butts. I couldn't have competed with them if I had tried.

On the beach by the Strand, showing off a newly toned body

Christy often watched me teach aerobics and saw that I had some rhythm. With her encouragement, I decided to try out to be on the L.A. Clippers Spirit Dance Team. I felt out of my league but flattered that she thought I was good enough to try out. In preparation for my audition, Christy showed me how to do my makeup (bold) and hair (high). I began to fantasize about making it onto the team.

The auditions were on the football field of Los Angeles Memorial Coliseum, where the 1984 Summer Olympics had been held. I wore my thong leotard with panty hose underneath. On the field there were about eighty beautiful girls, and I felt gauche and out of place. Here were all these sophisticated, knockout native Los Angelenos, and squeezed between them was little Laura Vikmanis from the Ohio cornfields, with stringy hair and flat boobs.

We all lined up and learned a routine, rotating so the judges could get a good look at each line. There was more head-flipping and hip-grinding than I was used to in Dance Theater Dayton. We had to learn the dance in minutes. After one round, the coaches read off the numbers of the girls who would stay. When I didn't hear mine, I was disappointed but not surprised.

My roommate in Hermosa Beach was named Melissa. She was sophisticated and from Manhattan Beach and she was dating one of the guys on the national volleyball team. She was a 1980s fashionista, and wore capri pants, shirts with oversized shoulder pads, and pouffy hair. One night she and a group of her friends took me to a party a few blocks from the beach. People were drinking and smoking pot and going off into rooms where I was certain they were snorting coke. I remembered my rebellious year in eighth grade, the drinking, black beauties, Sopors, and losing my virginity. I felt as though I had dodged a bullet when I gave it all up and got back into dance. Now I felt like I had to dodge another bullet.

It says something about my state of mind at the time that when I watched the young people at the party drinking beer, my first thought was, *Don't they know that a Bud has 145 calories?* I thought that if I drank two beers, I would not only get fat (immediately) but I would become an alcoholic. Beer might be my gateway drug to even harder drugs, the kind that people were doing in the back rooms. I could become an addict and wind up on the street. I was raised Presbyterian but I had the punitive mind-set of a Catholic.

My reaction was not completely irrational; whenever I thought of my dad, I saw him with a beer in his hand. And even if I would not have used the term aloud, I understood that I had an addictive personality because of the way I exercised, compulsively and even masochistically.

At the party with Melissa, I sat in a corner nursing one bottle of beer the entire night. When we finally left, I was relieved. I didn't go out with her again. It wasn't long before she moved out. I saw my choices in terms of extremes. I could abuse my body or improve it. I could be with bad people or good ones. Girls who went to parties were bad. Girls who did aerobics were good.

But teaching aerobics didn't earn me a living and as the end of college approached, I became apprehensive about my future. I hadn't realized when I decided to major in dietetics that it was one of the lowest-paying occupations in the country, partly because dietitian services in hospitals were so poorly reimbursed by insurance companies. Though they provided crucial preventive care and lowered healthcare costs in the long run, dietitians were (and still are) almost all women and weren't valued by the male medical establishment. I was worried that I wouldn't be able to support myself in expensive Los Angeles on a dietitian's salary. I was also concerned about the one-year internship I would have to do in order to become a registered dietitian. The programs in L.A. were famously competitive, and because I didn't have a lot of hospital volunteer experience or professional connections, I had doubts that I would be accepted into one.

I soon found the answer to all of my problems. His name was Brian Robb.

In the fall of my senior year I went back home to celebrate my twenty-second birthday. On September 10, 1990, I went out with Renee to a bar called George Newcom's Tavern in the Oregon District near the University of Dayton. A clean-cut guy came up next to me and offered to buy me a beer. He looked a few years older and he said his name was Brian. He looked at me very intently when he talked to me. He was from Dayton, too. When I said I was from Kettering but going to college in California, he was impressed. I liked the way it felt to be a big-time girl in a small-time town.

All night he remained focused on me and I soaked up the attention. My whole life I had felt like Lisa's little sister. But to this new man, I was the center of the world.

I never thought he was particularly handsome and didn't feel the kind of tingle you get when you're attracted to someone, but this didn't concern me. The attention he gave me was a different kind of high, not sexual but just as powerful.

Brian told me he worked in computer programming for a software company. With his technical job and overconfidence he reminded me a little of my father. He had bought his own house with money he had gotten from selling a computer game to RadioShack, and I was enormously impressed. He seemed like he had made something of himself at a young age. We went out again the next night and he was just as focused on me. I flew back to California wondering if I had met the man I was going to marry.

On my flight back I was exhausted because I had been out late every night on my trip. I was starting to drift off but the man in the seat next to me, a burly guy in his fifties, was chatty. I kept trying to indicate that I wanted to go to sleep, but he wanted a conversation partner. "You from Cincinnati or Los Angeles?" he asked.

"Cincinnati."

"You a football fan?"

"My family is. I follow it a little."

"How can you only follow it a little?"

"If you want to know the truth, I don't really understand it. It's fun to watch but I don't understand the rules." He frowned as though he was sad for me that I was missing out on something so wonderful. Football fans are like the newly devout; they want to bring the gospel to everyone.

"How can you not understand?" he said. "It's easy." I was shaking my head but he was already drawing a football field on his cocktail napkin. "So one team has the ball, see?" he said. "That team is called the offense. The other team is the defense."

"Yeah, I get that part," I said.

"The two teams meet at the center of the field. That's the fifty-yard line. After they meet, the offense has four tries to advance the ball at least ten yards. Each try is called a down." I had never understood that a "down" was a "try." A lightbulb went on in my blond head.

"If the offense doesn't advance ten yards or more after those four tries," he continued, "the defense gets the ball back. If the offense advances ten yards or more on any of their tries, they get another four tries. If they score a touchdown, they get six points. Then they get another chance to score by kicking the ball between the goal posts. If it goes in, they get one more point. If it doesn't, they just get the six."

"What's that extra point called?"

"An extra point. Then there's defense. The defense has one job, to prevent the offense from scoring. If the defense catches the ball—that's an interception—they can run the other way with it into the opponent's end zone and score themselves."

After five minutes, I understood the basic rules of football. From that night on, when I saw a game on TV, I didn't flip the channel the way I used to. I am a football fan today all because of my seatmate on a September 1990 flight from CVG to LAX.

Back in California, Brian called every day, saying things like, "I miss you so much." "I can't wait to see you again." "I want to be with you forever." I was on cloud nine. No man had talked to me the way he did. I felt like I was doing the drugs I had avoided at that party in Hermosa Beach. I felt the same exuberance I experienced teaching aerobics in a leotard and tights in front of a dozen women. I didn't do drugs or drink a lot but in Brian I discovered a new addiction to go along with my addiction to exercise. I was addicted to being loved.

He came to visit me in Hermosa Beach twice that fall and I introduced him as my boyfriend, despite the fact that he courted me almost entirely over the phone. I began to form a plan in my head, the same way I had formed a plan to lose the weight after my father made his comment, the same way I had formed a plan to go to school in California. Order conquered fear. I would apply for a dietetics internship in Ohio. The ones in Ohio were not as competitive as the ones in Los Angeles and I was certain I would be accepted. Brian was crazy about me and I could tell it was going in a serious direction.

At Christmas I went back to Dayton and met Brian's parents. They seemed stable and kind. His mom had always been a housewife. I found out later that she went to Brian's house every week to do his laundry and buy his groceries. I didn't yet know that he was looking for a wife who would take on that same role.

One night Brian and I were in his house, the big yellow one where he would one day lock me in a room. We were about to go out when he sat on the bed, opened a ring box, and said, "Will you marry me?" We hadn't known each other four months yet, and our relationship had evolved mainly over the phone. I was surprised. But I felt a click, the click of knowing that things were going according to plan. Brian was my escape hatch, my escape from the uncertainty of where to live and how to support myself on a dietitian's salary.

My mother had had her parents to take care of her, but she didn't have the kind of money her parents had so I couldn't lean on her, and I knew I couldn't rely on my father. I needed a husband with enough earning potential to support a wife and kids. I would marry Brian, raise children with him, and stay with him forever. Unlike my dad or "Except your legs" Joel, Brian would always have time for me. I said yes, feeling a little nervous that it was all happening so fast, but not wanting to have it fall apart by saying no. Afraid of ruining the moment, I wound up ruining my life.

The engagement ring was a marquise and looked big at first, but later, when I turned it on its side it looked thin and cheap. The night I got engaged I stared down at that ring on my finger, and saw only its big face. I had the idealism of a girl who had grown up in an intact family, at least for a while, and the codependence of a girl who always missed her father. I viewed my time in California, teaching at the club, auditioning to be a Clippers cheerleader, roller-skating on the Strand, as my college years. Now I was beginning my adult years. Time to get real.

A thousand times in the ensuing years I have lain awake at night wondering why I didn't say no when Brian proposed, or "Not yet." Wondering why I didn't try dating other men—or even dating Brian a little bit longer—before I made the choice to marry him. A thousand times I have replayed the night we met, imagining every variation of how it could have played out differently so that I didn't meet Brian. If only my back had been turned when he came in to Newcom's Tavern and he hadn't seen me. If only Renee and I had gone to a different bar. If only we had come two hours earlier, or later. If only I had met some other guy back in California after I returned. But none of those things happened. I walked into Newcom's Tavern and a man started talking to me and everything changed. We were on a collision course.

When I told my mother that Brian and I had gotten engaged, she was concerned. "But you're only twenty-two," she said. "Why do you have to marry him? Can't you just date him awhile and then decide?" She had been married at twenty-one and was thinking that I was about to go down the same path she had been on, giving herself over to someone else, putting her own needs aside.

I saw her doubt as a challenge. "I love Brian and Brian loves me," I said. I could not make people notice me by being outrageous like Lisa or brilliant like my dad or sexy like Christy Curtis Buss or Paula Abdul, but I could make people notice me by having a big, beautiful wedding.

I flew back to Los Angeles with an engagement ring on my finger, thinking I had it made. I would finish my last semester, move back to Ohio, and marry Brian Robb. My life was about to begin.

THE GASOLINE CAKE

DURING THE LAST SIX MONTHS OF SCHOOL I WAS OBSESSED WITH planning my wedding. While finishing my course work, I organized everything—bridesmaids, invitations, floral arrangements, the menu—almost as though I had left the state already. My father agreed to pay for the wedding but I had to call him or my stepmother, Chris, to ask approval for every expense. But he let me invite a hundred fifty people and the costs went up until they totaled $25,000, which was about as much as he had spent on my entire college tuition.

I was the first in my circle of Dayton friends to marry. I had already won admiration as the bold, brave one who had gone out to California for college, and now I was the first to wed. I relished the attention that my wedding brought me. I spent far more time thinking about that night than about the man I would be with once the reception was over. Lisa was working for Aunt Max's company, but she was single and spent her free time running around and having fun with her friends. Even though I was younger, I felt like the mature, sensible sister.

In the summer of 1991, in the thick of my wedding planning, Brian and I went to see the Arnold Schwarzenegger movie *Termi-*

nator 2: Judgment Day. It starred Linda Hamilton as Sarah Connor. She wore a black tank top with no bra and she had incredible biceps and knew how to use an assault rifle. I was reminded of Heidi from the yogurt chain. I wanted biceps like that and those cool, round Matsuda sunglasses. I thought about my dad, who used to point out women with big biceps admiringly. In the car after the movie I told Brian that Linda Hamilton looked amazing. "Women shouldn't look like men," he said. In one way at least, I had not married my father.

It was small, but one of many clues I got leading up to my wedding that Brian and I were nothing alike. Later that summer Brian and I went out with Renee and her boyfriend, Ted, to a bar in Covington, Kentucky, about an hour away from Dayton. It was a dance club barge on the Ohio River, with a view of Cincinnati. I was drinking beer and Brian had Sea Breezes. A disco ball spun around. The speakers blared the music of that era—Tone Loc, Madonna, Vanilla Ice, MC Hammer, C+C Music Factory, and Marky Mark and the Funky Bunch. As Brian drank more over the course of the night, he got meaner, his sulk deepening. The four of us were on the dance floor and Brian thought I was flirting with a guy. He started yelling at me, and before I knew it he shoved me down on the floor. A group of men pulled him off me. A few police officers appeared and then Brian was gone, being escorted out by the cops.

I was shocked, horrified, and scared. We went to the police station in Covington and they said he had to stay there overnight. I was told to get him in the morning. I was afraid he would be angry with me when he got out, as though somehow I had caused his arrest.

Renee, Ted, and I drove back to Dayton in silence, the excitement felt on the way to the bar completely lost now. I didn't call my mother or sister. I went to bed alone in the big yellow house, thinking about my wedding less than two months away. I didn't know if this incident was a red flag or typical male misbehavior. My invitations had gone out and we had booked a hotel in downtown Dayton. I had taken such pride in having graduated college, snagged a successful man with a nice house and an impressive job, and gotten engaged, all by the age of 22. In my traditional Midwestern world that meant a woman had Made It. I couldn't ruin everything by canceling my wedding.

So I told myself that what happened that night was a one-time thing. Brian had gotten drunk. Guys got drunk and did stupid things all the time. I had to let it pass. I buried the memory deep inside me until the night he locked me in the room, when it came crashing back.

In the morning I drove to Covington and picked up Brian at the police station. On the car ride back he said the police had blown everything out of proportion. The way he talked about it, it was as though he had merely tapped me on the shoulder and cops had appeared. I nodded silently. Even after he had been arrested he couldn't admit what he had done. It was the beginning of a pattern of denial that would last for many years.

Soon after the incident, Renee said that she thought I was making a mistake. She had thought I was going to call it off but then it became clear that I wasn't going to. "Are you sure you want to do this?" she said. "Marriage is forever."

"I know it is," I told her. "I love him and I'm marrying him. Do you have any idea how many people we've invited? This is happening, Renee!"

Later she told me that she figured I would talk to my mom and sister if I had real reservations. She didn't want to be the naysayer in my group of friends. But privately she never grasped what I saw in him. She didn't realize the extent of my need to be adored, so extreme that I was willing to look away from the fact that the man who supposedly adored me had pushed me down on a dance floor.

Brian had been raised Catholic and we were marrying in a Catholic church. He had wanted me to become a Catholic but I refused. He also wanted me to change my last name to his. I liked my unusual Latvian name and wanted to keep it, but he had an old-fashioned mentality. As a compromise I suggested that I be Laura Vikmanis Robb but he said no. So I kept my middle name, Lynette, and became Laura Lynette Robb. I was slowly erasing myself. After we were married, when I went to the DMV and Social Security offices to file my name-change paperwork, I felt like I was visiting a morgue.

Because it was required for our ceremony, Brian and I took a pre-wedding class with one of the priests at his church. He gave us a personality quiz and when he read us our results, he shook his head gravely. It was not a look you wanted a priest to be giving you. "You two are going to have to work very hard to have a happy marriage," he said. It was another warning sign, but I chose to ignore this one, too.

I decided to wear my mother's wedding gown, a scoop neck silk dress with long sleeves and seed pearls. It cost a thousand dollars in 1961, a fortune. My mother was delighted that I wanted to wear it, and I felt that I was getting a chance to "fix" her marriage. We all want to fix the mistakes that our parents make and I was doing it in the most literal way. (Today my mother has the dress tucked away in her closet and says that nobody will ever wear it again.)

At the reception I danced with my dad. He was in fine form—sociable, happy, and charismatic. I felt like he was proud of me for having found Brian. At one point during the reception, unbeknownst to me, Renee's mother leaned over to her, looked at Brian and me, and murmured, "I wonder how long this one's going to last." While no one was bold enough to mention it before we walked down the aisle, everyone thought that Brian and I were wrong for each other.

Following tradition, after the wedding I wrapped the top layer of our cake to be saved for our first anniversary. It ended up in Brian's mom's freezer, in her garage. A year later when we got it out to eat it, it tasted like gasoline.

The first year of marriage Brian and I were so busy with work that we didn't see a lot of each other. I was doing my dietetics internship at Miami Valley Hospital and working long hours on rotation. I worked in the cardiovascular unit, the burn unit, and oncology unit, helping patients understand the importance of healthy eating. I gave them prescribed diets according to their illnesses. It was often exhausting but I took comfort in the fact that I was helping people.

Brian worked late every night at the software company and when he was home, he was always on his computer. I soon began to see his personality. When we were in public, he had harsh words for two kinds of people: provocatively dressed women and overweight people. "She looks like a slut," he would say, if we saw a woman in a low-cut blouse. If we saw a heavy person, he would say, "That is disgusting. What's wrong with him? Why can't he control himself?" He said this even though my mother was heavy and I was a dietitian. I explained that some people had metabolic problems and others emotional ones but he saw extra weight only as a weakness.

Like my father, he always thought he knew the right way to do things and would not hear another idea. For example, he said to me, "If you're going to get the oil changed, you need to go to Jiffy and not anywhere else." As a result of his cocksure attitude, I began to doubt my own ability to make even minor decisions.

It soon became clear that he did not feel he had to pitch in around the house at all. His mother had done everything for him and now he expected me to. "You need to help me," I told him. "I can cook dinner and do laundry but this is a big house and I can't take care of it all by myself."

"I'm working, too," he said. "I make more money. Figure it out." I wanted my own checking account but he insisted we combine our accounts. All my credit card accounts were joint as well. I was just like my mother in 1961 but it was 1991. And so, while working at the hospital, I was also lawn mower, garbage disposer, laundress, housekeeper, cook, shopper, and cleaner. I tried to make healthy dinners from recipes that I found in women's magazines, but he hated them because I didn't cook like his mom and I stopped putting effort into dinner.

It was during our first year of marriage that I started to see more of his temper. He called me names and chipped away at my self-esteem. I hoped we might be able to be tender to each other in bed to make up for the ugly fights, but that turned out not to be true. Our sex was always missionary and I never had an orgasm. I had never had one with a man but had hoped that would change in marriage.

As our first Christmas was approaching, I spent a lot of time thinking about what I would buy him. I picked out clothes and electronic gadgets. When Christmas night arrived, my present from him turned out to be a plastic picture frame with the sample photo still inside it. It symbolized everything that was wrong with us. It wasn't even the cheapness that bothered me. It was the thoughtlessness. This man did not love me.

And then one night he locked me in the bedroom. That night I slept in bed with him, as far away as I could so I didn't have to touch him. The next day was a Sunday. When I woke up, he said,

"I'm so sorry. I'm sorry I hurt you. I won't do it again. I promise. I love you, Laura. I want to make you happy. Do you want to go shopping?"

We went to the mall together. I tried on clothes in front of mirrors that displayed the pink welts on my neck and arms. He waited for me outside the dressing rooms and then paid for my clothes. Later that day he bought me a bouquet of red roses. He always tried to win me over with red roses, and I have hated them ever since. "I promise you," he said that night at dinner, "I will never hurt you again."

When he said that, it was both true and not true. Never again would he kick, scratch, or hit me. Instead he chose to abuse me with words and insults. Over the ensuing years he called me names every day. "Retard," "idiot," "cunt," "ugly," "dumb-ass." He called me those names for small things, like tracking snow into the house. Whenever I threatened to leave him, he said I was incapable of living on my own. He said no one else would want me. He said that without him I would be homeless.

In response to the rain of hurt I checked out. I was there but not there. On the phone he ended conversations with, "I love you," and I replied in a singsong, "Love you, too." We stopped kissing and did not kiss again for the rest of our marriage, during sex or any other time. When I saw other couples nuzzling, I felt as if I was watching a movie.

Here are some things that I did not do with Brian, not even once, after our first year of marriage:

> Go on a romantic getaway
> Put my hand on his at a restaurant and stare into his
> eyes
> Buy him a surprise present just to make him happy

Make him breakfast in bed

Snuggle on a Sunday morning

Read the paper together

Listen to music

Dance

Sit down on the couch and talk about our days

Even though Lisa and my mom both lived a few miles away, I saw them rarely and didn't tell them how bad it was with Brian. But I knew that my marriage wasn't normal and I needed help. One night, soon after he locked me in the bedroom, I fished out one of my old psychology textbooks. I looked up *abuse* in the index and came to a page called "The Cycle of Violence." It was a wheel showing the three stages: Tension-Building, Abusive Incident, Honeymoon. It explained that conflict escalates until there is an incident of abuse, after which the abuser makes excuses, blames the victim, or tries to placate her. Then the incident is forgotten and there is a period of calm, the honeymoon. The chart said the victim doesn't understand that the honeymoon phase is part of the abuser's attempt to control her.

I got goose bumps. It was as though the author had been spying on Brian and me. I had always seen our honeymoon phases—our trips to the mall or dinners out—as signs that things would change. Over and over again I believed there would be no more name-calling or fighting. Now I was learning something different: Brian was trying to control me. He was my abuser and I was his victim.

But as soon as I put the book away I began to question what I had read. The chart had described physical abuse, not verbal. If he wasn't hitting me, could I call it abuse? Was name-calling wrong? Was name-calling even abuse? Were insults? He had fits around his parents, too, and they would just tell him to calm down. Maybe that was what I was supposed to do.

Brian and I eventually stopped socializing with other couples and Renee and I drifted apart. I passed my dietetics exam and began to work full time at the hospital, using work as an escape from Brian. I also used exercise. I became a Jazzercise instructor and busied myself with classes in church basements. I was comfortable in a leadership role with women but at home with Brian I was meek.

In front of the TV I did fitness videos like "Abs of Steel," "Buns of Steel," and "Arms of Steel." When I worked out, I didn't think about Brian and his hate for me. I felt the control I didn't have over my marriage, my feelings, my loneliness, and the intractability of my situation. Exercise allowed me to forget, for an hour, that I was imprisoned in that yellow house with a man who hated me but who I couldn't yet bring myself to leave.

In 1994 my father was diagnosed with a very rare form of skin cancer. By the time he and Chris called to tell me about it, it had already spread to his lymph nodes. In his typical tough-guy fashion, he wasn't gloom-and-doom on the phone. He said, "I'm going to get treatment. We're going to do whatever we can to beat this." Having worked in the oncology ward at the hospital, I knew his cancer would most likely kill him. I felt worried for him and the pain he would endure. I was losing him again, as I had many times before: when we moved to Kettering after my parents' divorce, when he married Chris, when Eric was born. It got me thinking about my own future and my own mortality.

During my last year of college Grandma Colleen had been diagnosed with kidney cancer. She received multiple rounds of chemotherapy. In the fall of 1994 she moved back home for hospice care. Grandma took morphine for her pain and became mostly unresponsive. One day, just before Thanksgiving, my mom called me. "Grandma is alert and oriented," she said. "Her nurse forgot to put a morphine patch on her. Come over and say goodbye." Lisa, my aunts and uncles, mom, cousins, and I all went over. I do not remember where Brian was, but the fact that he was not there says something about the state of our intimacy.

We each went in and had our time with her. She had a huge picture window with a bird feeder right outside so she could see them. That day the sky was super blue and it seemed as if every bird on earth came to that window. Grandma couldn't talk but was sitting up, trying to communicate. She held my hand and squeezed it and I talked about her birds.

She died later that night, with my mom and me by her side. In the living room, as my mother began to make funeral arrangements, I thought about my relationship with Brian. I felt like he was my family and I hadn't been treating him like family. I had given up on him even though I wasn't leaving. He still called me names but at least he hadn't hit or kicked me again. Grandma hadn't lived long enough to see me have a child, and I couldn't bear the thought of my mother dying before she had grandchildren. *I can do this*, I told myself. *I made my bed and I have to lie in it. Maybe when Brian and I have kids it'll be better.*

Soon after that I went off the pill but our sex was so rare, about once or twice a month, that it took a year to get pregnant. We never had a formal conversation about starting a family because there was no communication in our relationship. In the spring of 1996 we conceived a child. I didn't find out if it would be a boy or a girl because I wanted to be surprised. Just as my wedding had been an escape from L.A., my child would be an escape from the ugliness of my marriage. I began fantasizing about how different things would be when I had the baby. Once Brian and I had this child, we would fall back in love with each other. He would become the kind, doting, committed husband I had been seeking all along.

Brian didn't come to my ob-gyn visits with me, but he did come to childbirth classes, where I looked around at the other excited couples, the husbands kindly stroking their wives' bellies, and felt like I was the only one who was unhappily married. My mother and Lisa complimented my new, curvy figure, but Brian said things like, "Your body looks so weird."

Throughout my pregnancy I did my exercise videos, jogged, and watched my eating. My breasts got bigger, growing into healthy B cups. By the end of the pregnancy I had gained the recommended amount of weight, about twenty-five pounds, but no more. I was relieved because I had worried that the hormones would make me gain much more. I was looking forward to running more often, once I had the baby, so I could get in shape again.

One weekend morning in December when I was nine months pregnant, Brian and I were driving to get bagels. (I always drove because it made me nervous when he drove; he had a poor attention span.) A man coming toward us in his car had an epileptic fit, crossed the median, and careened into us, totaling our car. The airbag went off in my face. When I came to, I saw my lipstick smeared on the airbag about as big as an apple. My belly was cramping. I clutched it, terrified. Was the baby all right? Had it lived? Brian moaned, "Oh, my back! My back!" He didn't look over to see how I was or ask about the baby.

Searing pain shot through my knee. When I started to talk, my voice was a whisper. I opened the door and tried to stand to get help but it felt like my knee was broken and I sat back down. I realized I was having contractions. A police officer came, and ambulances. The ambulances took us to different hospitals because I was pregnant. I was relieved not to have to be with Brian one more second. I stayed overnight. The doctors stopped my contractions and when they said that the baby was fine, I was so happy I started to cry.

I had sprained my clavicle, shattered my left kneecap, and cut the right one. The doctors put a sling on my arm, a soft cast on my left knee, and stitches in my right knee. I was afraid the doctors were wrong and my baby would come out dead. Because of my knee, I couldn't be on my feet in the hospital. I had to quit work and stop exercising. My perfect pregnancy and postpregnancy fitness plan was falling to pieces and I was devastated. For the next two weeks, as I waited for the baby to come, I sat on the couch in the basement, growing more bloated and depressed, constantly feeling my belly for signs of life.

My due date was New Year's Day, 1997. On December 23, 1996, my mother drove me to my OB appointment. As soon as the nurse took my blood pressure, she laid me down, turned the

After the car accident, recovering before giving birth

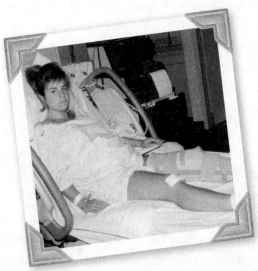

lights off, and told me to be quiet. She could tell that I had pre-eclampsia. The nurse got the doctor on the phone. He said, "Laura needs to go to the hospital now to have this baby by Cesarean."

"What are you talking about?" I said. I wanted a safe delivery but I was afraid of surgery. "I'm not having a C-section. I am not having this baby till January first."

We drove to the hospital and I was hooked up to the monitor and an IV. The OB came in. My blood pressure had gone down a little. "Please just wait till tomorrow," I said, sobbing. "If the baby isn't born by tomorrow, you can do it."

"I'll give you one more night," he said, "but I'm coming in at eight o'clock tomorrow morning and if your blood pressure hasn't returned to normal, we will have this baby."

At midnight I went into labor. The next morning Brian came, along with my mom and Lisa. Everyone wanted to be at the hospital for the birth and they were all off work because it was Christmas Eve. I labored throughout the day. I remember Brian being in and out of the room, which was fine with me, because I needed the labor nurses more than I needed him. I finally pushed out a baby girl around four o'clock. As soon as she came out, they whisked her away—it turned out her Apgar score was low—but when they brought her back they said she was fine. Despite all the odds, I had given birth to a healthy baby.

I had chosen the Latvian name Marija (pronounced like Maria) for a girl, in honor of my father's heritage, and surprisingly Brian hadn't put up a fight about it. While recovering in the hospital, I felt a strange new sense of pride in myself and my body. Before the birth, my feelings about my body had been those of self-loathing, fear of obesity, and fear of losing control. Now my body had delivered a baby, just the way it was meant to. Maybe the reason I had been born with those short, muscular thighs was so they could support a baby in the belly above them. Lisa, who had gotten married a few months before, had always said she never wanted children. I was supposed to carry on my family lineage so that Lisa could raise horses and race cars.

A few weeks after I came back from the hospital the doorbell rang. Carrying Marija and still wearing my leg cast, I opened the door to find a policeman there. He saw the baby in my arms and said, his voice choking up, "I cannot believe that baby is alive." It turned out he had been the first police officer on the accident scene and had seen it all: the totaled car and the hugely pregnant woman in the driver's seat behind the airbag. He was certain I had lost the baby and had come by to check on me. I was moved by his incredible kindness, and at the same time I felt hollow and sad. Here was this man who had come to my door to see if my baby had survived—when my own husband had been worried only about his own back.

I saw a wedding ring on the officer's hand. His wife was lucky to have him. How had some other woman wound up with this man when I had wound up with Brian? I hobbled back upstairs with my baby on my shoulder, wishing I could run off with the cop.

THE BIG CHECKBOOK

WHEN MARIJA WAS FOUR MONTHS OLD, THE SOFTWARE COMPANY that Brian worked for transferred him to Atlanta. I had taken my maternity leave and when it became clear that we were definitely going to move I quit. We sold the big yellow house and built a new house in a suburb of Atlanta called Roswell. I became obsessed with blueprints, tile, flooring, and cabinetry. It gave me something to focus on besides the routine of new motherhood and allowed me to believe that if the outside of a marriage—the money, the house—looked good then it meant the inside was all right, too.

If I had hoped that childbirth would improve my marriage, I was wrong. Fatherhood did not change Brian one bit. He now had a new excuse to work all the time—the added financial responsibility of a baby. He complained about changing diapers, he didn't throw in a load of laundry even during the perilous early weeks, and he wouldn't get up to tend to Marija in the middle of the night. That bothered me the most—Marija didn't latch on to the breast properly and was taking breast milk in a bottle, which meant that Brian could have fed her as easily as I did. As much as

I enjoyed the long nights, going into her room and feeding her in the moonlight, I felt like a single mother.

Despite the fact that I lost most of my pregnancy weight quickly, Brian often called me fat. He knew that body image was a sensitive issue for me. His new nicknames for me were "fat" and "useless," which was a funny one because unlike him, I was taking care of a baby all day and night. While my mother had put on weight to cover up her sad feelings, I put on big clothes to cover up mine. In Atlanta my outfit was the same every day: solid color baggy polo shirt, long khaki shorts, and tennis shoes. Everything was at least a size too big. I didn't want what lay underneath the clothes to be seen.

Our subdivision in Roswell reminded me of my family's neighborhood in West Bloomfield during the 1970s. The only difference was the size of the houses, which were fake Southern-style McMansions. One neighbor was completely addicted to *Gone with the Wind* and had decorated her basement like Tara, right down to the drapes. The men were Delta pilots, engineers, and doctors. The women were stay-at-home moms who socialized by playing Bunko, hosting progressive dinners, or joining the tennis team. Our house was spacious and expensive and would have been idyllic if it were filled with happy people, but instead it was just another huge prison.

One night Brian and I had company to dinner, a few other couples. We were all sitting around the living room chatting. There was a lull in the conversation and Brian leaned forward, pointed to my varicose veins, and said, "Laura, what is that on your leg?" I had developed the veins during pregnancy and they bulged out, dark and ugly. He knew that I was embarrassed by them, but here he was mocking me in front of our dinner guests. I was humiliated. He reminded me of the mean girl in high school who would tell a girl her hair wasn't brushed or her clothing didn't match. Beyond being embarrassed for myself, I was embarrassed for him. He had made himself look crazy in front of our friends. The guests looked around uncomfortably. I slipped out into the kitchen to get away.

After I had Marija, our sex life got worse. Sometimes I pretended to be asleep so he wouldn't touch me. When sex was over I felt relief that it would be a few more months before I had to do it again. With my joyless sex life I was convinced the problem was me. I went to the ob-gyn and he asked what I was using for birth control. I said I wasn't having sex very often. "Something's wrong with me," I said. I started crying. "I feel nothing in bed. I have no desire."

"Maybe you're depressed," he said. "You can go on a low dose of medication and it might make you feel better."

On the drive home I thought about it. I knew Brian wouldn't approve of antidepressants, and I also had the perverse fear that if they made me feel better, I might want to leave him. If I left him, I thought, I would have to go on food stamps or live in the street. I was living in a strange new city and my family was far away, so I didn't have a safety net. Brian had been telling me for years that I couldn't make it without him and I believed him. I had not returned to work, even part-time, since we moved to Roswell, and my darkest fear was that if I got divorced my kids would be in day care—as though day care was the worst possible ill that could befall a child. It all sounds ridiculous now, I know.

Though I was afraid of pills, I was open to talk therapy. When Brian came home that night after my ob-gyn visit, I said, "I think I'm depressed. I want to go into therapy. It might help me to talk to someone."

"Only weak people go to therapists," he said. I didn't agree but there was nothing I could do without my own money. Brian had me on a $2,000-a-month allowance for every single expense, and if I went over, I had to explain to him exactly why, just like a child would to a parent. I understood that my husband's unwillingness to pay for therapy was part of the reason I needed to be in therapy, but for the short term, at least, I was stuck.

Instead of seeing a therapist, I relied on my good friend Elene for support. She was a husky-voiced, brunette nutritionist turned stay-at-home mom who had recently moved from Connecticut to our subdivision. She was married to a DEA agent named Bob who traveled frequently and she had two babies, the older one just nine months older than Marija. The two of us would push our strollers around the neighborhood and complain about our uninvolved husbands. "He comes home at nine," I would say, "and I'm trying to bathe and feed Marija and he just waits for me to make him dinner. He can't even make himself a sandwich."

"Just let him wait," she would say.

"He says his job is to make money and my job is to take care of the kids and the house."

"You should call him the Big Checkbook," she said. I laughed. From then on whenever we talked about him we would refer to him as the Big Checkbook.

To make time pass, we often drove with the kids to the mall to shop. Elene liked designer bargains for herself, but most of my splurges were at Gymboree, for kids' clothes. I wasn't interested in adorning myself because I had lost touch with my body. I didn't want sexual attention from Brian or any other men because I was so depressed.

Elene and I often went to a Gold's Gym that had child care. I went there more to get to know Elene than to exercise; I walked on the treadmill, I didn't run. Elene worked with a trainer but I couldn't afford it. I failed to consider the possibility that real, vigorous exercise might improve my mood. When it was time for us to fetch our children, we would walk very slowly to the child care room to stretch out our limited period of freedom.

I told Brian several times how miserable I was. "This marriage isn't working," I said. "I need some time for myself. I need you to help me more with the kid and the housework. If things don't change, we're headed for a divorce."

His face would get red and he would explode, "Don't say the D-word! I can't believe you're saying that! Do you want to ruin the family?" He didn't want to know why I was unhappy or what he could do to make things better. It was as though the mention of divorce could make it happen, and he was too traditional to consider it.

To console myself about my unhappy marriage I turned to food. Oreos, processed-cheese sandwiches, Ben & Jerry's New York Super Fudge Chunk—not foods a registered dietitian should be eating on a daily basis. Unlike my teenaged years, there was no extreme exercise after my little binges to wipe away the calories; my treadmill walks didn't burn anything off. I didn't care what I looked like or what I put into my body. I kept a one-pound bag of peanut M&Ms in the house and nibbled on them when I felt sad, sometimes consuming eight hundred calories a day in M&Ms alone. I had given up on cooking, also embarrassing for a dietitian. I ate with the baby, simple food like pasta and steamed vegetables, and left Brian frozen food or a sandwich at night. One of my greatest regrets, even today, is that I am not a confident cook, because I still associate meal preparation with rejection.

One night when Marija was about twelve months old and weaning off breast milk, Elene and some of the other Roswell mothers organized a progressive dinner. Brian and I went. Cou-

ples went from house to house, eating different courses and socializing. Between my pregnancy and the pumping I had not had an
alcoholic beverage in two years, but that night I ended up drinking
a lot of wine. My system wasn't used to it and I came home drunk.
Brian and I had sex. In the morning I could barely remember it.
He told me he pulled out but nine months later I had Courtney. I
had always dreamed of having two children but because my marriage was so troubled, when I told Elene I was pregnant, I said it
like I had contracted a disease.

With two children under two I yelled. When Brian heard me
lash out he would say, "You yell at the kids a lot. You're a bad
mother." But he still didn't offer to help me or take them.

Despite my occasional flare-ups, for the most part I loved
stay-at-home motherhood. It satisfied me in a way marriage had
not. I was able to nurse Courtney and was relieved to have the
closeness of breast-feeding after not having been able to breast-
feed Marija. I read books on child rearing, thinking about how to
deal with the different phases and challenges. I fed them well and

*My girls were the best
thing in my life.*

Courtney, like her sister, slept through the night by three months old. It helped that I could do everything on my own terms and didn't have to consult Brian; the only upside to having an uninvolved husband is that you have total autonomy when it comes to how you raise your kids.

Brian was not wholly absent as a father. He was loving with the girls, not contemptuous of them the way he was with me. We had a swing set in the back of the house and he would go out with them and push them on it. We went to the community pool together and he splashed around with them, but I never let him take them to the pool without me because I was afraid he wouldn't watch them closely. I could not relinquish control even though my need for it was keeping me imprisoned. When Brian came in at night he kissed them hello, engaged them for about half an hour, and soon disappeared into his home office to work on his computer. When one of them misbehaved he would get officious, very Ward Cleaver, but he didn't know what time they went to bed or what shelf the pajamas were on.

After we had been in Atlanta for four years, Brian's company transferred him to Austin. It had a thriving music scene on Sixth Street and would have been a great city for someone like me, who had once loved to dance to live music, but I was so consumed by child care that I could have been living in any small town in America. I was in a pop cultural void, like a prisoner or someone in a cult.

But I was desperate for companionship and to make friends and build some independence for myself. I soon got involved with a direct-sales home decor company called Southern Living at HOME. I didn't like the shabby hand-me-down furniture Brian and I had, and I thought that if I sold the Southern Living products, I could make enough money to buy better things, and at a discount. I was intimidated by the idea of selling products to strangers, but as I attended more sales demonstrations my confidence grew. I made new friends and started dressing differently—Talbots sweater sets instead of gym shirts. At my peak I made about one thousand dollars a month from the sales. Instead of saving for divorce, I spent all the money on clothing for the girls or new furnishings.

One year the company entered a partnership with an organization called Cut It Out, which trains hairdressers to recognize signs of domestic violence. A dime from every dollar of sales would go to Cut It Out, and at the end of our demonstrations, held in different women's homes, we would make an announcement about Cut It Out. Every time I had to make the announcement I started to sweat. I worried that the women would figure out that I was in an emotionally abusive marriage. If they did, how would I explain why I was staying? I didn't know the answer myself.

Through Southern Living I earned enough points to go on a trip to the Bellagio in Las Vegas with the other consultants. My mom flew to Austin to take care of Marija and Courtney while I was gone, because Brian was working. At the hotel my bed was so comfortable and soft that I laid in it for an hour when we first checked in. It was my first overnight without my children in five years. I did not call home for three days because I knew my mom would call me if she needed to. I wanted a break from motherhood and marriage.

One night the Southern Living ladies and I went to *Jubilee!*, the long-running Las Vegas showgirls show, with Bob Mackie costumes. At the behind-the-scenes tour I looked at the enormous headdresses and sparkly skirts and jewels and felt like I was in heaven. They reminded me of our costumes for the plays in Dance

Theater Dayton. They reminded me that women could choose to make a living as performers; they didn't have to marry men and live off them.

Part of the show turned out to be topless, but the production was so classy that I was transfixed. I remembered my own dreams for myself, my drill-team and dance-class days. Here were all these women who had probably started out just like me and now they were realizing their dreams, doing a glitzy show in Vegas while I was sitting in the audience with a bunch of housewives. Why wasn't I up onstage wearing a huge feather headdress? I felt like life was passing me by.

After September 11, 2001, the city of Austin imploded financially. The tech company Dell, which was based in Texas, had already begun laying off employees and Brian's company was downsizing, too. We began talking about moving to a smaller house in case he lost his job. I got in the habit of watching CNNfn. I had received eighty thousand dollars in a settlement after the car accident in Ohio and Brian had invested it all in stocks. One day as the markets were plummeting, I called him up. "Take my settlement money out," I said. "I can't take this anymore."

"It's already gone," he said, with a strange, knowing tone, as though I was silly for thinking he would protect my money. I felt betrayed. I couldn't believe he had been careless with money that wasn't even his. Now my rescue boat was gone.

That was a changing point in our marriage. The next time my mother came to Austin to visit she could see that things were different between Brian and me. I had stopped covering up for him. He would get upset about something silly and I wouldn't placate him or make excuses. I would say, "He's crazy" in an even, dull tone. She and I talked about how I had to get back home to Ohio. Though we weren't spelling it out I felt she understood that I needed her close in order for me to leave him.

I began my campaign to convince Brian that we needed to move. At first he was hesitant but I appealed to him on personal and financial grounds. "Your parents are getting older," I said. "They're going to need you close by. It's better for us to be near them." With the economy crashing and his job increasingly insecure, I said, "If we're going to have to buy a smaller house anyway, why not do it in Dayton, where we have family?" He was thinking about starting his own software company and I reminded him that he didn't need to be in Texas to do it.

Miraculously I convinced him. We sold the house in Austin and moved to Springboro, a suburb of Dayton, in August 2004. The girls were seven and five. I boxed up all our possessions while he was at work. His father and brother came down to help us. We hired movers to help us load but not drive so that we could save money. Brian's father and brother took off in two moving vans, Brian drove our Taurus by himself, and I drove our Expedition, with the girls inside it and a U-Haul trailer behind us. I was moving back to Ohio, back to my family, for the safety and support I knew they could provide, just as my mother had done nearly thirty years before. I was going to leave Brian. I just had to figure out how.

DESPERATE HOUSEWIFE

BACK IN DAYTON I STARTED WORKING PART-TIME AT THE HOSPITAL again, the same one I had worked in during the first years of my marriage. Even though the low income and part-time hours meant that I barely brought in ten thousand a year, it was my way of beginning to build something for myself financially. At the hospital, I was once again surrounded by a group of women dietitians. Some were the same women I had known a decade earlier. They were happily married and once in a while they would make sex jokes or talk about their husbands in a kind way: "You won't believe what Mike did on Mother's Day. He and the kids made me breakfast in bed and then he took them out and I went back to sleep." Or, "I was running late from work and Hank got all the grocery shopping done and had a spaghetti dinner ready when I came back." I would sit there silently in the hospital cafeteria listening to them, my mouth a thin line.

At night I watched a new television show called *Desperate Housewives*. I fell in love with Teri Hatcher's character, a plucky divorcee, but my favorite housewife of all was Eva Longoria, who was having an affair with a hot young gardener. I thought she was sexy and brave to be having an affair. When Brian would come in the family room and see me watching it he would say, "Why are you watching that? It's so trashy." He was beginning to suspect my own desperation.

We bought a Chihuahua named Penny so I could teach the kids about responsibility and caring for a pet. I had missed having a family pet but didn't want to get one until the girls were older and could help me. Penny was more like a cat than a dog and would sit in our laps and snuggle for a long time. When I was stressed about the future I would take Penny for long walks and when I came back, I felt calmer.

I started running as another way to clear my head. But there was an addictive quality to the running, too. I began to weigh myself every morning or after a long run, as hyperaware of my weight as I had been when I was a teenager. Alone and in crisis, I was in danger of reverting to the same compulsive attitude I had had toward exercise nearly twenty years before.

One day in the winter I met two women in the neighborhood who were also runners, Carmen and Aimir. They were training for the Dayton River Corridor Classic half-marathon in the fall of 2005 and I decided I would run it, too. We started going out together and they became like therapists to me. Carmen was going through a divorce and though it was difficult for her, I saw that women could survive the end of a marriage.

Sometimes when I ran alone, I would play out different scenarios in my mind. *Would you care if Brian dated someone else?* No. *Would you care if he got married?* No. *Would you care if he had more children with another woman?* No. *Would you care if he moved away?* No. *Is there anything about him that you would miss?* No. I would try the same game the next day to see if I had another answer, but the answer to all the questions was no, no, no.

All of the running led to the shedding of pounds. With a leaner body, I fantasized about getting breast implants; my breasts had gotten smaller from pregnancy and breast-feeding, and when I stood sideways in the mirror, they looked like Dutch clogs. But I had no money of my own to get surgery. Maybe someday I would.

I began dressing differently: in platform heels and cute jeans. After seven years of hiding my body and barely exercising, I felt like a turtle coming out of its shell. Sometimes I took the girls shopping with me. We'd go to the girls department of Macy's and get outfits for them and then to juniors for me, because the clothes fit me, they were sexy, and the prices were better than women's. In the dressing rooms we critiqued one another, pretending to be runway models. My girls were discovering the advantages of having a newly body-conscious mom. I moved my Talbots stuff to the back of the closet to make room for my hot clothes.

My mom and Lisa both worked for Aunt Max's company and they had a personal trainer who came to their office building to work with employees. Sometimes when he had free time he would train me for free. He was young and cute and I watched his eyebrows go up when I wore my new heels and jeans. We bantered when I worked with him and I realized that there were men who might be interested in dating me if I left Brian. Turns out I wasn't invisible to men. In September I ran the half-marathon and finished in decent time.

Our first fall in Springboro I had signed up Marija for the peewee cheer team at her school. The idea of third graders cheering was foreign to me, but I learned that modern-day cheerleading was a combination of tumbling, choreographed dances, and sideline, with serious citywide competitions. When I was growing up, cheering had nothing to do with gymnastics and very little to do with dancing. This was both. It was something new, a hybrid sport, and even though Marija was very young, I was impressed by the skill level. Girls who were really good at it and stuck with it could get cheerleading scholarships to college.

It turned out that there was an entire class of women who lived vicariously through their daughters' cheering: Cheer Moms. Many were former cheerleaders themselves and they wore T-shirts that said "Go Boro" (for Springboro) or "Cheer Mom" spelled out in rhinestones. They brought water bottles filled with marbles and shook them at competitions so their daughters' teams scored high on crowd involvement. I wanted them to like me. There were a couple of Cheer Moms who would drop off the kids to practice and return an hour early to watch and correct their daughters from the sidelines, which the coaches hated.

Despite the Cheer Moms, competitions, awards, and high level of skill, competition cheerleading was still a victim of its sexist past. None of the girls' athletic teams had cheerleaders—so girls were taught from a young age that girls cheer for boys, but no one cheers for girls. At the older levels, competition cheerleaders had to put in time to do sideline cheering in addition to their competitions, like a mother fixing dinner for her family after a hard day's work. I wondered if competition cheerleading would someday evolve from its sexist roots into a legitimate sport like gymnastics, with Title IX funding. It deserved to be considered a real sport, but I wasn't sure it would happen by the time my kids went to college.

During Easter 2006 I had one of those eureka moments when life veers off in a new direction. We had been living in Springboro for almost two years and I still hadn't taken any action to end the marriage. My old excuses about the girls being too young to be cared for just by Brian during his visitation time weren't true anymore. They were nine and seven now. My self-esteem was higher than it had been in Austin or Atlanta. I was happy to be living near Lisa and my mom, who were building close relationships with the girls, and I knew I could keep my job once I divorced. I was sitting at the table dyeing eggs with the girls, thinking about how I would have to hide the eggs myself and buy candy myself just like every other year. *Why am I so afraid of being a single mom?* I thought. *I've been a single mom this entire time.*

Lisa and my mom weren't surprised when I told them. They found me a divorce lawyer named Stevenson, a no-nonsense, gruff man with white hair. I went to see him before I said a word to Brian. "Can you tell me how divorce works exactly?" I asked. This was a new world to me and I wanted reassurance that Brian couldn't take the girls away from me.

"What's most common in the courts now," Stevenson said, "is shared custody and shared parenting time. Custody means decision-making power: educational, medical, and so on. Parenting time means how many nights the children stay with each parent. The dominant belief now is that children need time with both parents, especially as the children go through adolescence. Unless one parent has shown himself or herself to be grossly negligent, on drugs, or physically abusive, you'll probably get shared custody and shared parenting time."

I swallowed hard. I imagined Brian letting them ride in the front seat of the car. I had been with them virtually nonstop since they were born, and if I wanted a divorce, I had to accept that that would change. At the same time, I had a vision that divorce might force Brian to step up to the plate as a father. In the past he had practiced "learned helplessness." Without me around, he couldn't afford to be helpless. He would figure out how to fix the girls' dinner, get them to doctors' appointments, play with them, bathe them, and put them to bed. It wasn't rocket science.

"As for your assets," Stevenson continued, "they will be divided equally. Spousal and child support will be determined according to a formula based on the visitation schedule, your income and his, the number of years you have been married, and your employability. Since you have a degree in dietetics, the court will estimate how much you could reasonably make and factor that in to the spousal support that they award."

After that conversation, divorce no longer seemed foreign to me. I probably wouldn't wind up poor, and, according to Stevenson, it was unlikely that Brian would get sole custody. I had Stevenson draw up the papers but I didn't sign them. At his suggestion I took out extra cash in case a court froze the account. I knew my legal fees would be expensive but my mother had offered to lend me money to pay them.

One night a few weeks later, when the girls were in bed, I did the dishes and cleaned the family room. I sat watching TV for a while. Brian was downstairs in his office on the computer. I shut off the TV, went down to his office, and said, "I need to talk to you about something." I knew I was doing the right thing but I was nervous about how he would react. "I am so unhappy," I said, "and I don't want to be with you anymore. When the kids are older and gone, I just can't see us being together. We've grown apart and we don't know each other. I feel like this marriage is over."

His face got red. "What are you talking about?" he said. "This is crazy. Let's sit down and discuss this."

But then, almost immediately, he got upset. He seemed to be at war with himself, trying to determine how to respond. "What the fuck?" he said. "What are you doing? How can you be such a selfish bitch? Why are you doing this to me? You want the kids to grow up with divorced parents?" I had taken a huge strike at his huge ego. Despite our many obvious problems, our total lack of intimacy, and our mutual lack of respect, he apparently saw us as a perfect family—husband, wife, and two adorable kids. It was a dream that had existed only in his mind, but now that I was shattering it he was clearly frightened. He paced back and forth in his office, vacillating from hurt to anger over two hours. I was scared that he might hurt me, but he was in too much shock to do so just then.

"Where is this coming from, Laura?" he said. "You never told me you were unhappy."

"I've told you many times that I'm unhappy," I said angrily. "You don't seem happy either. This marriage hasn't worked in a long time. I'm going to the attorney on Friday to sign the papers."

That night I stayed up very late and slept in the guest room. Before I fell asleep I realized that from my wedding night until now, it had been fourteen and a half years. My marriage had lasted as long as my mother's. We had both married overconfident, domineering men, worn the same wedding dress, had two daughters two years apart, and now my marriage was crumbling at the same time hers had. We truly were cut from the same cloth.

The next morning when I woke up, Brian was gone. He never left before I woke up. Something was strange.

A day later I went out running and he followed me in my car. He gave me a hundred dollars and said, "Go buy yourself something," as though I might change my mind about getting divorced if only I bought some new clothes. I took the money and saved it because I knew I would need it. The next night he came home with an enormous shopping bag from the Hustler Hollywood store in Cincinnati, filled with porn videos, huge dildos, and vibrators. "I thought we might enjoy this," he said.

I looked at the bag. Beyond the fact that our sex life had never included any of these things, it was completely devoid of pleasure and fun. I laughed out loud at the idea that our miserable fourteen-year marriage could be repaired by the contents of this bag. "Are you kidding me?" I said. "You disgust me."

But when he asked if I would go to couples counseling, I agreed. He had been against the idea of my seeing a therapist in Atlanta, and now he was suggesting we see one together. It was like he was grasping at straws. I thought, *Too little, too late.* I knew I wasn't going to change my decision, but I was curious as to what the therapist might tell us. We sat there on a couch talking to him, and he said, "You two should have been in counseling years ago. Everyone waits till a marriage is already over and clearly this is already over." Brian was in shock. He didn't say anything but I could tell that the reality of the situation had set in. That was a huge moment for me: After only twenty minutes, an outside party had given our marriage a vote of no confidence.

Aside from that first night, we continued to sleep in the same bed. I was afraid of what he would do to me if I moved into the guest room. My hope was that when he finally accepted that it was over, he would move someplace temporary and I would have some peace while we went through the divorce.

It didn't work out like that.

One night I was putting the kids to bed around nine o'clock when the doorbell rang. They ran down to see who it was. I opened the door to find a sheriff. The girls were behind me and they were scared. I knew what was happening. "I'm so sorry to have to do this in front of your children," the sheriff said, handing me divorce papers. "You have to sign for them." He shook his head, looking at the girls. "This is really awkward," he said.

It turned out that after I had told Brian I wanted a divorce, probably the morning he had risen early, he had gone to his attorney to get the papers drawn up himself. The sheriff had been following me the whole day trying to serve me.

I remembered the way my parents had told Lisa and me that they were divorcing, sitting us down on that turquoise couch in West Bloomfield. Even in the midst of what was the bleakest period of their lives, they treated us with respect. In all the scenarios I had played out in which I told Brian I was leaving him, I had never imagined that the girls would find out about it from a sheriff coming to the door to serve me.

"What's going on?" the kids asked.

"Go upstairs," I said. "We'll talk about this later." I went into the family room where Brian was pacing back and forth. The girls followed.

"This is how you're going to do this?" I said to him. "You had to serve me in front of them?" The girls were standing behind me, begging to know what was happening. "Your dad and I aren't going to be together anymore," I said. They started to cry.

"I filed before you," he said, "and I'm going to get full custody. You're not going to get a dime of my money." Despite what Stevenson said, I was scared that Brian was right.

The next few days were the most terrifying of my life. Brian stalked me inside the house, pacing, arguing with me, and keeping the lights on when I wanted to go to sleep. The only thing that stopped me from losing my mind completely was running; when I ran I had an outlet for my anxiety. In the midst of the terror of living with Brian, I ran a Cincinnati half-marathon called the Flying Pig. I ran it in about two hours but they went by in a blur because I was thinking nonstop about my future if I ever got Brian out of the house. I wanted the race to go on forever because I knew that at the end I would have to return to the chaos at home.

One night I called my mother and said, "I'm worried he's going to hurt me. Can I come over?" When I got to her house, it was past one in the morning. We called Stevenson at home, waking him up.

"If you're really afraid, Laura," he said, "go home and get the girls. If you're not, then you need to try to live in the house until the divorce is settled."

I didn't know what to do. I was scared to leave Brian alone with the girls because I didn't want him to take out his anger on them, but I was scared to be in it with Brian. When I got home, he had locked the door that connected the garage to the house. I didn't have the key for it so I banged and banged but he kept saying, "You're not coming in," and finally I called the police. It was humiliating to have a police car come to the door in our subdivision, where all our neighbors could see what was happening. In the house the two cops interviewed us separately. "Until you work out your divorce," said one cop, "you both have to live here. You can call us every night if you want to but you have to live together."

The cops left and I went upstairs to bed. A short while later, Brian came up, tore off the covers, and turned the light, fan, and radio on. He jumped on the bed, screaming, "Fuck you, you're a whore! You're tearing up the family! Only whores tear up their families!" I was crying hysterically, exhausted. I didn't sleep the whole night. My mind was racing with new fears: Was he going to hurt me? Would I lose the girls? Would he kill me?

In the morning I went to Stevenson with my mother. I told him that Brian was scaring me. He asked if he was hitting me. "No," I said, "just threatening and calling me names."

"It's hard to prove that in court," Stevenson said.

On my way home I decided that the only way to prove it was to record Brian. I went to RadioShack and bought a mini digital recorder. Over the next two weeks I kept the recorder on all the time, hidden in my underwear. Every night as soon as Brian came home I started recording, careful not to let him get too close for fear that he would figure out I was doing it and hit me, or worse.

The recordings are a document of the dysfunction that was our marriage. One night he got upset that I had stopped doing his laundry but was continuing to do the kids'. He ripped the sheets and comforter off the bed so I couldn't sleep and said he would break the laundry machine. He said he would slash my car tires so I couldn't go to work in the morning. I threatened to call 911 but he said if I did that he would say I was beating him up.

On Mother's Day, he threw all my clothes and shoes into the guest room, stacked on the bed and the floor, and I moved in there. Another night he threatened to bug my phone, convinced I was dating someone else, which was laughable. He said he was going to get a restraining order against my mother. He said if she came by the house someone would get shot. He kept two rifles in his office and I was afraid that he was going to use them.

As I made the recordings, I gave them to Lisa and she saved them on her computer as backup and then I took the recorder to Stevenson's office, where he made copies. I was under so much stress that I needed help making decisions. I was like a marionette and Lisa and Mom were pulling my strings. I began losing more weight because of my anxiety. I took Benadryl every night to sleep. I was so worried about the kids and the impact of all the stress on them that I often sent them to the backyard to play with Penny. I let her sleep in their beds when they asked. I wanted Penny to provide them with the comfort I didn't always feel I could give.

A week and a half after I moved into the guest bedroom, Brian came into the room late at night. I had the recorder on. I begged him to let me sleep but he stayed, trying to get me to promise not to call Stevenson in the morning. This went on until almost two A.M. Every time I tried to leave, he blocked the door. I finally got through and ran to my home office downstairs, the farthest room from the guest room, my cell phone grasped tightly in my hand for protection. He followed me in and blocked my way. As I tried to push past him, I said I was calling the police. He grabbed my arm and shoved me hard against the wall. "I will fucking kill you if you do that crap," he said. I was more scared than I had been in the bedroom of the yellow house. I thought he was going to kill me.

Two days later I raced down to Stevenson's office. I gave him the most recent recording. "You have to do something," I said, shaking. "I can't take this anymore. I can't live in this house with him. You have to help me."

He sat and listened to the increasing threats of harm to my mother and me, culminating in the marathon fight that went on till two in the morning. As soon as Brian said on the recorder "I will fucking kill you," Stevenson said, "Let's go."

"Where?"

"To court." The hearing was scheduled for a few hours later and Brian was not required to be there. The judge heard all the recordings and granted a decision on the spot to issue a protection order against Brian. "What exactly is a protection order?" I asked Stevenson on our way out of the courthouse.

"Brian will be violating the law if he comes within a hundred yards of you or the girls," he said, "or calls or attempts to contact you or them."

"He's not going to come back to the house anymore?" I asked.

"He's not supposed to but he could. You have to remember that these are just words. It's not a force field. They'll serve him with papers at work and then he can get some things from the house. After that, he's supposed to obey the order. But he may not care."

I knew that he would be angry and humiliated when he got served at work. Would he come to the house at night and try to hurt me in revenge? Later that day I called the sheriff's office.

Brian was being escorted to the house to get his things. I drove down our cul-de-sac and waited in the car behind a row of hedges. I saw the police car arrive and the cops escort him in. They were inside for a long time. My grandmother's cabinet was in the house, with china and crystal that I had inherited from her, and I worried that he would destroy it all.

Finally he and the cops came out. The police were carrying his guns and Brian had a few items in his hands that I couldn't make out. The police drove him away. I went inside the house, expecting to see wreckage. Instead not a thing had been touched. In his closet there were some empty hangers, but that was it. It was as though in his mind he would be back any day. I was so afraid he would come back that night to kill me that I checked into a local hotel with the girls. It had a pool and we went swimming. I tried to make it seem like a vacation.

Two nights later we went home. I had a copy of the restraining order with me wherever I went, within arm's reach, like a gun. I tried to get things back to normal for the girls—the new normal, which was Daddy not being allowed to live with us or to talk to them. I said that Daddy and I were getting a divorce because we weren't getting along and when we fought, we couldn't make up, but it would work out and we would all get through it together. I wanted to give them more of an explanation than my mother had given me, but I tried to be matter-of-fact and calm, so they didn't panic. I didn't tell them what he had done to me. I said they would see their father again, but I could see the trepidation in their eyes, their fear that it wasn't true.

With Brian out of the house I began to feel less afraid. The next hearing was scheduled for late July, a month away. Stevenson said, "Meet me in the parking lot because we don't know what he will do if he sees you." I was rigid with fear. In the parking lot he explained that our magistrate, Magistrate Wilson, the same middle-aged woman who had issued the restraining order, could either drop the order or issue a longer one. "Even if she does issue another," he said, "don't expect it to be for more than a year."

Within hours, my restraining order would possibly be no longer valid. Brian could hurt me again. Maybe he could even be back in the house. As we headed into the courtroom, I couldn't look at Brian I was so angry. I was questioned about the events that had happened in May, after I said I wanted a divorce. I talked about the violence, menacing, and harassment. I talked about my growing fear and sense of endangerment. When Brian got on the stand and Stevenson questioned him, he denied everything that I had said, denied hurting me, threatening me, or harassing me.

"All right," Stevenson said. "Let's play the tapes." I was relieved there was a bailiff in the room. Stevenson played snippets totaling about a minute of Brian threatening to hurt me and kill me. Brian was stone-faced as he listened. Stevenson asked Brian if that was his voice. Brian said yes.

The hearing was adjourned and Magistrate Wilson granted me a restraining order that was good for five years, until July 2011. I exhaled deeply and began to cry. Brian wouldn't be back in the house for five years. This was even longer than the order that Stevenson had imagined she might issue.

The conditions were very strict: I was given exclusive possession of the house and he couldn't cancel utilities or the insurance, or interrupt phone service or mail delivery. He could not enter the hospital where I worked. He had to stay one hundred yards away from me. He had to vacate the house for good and, on top of that, he could not harm, attempt to harm, threaten, molest, follow, stalk, bother, harass, or annoy me. After all those years of emotional abuse, I was astounded to see these words on a piece of paper as against the law. It meant that his verbal abuse was just as illegal as physical abuse.

But while the original restraining order had not allowed Brian contact with the girls, the new one did. I was given temporary custody of the girls but Brian could pick up and drop off the kids for parenting time. He had to remain in his car curbside while I stayed inside. We could have email contact, no phone contact, to discuss child-related issues. He could talk to the girls by phone and attend their activities but he wasn't allowed to approach me.

The kids were confused as to why he couldn't come in anymore. I said it wasn't good for Daddy and Mommy to be near each other.

Though Brian soon proved himself capable of taking care of the girls, there was a price to pay. It seemed that he was trying to poison their attitude toward me. After one visit, Marija came home and said, "Daddy said you're a bad mom and you don't want us to see him ever again." It didn't surprise me that Marija was telling me this. My children were opposites in every way: Tall, brunette Marija was energetic, in the moment, spontaneous, and hasty. It felt like a tornado was following her. Tiny, blond Courtney was quiet, always absorbing everything going on, a listener more than a talker.

"That's not true, honey," I said. "We're not getting along but I would never stop him from seeing you."

Every time they came back from a weekend with him, Marija would tell me the awful things he had said about me. I tried to be quiet when Marija reported Brian's negative talk because I didn't want to denigrate him the way he was, apparently, denigrating me.

He began buying them lots of clothes and toys. "Mom," Courtney said, "how come you don't buy us stuff like this anymore?" I was living off credit cards and I had no child support until the court worked out a temporary arrangement.

"I can't buy you very much right now," I said. "But I love you as much as Daddy does. Just because someone buys you more it doesn't mean they love you more."

Though Brian had been largely absent as a parent since the girls were born, he decided to fight me on every single aspect of our divorce: custody, visitation, spousal support, and child support. We would be in court on and off for the next year and a half and my divorce would wind up costing me fifty thousand dollars in legal fees.

Because of the police car they had seen in my driveway, my neighbors treated me like I had leprosy. Some were religious and opposed to divorce. They avoided making eye contact on the street and drove past me without waving, pretending not to see me. There were three other splits within a year in my subdivision and people thought divorce was contagious. Some married women confided in me that they were unhappy, too—knowing that I was one of the few people who wouldn't judge them. One woman and her husband were swinging and she became disillusioned and left him. Renee had gotten married and divorced. Elene and her DEA husband Bob were having problems and would later begin divorce proceedings. Everywhere around me marriages were falling apart, but I took no joy in the company. I felt sad for all of us.

My own father was very ill at this point from cancer. I knew he wouldn't be alive much longer and I wanted to tell him what was happening. I called and said that Brian and I were divorcing. He was very quiet and he asked, "Are you sure about this?"

"Yes," I said.

My father had known nothing of my marriage, even less than

my mother had. I had seen him only a handful of times since my wedding. He didn't know the names Brian called me. When we spoke on the phone I was always "up" and he had no reason to suspect that my relationship was troubled. After I told him about the divorce, he paused and said, "Okay. If there's anything we can do, let us know." It meant a lot to me that he didn't try to change my mind. I felt that I had disappointed him but I also felt that he wanted me to be happy. We finally had some of the closeness I had craved as a child, but it hadn't come until my world collapsed.

One night that summer, my neighbor Sally invited me to a barbecue at her house a few doors down from us. She was married with kids and said I could bring the girls. When the girls and I got to the barbecue, Sally said, "Oh, by the way, my husband's bringing a friend. A single guy he's known for a very long time."

"Okay," I said. Seeing a funny look in her eye, I asked, "Is this a setup?"

"No," she said. "Matthew's an eternal bachelor anyway. He's never had a relationship that's lasted more than three months. He's an expiration dater."

I was in a ponytail and long khaki shorts. I was the furthest thing from ready to meet a man, physically, emotionally, and mentally. But Sally had said it wasn't a setup. I didn't need to worry. The door opened and her husband, Tom, came in with Matthew. He looked to be my age and he was cute—bigger and taller than Brian. We started talking and he seemed to be checking me out, focusing on me. We all sat in the yard sipping beer and eating chips, the kids playing. I noticed that Matthew was directing his conversation to me. After dinner, Tom got a fire pit going and it was getting dark. At one point Matthew looked at Tom and said, "Hey, do you want to see Pearl Jam next Saturday? I have tickets."

"I can't do it," Tom said. "I'm out of town."

"I'll go," I heard myself say. "I'm free." The words hung there in the air. I *was* free. I wanted the experience of going out again. I wanted to live after having been dead for so long. After the stress I had been through, he could have invited me to observe an appendectomy and I would have said yes.

"Really?" Matthew said. "You want to go?"

"Sure I'll go!" I said.

The night of the concert, hearing the songs, I remembered all the old Pearl Jam music I had listened to in my car in Hermosa Beach. I got excited to be there, with a guy who liked me, having fun for the first time since I could remember.

After the concert, he drove me back to his house, where I had left my car. He asked if I wanted to come in for a drink. *Oh God.* I didn't know what was going to happen next, whether we would make out. If he did touch me, would I clam up and run out of the house? But there was something about Matthew that made me feel comfortable. He was a big guy, but cuddly and warm. I had the feeling that no matter what happened between us tonight, he would make a good friend, and I was going to need friends.

Inside his house, Matthew showed me around. It was clearly a bachelor pad: one couch, one armchair, a huge TV, and no knick-knacks. We sat on the couch talking for a long time and then he kissed me. I realized that Brian and I had not kissed in thirteen years. I went into a trance. I hadn't felt sexual with a man in so long. I figured Matthew would try to have sex with me because he seemed attracted to me and Sally had told me he was a perpetual bachelor, which meant a player.

As we continued to make out, slowly he took my hand and guided it toward his pants. I had a moment of panic but didn't pull my hand away. We got up from the couch and moved to his bedroom. After much foreplay, I was close to the edge by the time we made love. I wasn't used to a man caring about my pleasure. We had sex in his soft bed and I was surprised to enjoy it, and further surprised when I came.

Afterward I was so exhausted from the intensity of my new feelings that I fell asleep in his arms. In the morning I woke up but kept my eyes closed because I didn't know if he was awake. I had never had a one-night stand. I wondered if he was going to kick me out like those guys on *Sex and the City* did. I was shocked and embarrassed, but glowing. I loved what we had done the night before. Who was that girl who had slept with a man after a Pearl Jam concert on the first date? Was she really me?

I wanted to see Matthew again but thought that maybe he wouldn't want to see me, since to him this was casual sex. I opened my eyes. He was awake, and had a crazy smile on his face. I laughed. "I've never done anything like this before," I said. He smiled wider. "What is it?" I said. "Why are you looking at me like that?"

"I think I'm in love with you," he said.

LIVING DEAD GIRL

FROM THAT FIRST MORNING ON, MATTHEW WAS CALLING ALL THE time and sending texts like, "Good morning, beautiful." We saw each other nearly every weekend that I didn't have the girls; he was independently wealthy and worked only minimally. I would drive out to his house in Cincinnati about forty minutes away and we would end up spending the entire weekend together. When I was with him I felt like I was on a little tropical island, far from the stresses of my divorce.

What I felt for him in those heady early months was infatuation, of course; I had the emotional maturity of a young woman. Lisa, who had gotten divorced and was happily remarried, told me that after you divorce, in your mind you revert to the age that you were when you first married. Emotionally I was about twenty-two, the age that I had been when I met Brian.

But the strange thing was that Matthew seemed infatuated with me, too. We kissed all the time and couldn't keep our hands off each other. It was everything I had missed during my marriage, the same intense attention that Brian had given me at the beginning—without the verbal abuse that came later. Matthew wanted to hold my hand every second—in the car, on the couch, and in bed. Unlike Brian, Matthew was independent. He did his own laundry and cooking and knew how to take care of himself. I was slowly coming to realize that not all men were like Brian. Many were self-sufficient and capable. It gave me hope that whatever happened with Matthew, there were kind, respectful guys out there who wouldn't treat me like a slave. I kept my relationship with Matthew separate from my relationship with my daughters. Because I didn't know how serious it was going to be and because it was way too soon to involve someone else in their lives, I only introduced them to Matthew a few times and he never slept over when they were in the house. In their minds he was just Mommy's friend. I didn't want to complicate their feelings about the divorce.

When I wasn't with Matthew or the girls I relished the quiet and peace of my empty house, though it was still tarnished by memories of the ugly weeks after I told Brian I wanted out. I was working only part-time, so I had time to do errands, take care of myself, and run. After virtually ten years without solitude, I discovered that I could tolerate it and even like it.

In July the girls went off to horseback riding camp. My relationship with Matthew was getting more serious. Despite the fact that he lavished attention on me, as we started to spend time with his friends, mixed groups of men and women, I became compulsively jealous. Some of his female friends were women he had dated. I hated the idea that he had a romantic past, even though he was in his late thirties and there would have been something wrong with him if he didn't. When he told me a girl was an ex-girlfriend, I would imagine him leaving me for her. On the way home from a party I would say, "Did you guys date before?" "You probably think she's prettier than me." "How long did you date?" I kept remembering what Sally had told me about Matthew being an expiration dater.

My angry, jealous words felt familiar to me. I was turning into Brian. But whereas Brian's harsh language came from his ego and overconfidence, mine came from total insecurity. I was so self-doubting that I was terrified of anything—like an attractive woman—that appeared to threaten my new happy world with Matthew. His positive attention was like a glucose drip and when he withdrew it, even for a moment, I felt like I was dying.

My emotional insecurity was coupled with physical insecurity. Though I was slim and fit from my running I kept comparing myself to other women. I was still insecure about my breast size, certain Matthew thought my boobs were too small even though he never complained about them. I thought more often about getting implants but I couldn't do anything until I had a settlement.

One weekend morning Matthew and I were lying in bed together, chatting. He was a big Howard Stern fan and we soon moved from the subject of Howard to the subject of *Playboy* magazine. Matthew mentioned that he was a longtime reader of *Playboy* and saved the issues with pictorials of his favorite celebrities. He took a stack of *Playboy*s from his side table and began flipping through them. I was deeply uncomfortable but tried to act nonchalant. I felt like Superman seeing Kryptonite. Finally I couldn't bear it anymore. I told him what had happened at my dad's house when I was twelve. I told him of my insecurities around porn and body image. "I don't handle this well," I said.

"I'll move them to the basement."

"Why don't you just throw them away?"

"Fine, it's no big deal."

I didn't believe him but I knew he wouldn't keep them near the bed anymore.

Now that I was having frequent sex, I was concerned about birth control. My relationship to sex had evolved from terror at age fourteen to dread during my marriage to elation with Matthew. But pregnancy scared me. I had no financial footing and no idea when I would. And I thought it could be dangerous to become pregnant in my late thirties. I felt strongly that I didn't want to start over with motherhood at this point.

While I was pregnant with Courtney, my mother had had a pulmonary embolism and had to be hospitalized. She recovered well, but I didn't want to go on the pill because of the clotting risk. I didn't want an IUD because I wanted irreversible birth control. Without telling Matthew, I made an appointment with my ob-gyn. "I want to get sterilized," I said.

"Sterilization is permanent," the doctor said.

"I promise you, I am never going to want more children."

"What if you meet someone new and change your mind?"

I thought about Matthew. I knew there could be other men in my future even if he and I broke up, and I realized that I might be ruining my chances with a man who wanted children. And then I thought that no matter how perfect that man might be, he would have to find someone else. "He'll just have to accept it," I said.

The gynecologist realized I was serious. He told me about a new form of sterilization that involved coils placed in the fallopian tubes. The coils cause scar tissue to build up and sperm can't reach and fertilize the egg. The procedure was nonsurgical and took about half an hour. I made an appointment.

When I walked out of the hospital after it was over I was a

little sad that my childbearing years had ended, but I also felt that I had made a positive choice about my body. The days of existing purely for other people—my husband and my daughters—were over. I would never have more children. My life could now begin to be about me.

I was running more seriously now, training for the Flying Pig half-marathon again in the spring. But I wasn't excercising manically, the way I had been when we first moved back to Dayton. Because the running made me feel healthy, I became more conscious of what I ate and how different foods made me feel. I was also extremely conscious of the fact that Courtney and Marija would model my behavior. I had educated them about the different food groups but I knew what I did was far more important than what I said. I ate processed food infrequently, tried to make my treats healthy, had a lot of protein, and tried to stop eating when I was full. Over time I noticed that the girls learned to regulate their own behavior. They might binge on Oreos for a day but the next day they would get sick of them and make healthier choices on their own.

Because of my running and my healthier eating, I soon dropped from a size ten to a size six. One day a neighbor named Donna, who had started running with Carmen, Aimir, and me, asked me to help her do weight training at our local gym. "I haven't trained anyone in almost twenty years," I said, "but sure." I started working with her for free, and that inspired me to start lifting weights myself and getting back in touch with my own fitness. My body became stronger and leaner. I had abdominal muscles. I liked this new figure. I wondered what Heidi of Heidi's Frogen Yozurt would think if she could see me now.

In September 2006 after we had been dating for a few months, Matthew took me to a Bengals-Browns game. He had season tickets to the Bengals and was excited about the game because of the Bengals-Browns rivalry. "Football is a really big deal for me," he said. "I watch the game. I don't just go to socialize. And I want you to know, I usually don't take girls to games."

I was flattered that he was inviting me into his elite macho world. We had a good time tailgating with his friends, and when we went into Paul Brown Stadium, where the Bengals had moved in 2000, the crowd was roaring. I saw the green FieldTurf and the hash marks and video screens. I saw thousands of people in Bengals jerseys, hats, and paraphernalia. I loved the fact that the fans were so loyal even though the Bengals had never been a top-ranked team. Since 1968 the Bengals had never won a Super Bowl, they played only two, made only nine playoffs, and had had winning records less than a third of the time they had been in existence. Cincinnatians like Matthew and my sister Lisa and my mom never lost faith. They showed up year after year, hoping things would change.

As much as I enjoyed watching the players, it wasn't until the Ben-Gal cheerleaders came onto the field to do their opening dance number that I was truly riveted. I could not take my eyes off them. For me the players were a mindless distraction from the pretty, glamorous cheerleaders. "I love that dance they just did!" I kept shouting. "Oh, that is so cute! Did you see that kick?" Matthew kept shushing me so he could focus on the game, which turned out to be exciting because the Bengals actually won, 34–17. Quarterback Carson Palmer threw for 352 yards and got two touchdowns. Chad Johnson got his first touchdown of the season and did the Chicken Dance, and Chris Henry had five catches for 113 yards.

As I watched the Ben-Gals strut their stuff, cheering for a team that was probably going to win, the beer went to my head. I went from admiring the cheerleaders to thinking I could be one.

I want to do that. . . . I could do that. . . . I think I could do that. . . . I could definitely do that!

"I want to be one of those cheerleaders," I said to Matthew.

He shook his head with a patronizing smile and said, "Honey . . . You're too old." I felt a flash of hurt but then decided he was being honest. I was thirty-eight years old. It was ridiculous to think I could be an NFL cheerleader.

That summer my half-brother, Eric, had gotten married in Connecticut. My father was so frail from the cancer that it was a struggle for him to walk down the aisle. He moved like he was eighty years old even though he was only in his late sixties. It was heartbreaking. I sat with him on the porch of his house in Connecticut, thinking that it could be the last time I saw him alive.

One day in October, Lisa called me in the middle of the night. "Dad's gone," she said. He had gone into the hospital a few days before. I felt relief that he wouldn't have to be in pain any longer, but I grieved for the father I had barely known.

Matthew drove twelve hours with me to the funeral, reminding me all the while that he never did stuff like this with girls he dated. During the service I realized that Dad had seen Marija and Courtney, his only grandchildren, just a handful of times. Though Connecticut was a long distance from Atlanta and Austin, I felt he could have been more involved. I was sorry that the girls would never get to know their grandfather. I felt the pain of having loved him and never being loved back quite enough. And yet my grief was blunted by the fact that we'd barely had a relationship when he was alive. In some ways it was as though he had died years before.

Though Matthew and I were saying "I love you," the insecurity that had built up during my marriage caught up with me. I could not accept that Matthew cared about me. I became more needy around him. My jealousy reared its ugly head every time we were in the company of other people.

At one party Matthew introduced me to a friend of his named Val. I liked her immediately. She was single, friendly, and she looked like Fergie from the Black Eyed Peas. I thought we could be best friends. The three of us found ourselves at a kitchen island, on barstools. Matthew was on one side of me and Val on the other and I sensed electricity between them. On our way home I said, "It seemed like there was something between the two of you. Do you guys have a history or something?"

"We've always been really good friends," he said. "We hooked up a few times but it was so strange we just went back to being friends." I didn't hear the "friends" part—only "we hooked up a few times." It stung. Because I had felt a kinship with her, I be-came convinced that he would replace me with her. From then on, every time I saw Val I was rude to her. I went on jealous rants about her and nothing he said could calm me down. "Laura," he would say. "You're not being logical. You feel this way because you don't have any self-confidence. You need to talk to somebody."

He was right. I had been thinking that my girls should see a therapist to help them cope with the divorce, and when he sug-gested that I see one, I realized I wasn't coping very well either. Stevenson recommended a psychologist named Rose who had ex-pertise in family therapy. The girls and I each saw her separately and sometimes we saw her together. She was like a movie star from the forties—she looked to be in her early seventies and she had a smoky voice and slim figure. She had a Shih Tzu named Bethany that wore barrettes and stayed in her office during sessions.

During my own appointments with Rose I began to talk about my marriage. It was a relief to tell someone my story, to talk about the pain, anxiety, and helplessness I had felt. Rose said that my marriage had given me post-traumatic stress disorder. I didn't want to think of myself as having a disorder, but if there was a name for what I had, then I could work through it. "The whole entire marriage you were told how dumb and stupid you were," Rose said, as Bethany panted in the corner, blinking at me with her black eyes. "You had no reinforcement of your attractiveness, intelligence, or worth as a person. No wonder you feel this way with Matthew. He is fulfilling needs you have never had fulfilled. That's why your insecurities come out when he's directing attention away from you. You become afraid he's going to abandon you, just like your father did."

When she said that, I was shocked. Not only did I have PTSD, I was abandoned. But an abandoner was a man who walked out on his wife before the baby was born. That wasn't my father. Dad hadn't been *completely* absent during my childhood; Lisa and I had had our long vacations with him. But he had made a choice not to live near us, and I realized that was a form of abandonment. Whether it came from anger at my mother, ambivalence about being a father to girls, or loyalty to his new wife, it didn't matter. He hadn't been there for us in the important, day-to-day way that children needed. I understood, in a deep and painful way, that my father had inflicted a wound on me by choosing to stay in Michigan and that this had affected me more deeply than any other event in my childhood.

There was a direct line from my relationship with my dad to my relationship with Brian to this recent one with Matthew. Ever since my parents divorced I had been desperate for male love, and that was why I had rushed into my marriage. Rose said that I had believed the negative things Brian had said because they confirmed my suspicions about myself. She was right.

But even with my slowly building awareness, I couldn't stop being jealous in my new relationship. In May Matthew and I went to the Taste of Cincinnati, a big culinary festival in the streets of the city. We were with a friend of his named Hendricks and while we were all walking, I heard a girl's voice say, "Hi, Matthew!" We all looked across the street and there was Val, waving. He waved back nervously because he knew I was going to go ballistic. I stopped. The men kept walking ahead and realized I wasn't with them.

"What's going on?" Matthew said.

My breath was short. I thought I was going to have a panic attack. "That's it," I said. "I'm gone." I knew I was acting crazy but I couldn't stop myself. My therapy sessions with Rose went right out the window. I started walking in the opposite direction. I had no cell phone and no money because my purse was in his car, but I didn't care. I wanted to get away but I also wanted him to follow me.

After a while, Matthew caught up with me in his car, Hendricks sitting beside him. "Do you know where you're going?" Matthew said. "The worst part of the city. You're going to get killed." I had been heading toward a rough neighborhood called Over-the-Rhine. "Get in the car."

We drove all the way back to his house not speaking. Hendricks got out to give us privacy. "I'm getting your stuff," Matthew said. "You're getting out of here. You have got to fix yourself, Laura. I cannot fix you. You have to do it yourself." I was crying. It was a self-fulfilling prophecy. Because of my neediness, I had made Matthew leave me. He was sand and I had squeezed him so hard through my fingers that he had slipped through.

I got into my car and popped my trunk, tears running down my face, while he went in and out of the house loading my clothes and toiletries into the car. Through my hurt and shock I heard a still, small voice within me. What he had said was true. I couldn't tie my self-worth to someone else's perception of me. No one else could save me. I had to save myself. I decided that if I met another man someday, I wouldn't try to force him to love me and I wouldn't tell him how to act. That was what Brian had done to me. I was never going to become someone else's Brian.

Around the time Matthew broke up with me, the property portion of my divorce was settled and I was allowed to sell the house and find a new one. I didn't want to continue to live in that redbrick house, with the frightening memories, violence, menace, and rage. And I needed something cheaper. The house sold within a week.

My mother helped me buy a house close by. She was there for me just as her own parents had been for her. I had temporary spousal support but nowhere near enough for a down payment, and I didn't know how much I would be earning once I started working full time. School had ended and the girls, ten and eight, were off at summer camp again. To save money I moved most of the boxes myself, and though it was exhausting it felt therapeutic. Little by little I was moving myself away from Brian. As my new house began to fill up with boxes and the old house got emptier, I began to feel calm. This move felt nothing like the move from Austin to Dayton, two little girls and a trailer behind me. It felt victorious. I was going to get a fresh start.

One early evening I sat down on the couch in my new house, looking at all the boxes. It was a hot June night. The sun was starting to set. The cable had not yet been plugged in. My only company was Penny, the nine-pound Chihuahua. I pulled the blinds closed. Everything decompressed. I hadn't realized how wounded I was from my marriage but I didn't have to be that way anymore. I wanted to find something to do that didn't involve a man.

Go back to the beginning, I heard a voice say. *What made you happy before Brian? What did you like to do?* I thought about roller skating down the Strand in Manhattan Beach. I remembered the dance company, Jazzercise classes, the health club, and teaching aerobics. *If I could start my life again*, I thought, *I would do something with dance.*

And then I realized I *could* start my life again.

I went to the computer and Googled "dance classes Dayton Cincinnati." All the listings were for children's classes. I specified "adult." An entry came up called PoleKittens. Curious about the name, I clicked on the site. There was a comic book–style graphic of a voluptuous woman in a tight magenta tank top, green short shorts, and white knee-high platform boots, her body wrapped around a stripper pole. It was a fitness class for women who used poles to build core strength. The address of the studio was on Vine Street in downtown Cincinnati, not in the ghetto, but near it. In my head I could hear Brian's judgmental voice. *PoleKittens? That's disgusting. Only sluts dance on stripper poles.*

The next day I drove down and pulled up to the address. It was a tattoo parlor. I checked my printout, certain I had the wrong address. *Don't be scared. Just park the car, go inside, and ask if it's the right place.* After I parked, I walked past a head shop and an adult video store back to the tattoo shop.

I had never gotten a tattoo before, I didn't have any close friends with tattoos, and I certainly had never been inside a tattoo parlor. I felt like Alice going through the rabbit hole. The parlor smelled of incense. There was weird music playing and tattoo designs on the walls. A man with spiky, gelled hair and piercings in his nose was tattooing another guy. He looked up.

"I'm just wondering if there's a pole-dancing place around here," I whispered.

"What?" he said. All the men looked up at me.

"Is PoleKittens here?" I said, a little louder.

"That's my girlfriend's class," he said. "It's upstairs."

I took the stairs and emerged into a narrow hallway. One side was black and the other was white. It opened up to another tattoo parlor. More tattoo artists were sitting there with their clients, looking through books. One guy looked at me and said, "Pole dancing? Keep going, one more flight."

As I climbed the final flight of stairs I had a horrifying thought. What if this wasn't really PoleKittens? No one knew I was here. The girls were away. I hadn't told anyone where I was going, not even Lisa or my mom. These scary tattoo guys were telling me to go upstairs but maybe it was a ploy to follow me up and kill me. Then I decided, *Screw it. I'm going to find out what's up there.*

The stairs led to an attic. T-shirts reading POLEKITTENS in rhinestones hung on the hot pink walls. There were fuzzy green chairs, mirrors and velvet curtains. A curvy tattooed woman in her early forties materialized and said, "Hi, I'm Victoria." She was sexy, but in more of a Goth way than a stripper way, and because she was my age, I was less nervous than I might have otherwise been.

Over the next fifteen minutes the other women arrived, all in short shorts and sports bras, mostly in their thirties. I was in a tank top and longer shorts. "I didn't know what to wear," I said to Victoria, embarrassed.

"You can buy a pair of my shorts if you want," she said. So I bought a pair of shorts that said POLEKITTENS on the butt and changed in the powder room.

When I came out, the other girls were putting on stripper-style six-inch platform shoes. I had on flip flops. Victoria saw me staring at the other girls and said, "You're a beginner, so you should do it barefoot."

During the lesson I was sweating so much that my hand kept slipping on the pole. We had never done anything like this in Dance Theater Dayton. The only time I had seen a strip club was in R-rated movies or on *The Sopranos*.

Victoria showed us the beginner moves, such as the Fireman (coming down), Scrapping the Barrel (a grinding hip circle), and Dorothies (where you lean over and click your heels together like Dorothy and your butt claps). I definitely wasn't in Kansas anymore. I hadn't realized it took such great upper-body strength to support your own weight on a pole. My arms and shoulders were sore. Suddenly I had incredible respect for the physical prowess it took to be a stripper.

"Wow, you're really strong," Victoria said as I was doing a spin. I felt the same glow I used to get in the dance company when Debbie liked my arabesques.

At the end of class we sat on the floor. "It's time to freestyle," Victoria said. "Each of you will do your own pole dance for three minutes, using the moves that you've learned today. We'll start with Laura."

Oh, no. Not first. "You go first, Victoria," I said. "Please? I'm really nervous." Rob Zombie came on, singing "Living Dead Girl." Victoria did an amazing performance, with much more advanced moves than we had learned. I was in awe. I wanted to learn to do everything she did.

When it was my turn, I hesitated again. "Just dance for one minute," Victoria said. "You can dance for one minute, can't you?"

I stood up in front of my classmates, insecure in my tiny shorts, and not yet comfortable with the moves. They were so close and I didn't know them. Slowly I walked around the pole and did my first spin. I vamped for longer than a minute, kicking back and enjoying myself, and when I finished, my classmates said I was great.

I loved it. I drove home with a big smile and decided to take the class as often as I could. I ended up driving to the Vine Street studio three times a week.

My days became fuller—with work, PoleKittens, and taking care of the girls. I spent a lot of time reading with Penny snuggled against me. She made me feel less alone at night and safer; she would bark when strangers walked past the house. I read *The Complete Idiot's Guide to Football* because I had gotten curious about the Bengals from going to that game with Matthew. I also read a lot of self-help because I wanted to "fix" myself: *The Rules* (though I now think that that book is the opposite of self-help); *Living Alone & Loving It; Act Like a Lady, Think Like a Man;* and *Ten Stupid Things Women Do to Mess Up Their Lives.* I also read a book called *302 Advanced Techniques for Driving a Man Wild in Bed*, which I highly recommend.

After Marija and Courtney returned from camp, they had a few long stays with their dad. I was trying to figure out how to fill my days and nights and felt out of place in my neighborhood as a separated mom. I felt like I wore a scarlet letter. I wanted to make new friends.

While Matthew and I were dating, he had taken me to a sports bar–restaurant in Cincinnati called the Porch of All Sorts. One night I decided to go by myself. When I walked in that door, my mouth was dry and my hands were shaking. I had never gone to a bar alone. *Am I dressed right? Are they going to think I'm weird because I'm a single woman in a sports bar? Will anyone talk to me? Do I want anyone to talk to me?*

I glanced around the room. It was about six o'clock so it wasn't crowded. *You can do this.* People were watching sports games on TV, drinking, eating, and playing pool. It wasn't rowdy or seedy, and there were a handful of women there, too. *I'll just have one drink. If I don't like it or someone hits on me, I can always walk right out that door and go home.* I sat down and ordered a beer, and the bartender, a middle-aged guy, said, "Great to see you again." I giggled. He didn't know me but he was pretending to, and his joke was exactly what I needed to relax. The bartender, Christian, turned out to be a married guy who was putting himself through pharmaceutical school by working as a bartender. As I started to visit the Porch more often we became friendly and I looked forward to going to the bar to talk to him, partly because I felt he protected me.

Soon I was going every weekend that I didn't have the girls. I made friends with a group of other regulars, women and men. Christian gave me free beers sometimes. I was having the college days I'd never had in California. Inspired by Christian, I considered becoming a bartender part-time but rejected it because of my visitation schedule.

When I met people at the bar my opening line was always, "So tell me your story." They turned out to be literally all sorts, some single, some divorced, most without kids. When people asked my story, I told them I was a single mom with two beautiful, healthy girls. At first I felt like a failure when I said I was going through a divorce, but it got easier. People were understanding.

At the Porch I spent a lot of platonic time with men. I wanted to get to know guys as friends so I could think about what type appealed to me. I talked to men who had tattoos, businessmen, and sporty guys in Ohio State shirts and ball caps. I wanted to know what made them each tick. One of the other married bartenders liked to check out every good-looking girl who came in. It bugged me but for the first time I had an opportunity to ask a man about it instead of judge him. "Why do you do that?" I finally asked him. "Why do you undress them with your eyes when you're married?"

"It's just about variety," he said. "Men are visual and we like to look at different things." I started to understand. He still went home to his wife and he wasn't cheating but he liked the eye candy. It made me accept that men and women operate differently. It made me more forgiving of Matthew's *Playboy*s. Just because a man liked porn or attractive women it didn't mean he was a cheater.

Sometimes men at the bar would hit on me but I was still wary of casual sex. I dated only one man that summer, and only for a few dates, before we realized we were incompatible. I didn't visit the Porch to get laid. I did it to regain the social confidence that Brian had stolen from me. I didn't want to be the old Laura anymore, the meek, tired person I had been in the marriage. I wanted to be the kind of woman who is comfortable around guys, who can make them laugh, and beat them at pool. At the Porch that summer I learned how to banter. A guy would make a dirty joke and I would have a comeback or a tag line that could get a group of people laughing. I felt like I was on *Cheers*.

The old Laura had been withdrawn and numb. She doubted her intelligence, she was intimidated by men, and she certainly wasn't funny. But that Laura was gone. The new Laura was boisterous and funny, a guy's girl.

She was Lisa. Everything about my new personality had been learned from watching my sister. Without a self, I needed to mimic someone else. The real Laura wasn't Lisa any more than she was the Laura who had stayed in an abusive marriage for fourteen years. Though I wasn't yet sure who the real Laura was, I felt like I was getting closer to her. I wasn't afraid of people, I liked my body, and I could strike up conversations with strangers without being nervous. I didn't yet have Lisa's boobs but I was going to do something about that, too.

. . .

One day I took a trip to the Hustler Hollywood store in Cincin-nati. I had decided to buy a pole for myself so I could practice my pole-dancing at home. I had a fantasy of getting certified as a pole-dancing instructor (yes, it's a real certification) and teaching my own classes in a private studio.

As apprehensive as I was about going in, I decided to play the role of a woman who shopped at Hustler on a regular basis. I had passed the store every time I drove to Cincinnati because it's on the way there off I-75, and I had always wondered what it looked like inside. As disgusted as I had been when Brian brought home the bag of sex toys, I had wondered, *What else do they sell in a store that carries those?*

It turned out to be like a Spencer's novelty store in the front, and a sex den in the back, well-lit and not at all seedy. In the front there were T-shirts and shorts, bathing suits, and men's clothes, plus lingerie and bachelorette-party items. The back had dildos, sex toys, and magazines. The poles marked the division between the two sections. I finally got up the nerve to ask one of the women behind the counter if she could show me the poles. She gave me the specifications of the different poles, just like I was buying a tennis racket. It was painless. I came home and installed it in the storage area of the basement, next to the family room.

Courtney and Marija had been away while I was at PoleKittens, so I hadn't told them about it. One day after I had put in the pole, Courtney came upstairs from the basement and said, "Um, Mom? There's this pole. Like for a fireman. What is it doing there?"

"Marija!" I called out. "We're going to have a chat." Marija came down from her bedroom. They looked at me warily. "Girls," I said. "I've been taking these dance classes over the summer. It's called pole-dancing. And it's a really good form of exercise for the upper body and abdominal area."

"Oh my God, you're a stripper," Marija said.

"I am not a stripper!" I said. "It's just a dance class. It's all women, and it's purely for exercise. You are right that there are women who take their clothes off and dance on poles in clubs and that's not good, but that's not what I do. I have a female teacher who's even older than I am."

"Ewwww!" they both replied at once.

"We're all wearing clothes and we do it to stay fit. It's fun. Come on. I'll show you." I took them downstairs and showed them some of my moves. "Now you try," I said. They could barely lift themselves up and they realized how difficult it was. We spent about half an hour spinning around, giggling, and making fun of each other.

I realized that it was the first time in a long time that they had seen me laughing. Our house had become less tense without Brian. They were seeing a side of me that they hadn't seen before, a joyous, playful side. Brian had been out of the house a year and none of us had to live with emotional violence.

That night we were watching TV together and Marija said, "You know what, Mom? You seem happier than you were before."

"You think so, sweetie?"

"You're so much more energetic now. You're not angry all the time the way you used to be. I didn't know you were like this."

"I am like this," I said. "I've always been like this. It's just that for a while I . . . forgot."

Later that summer my PoleKittens classmates and I visited a high-end strip club in Cincinnati called Deja Vu Showgirls. There was a featured pole-dancer there who had come from Florida and we wanted to see her. It was like a dirty field trip, but fun. At the club we all sat together, trying not to giggle. The strippers were young and beautiful, with a surprising variety of bodies, from small breasted to large breasted. I thought the naturally large-breasted ones were the prettiest of all. I loved watching the strippers when they were on the poles, with their strong muscled bodies, but when they did floor dancing, legs wide open, their crotches just inches from the men's faces, I thought, *Eew*. The whole night I flipped back and forth between fascination and apprehension.

When the men watched the girls, their mouths hung open, their heads were cocked, and they wore slightly smug smiles. A man in a booth got a lap dance. He was smiling gleefully, and the stripper looked bored.

But some of the other girls seemed to enjoy what they were doing, enjoy their power over the men. It was like a *National Geographic* special on gender relations.

On my way home from the club I thought, *Maybe I should be a stripper. I really like pole-dancing and I love to perform.*

Then again, I'd have to stretch my own butt cheeks for strangers on a nightly basis. Why can't I just dance with my clothes on like the girl in Flashdance?

Because there are no bars like Mawby's anymore. If I want to dance like that, I'd have to be topless.

But there's always something about a job that you don't like.

Laura, get real! Who's going to hire a thirty-eight-year-old stripper?

Maybe someone would. The money would be good and I really need money.

It wouldn't be setting a very good example for Courtney and Marija.

It was one thing to shop for hip clothes with Marija, or doodle imaginary outfits on a sketch pad with Courtney, who dreamed of becoming a fashion designer. It was another to go out every night and strip for money and then come home to them. As disappointing as it was for me to admit it, I didn't have it in me to be a stripper.

But something had happened as I allowed myself to fantasize about it. I realized that I could do whatever I wanted; I didn't need to be limited by Brian's ideas of propriety. I could be a bartender like Christian, or a pole-dancing teacher like Victoria, or a professional fitness instructor. There were no rules.

After I went to Deja Vu and saw how bare the strippers were down there, I got the idea to get a wax. I went to a professional salon and asked for a Brazilian, thinking that meant a very narrow triangle. In the room I stripped from my waist down, nervously. Even at the ob-gyn they gave you a gown. The waxer said, "Flip over." I laid flat on my stomach and she said, "No, on all fours." I had no idea what she was going to do to me.

She put the wax on my butt and then stripped it off. I was shocked but it didn't hurt. Maybe the rest wouldn't be painful. I flipped over onto my back and she said, "Spread your legs open." I did. "You want everything off?" she asked. I didn't quite grasp what she meant by "everything."

"Sure," I said. It turned out that a Brazilian wax meant the whole kahuna, all the way to the inner portion of the labia. What followed was the most painful thing I had ever experienced besides childbirth. As Jerry Seinfeld once said, "I will never be able to understand how a woman can take boiling hot wax, pour it on her upper thighs, rip the hair out by the root, and still be afraid of a spider."

But when the waxing was finally over, I loved it. It felt sexy and new. My outer self was beginning to resemble my inner self.

One afternoon, as I was leaving PoleKittens class, I noticed Sherri, one of the other students, putting on tennis shoes with Bengal tigers on them. "I really like your tennis shoes," I said.

"Oh, I used to be a Ben-Gal cheerleader," she said.

"You did? My whole family is Bengals fans!" I told her that I had tried out to be an L.A. Clippers cheerleader when I was nineteen but didn't make it.

"You know what?" she said. "*You* should be a Ben-Gal."

"What are you talking about?" I started to laugh.

"I saw you dance. You dance really sexy. They would love you. You should try out. You can't do it now because they picked the girls in May, but wait until the next tryouts. Look on the website in the winter for the clinic dates." A real Ben-Gal was saying I could do it. Sherri wasn't that different from me except for her age. I had seen her on the pole and knew I could dance as well as she could.

That August a coworker at the hospital mentioned that she was going to a Bengals-Saints game. Thinking about the Ben-Gals, I said I wanted to go but I couldn't get tickets in the same section so I watched the game alone. My eyes were glued to the Ben-Gals.

It had been nearly a year since that Bengals-Browns game with Matthew and I wasn't the same woman I had been then. Now I was dancing again, even if it was on a stripper pole. I knew how to move like they did. More important, I wasn't afraid to try something new. I stared out at the cheerleaders, hearing Matthew saying, "Honey . . . you're too old."

You think I'm too old? I heard myself telling him. I wasn't just talking to Matthew. I was talking to Brian, my dad, and the old Laura, who was afraid of everything, afraid to breathe, afraid to dream.

You think I'm too old? I told the voices in my head. *Well, watch this.*

OLDILOCKS

ONE NIGHT JUST BEFORE LABOR DAY, I WAS AT THE PORCH OF ALL Sorts, talking to Christian, when three young guys walked in. One of them was tall and handsome and looked like John Corbett from *Sex and the City* crossed with the comedian Dane Cook.

"That guy is so cute," I told Christian. The guys sat at a table behind me, talking about what food to order. The cute one came up to order a drink, leaning his elbow on the bar. I stared at him and he smiled, but I was so attracted to him I couldn't speak. After nonstop talking at the Porch all summer, I was at a loss for words. The cute guy's friend stepped up to the bar between us to order a drink. I started talking to the friend just so I could relax. When they went back to their table, I heard them discussing the menu. I took a deep breath, went over, and said, "You want me to tell you what's good here?" One of the guys was talkative, but the cute one was quiet. His name turned out to be P.J.

They asked me to stay at their table and I wound up sharing their pizza. They stayed at the bar a long time, a few hours. We shot pool. P.J. and I were talking and flirting. "Do you want to go over to the hotel next door?" he asked in a very joking tone. I laughed but after I thought about it I realized that if I said yes he might have followed me right out the door. I had jumped into bed with Matthew and I wasn't going to make that mistake again. My therapist, Rose, had told me I needed to slow down the next time I met a man, so I could get to know him and decide for myself if he was worthy. It was a new way of thinking. I could decide if a man was worthy of *me*—and not the other way around.

"You sleep with me tonight," I told P.J., "you're never going to talk to me again."

Later on, as he was leaving with his friends, he came over and handed me a business card with his name and cell phone number written on the back. His handwriting was so tiny I could barely read it. I put the card in the back pocket of my jeans.

On my drive home I reached for the card. It wasn't there. Had I dropped it in the bar? Was it in the car? When I got home I crawled on the floor of the car like an alcoholic trying to find a few drops of liquor but the card was gone. That night I couldn't sleep, trying to remember the name of his company. I knew it was a flooring company but for the life of me I couldn't remember what it was called.

The next day, Labor Day, at the pool, I wracked my brains. He had told me which strip mall it was in. I had been there and I tried to remember the sign. I was thinking of driving to see for myself and then the name of his store flashed in my head.

I called the number. He answered the phone with the store name and said, "P.J. speaking." I was so shocked that he had answered the phone, I hung up. I suspected immediately that he was single; no married guy would be working on Labor Day. I called back a second later. "I don't know if you remember me," I said, "but my name's Laura. We met at the Porch of All Sorts. I lost your cell phone number but I wanted to give you mine in case you wanted to go out."

A couple of days later we went to a restaurant called Silver Spring House in Cincinnati. We sat in the outdoor seating area in the hazy night, eating appetizers, and I told him everything, about my marriage, divorce, and kids. "I probably shouldn't be telling you all this on a first date," I said.

"I'm not interested in people who haven't been through some stuff," he said.

He didn't seem scared by my past or my complicated life or even my age. (He turned out to be twenty-eight.) Afterward we drove around, wanting to spend time together alone. He smoked cigarettes but blew the smoke out the window. I hadn't contemplated dating a smoker but somehow it didn't concern me. Even though I was a health professional I liked him too much to judge him.

We stopped at a soccer field behind a church, went out onto the field, and kept talking on the grass. It reminded me of those summer nights on the Dayton Country Club golf course. We started kissing and made love under the Ohio sky. (Guess my "don't sleep with him too early" plan hadn't worked so well.) I felt more confident in my sexuality because of PoleKittens, and at the Porch I had learned how to talk to people. If I had been about twenty-two emotionally the night I went to Pearl Jam with Matthew, now I was about thirty. Not quite my real age, but getting there. We laid there looking at the stars and I thought, *This is the best night I've ever had.*

P.J. and I found it easy to talk to each other. I wasn't as needy as I had been before and I began to trust that he cared about me. I learned how to read his moods, which was tough, because he was private. I could see he was guarded and I tried not to rush our closeness, which gave me time to think about what I wanted.

There were a few hiccups early on; because of his own issues he was afraid that I might hurt him, and he would sometimes distance me. I got jealous and angry but then I remembered how I had acted with Matthew and realized I had a chance to be different. If P.J. and I took a few days off from each other, I had to trust that he would come back to me. And he did.

As our relationship deepened I realized that I was a serial monogamist. I had gone straight from my marriage into the relationship with Matthew, and I'd been single for only three months before I met P.J. Now I was getting involved again. It was scary. But I liked him and didn't want to stop seeing him.

Tailgating before a game
with P.J.

P.J. nicknamed me Oldilocks. He could not believe I had seen *Star Wars* in the theater. I would mention old TV shows like *Good Times* or *Welcome Back, Kotter* and he wouldn't know what I was talking about. Sometimes at restaurants the hostesses would glance from me to P.J., my sun-damaged skin and crow's-feet, his big eyes and boyish grin, and I was certain they thought we were mother and son. It got to me. One night P.J. had a party at his house. A lot of late twentysomethings and early thirtysomethings were over and a band was jamming in the basement. It was like what we used to do in high school, but I was the oldest one there. I questioned whether I was trying to act out by dating a man ten years my junior. Was I having a midlife crisis? Maybe I was, but wasn't I entitled after what I had been through?

My kids often teased me about the age difference between P.J. and me. "Mom, you were fifteen when he was five. You could have been his babysitter! That is so disgusting!" As he spent more time at my house, he began to get to know them, coming over for dinner, or going bowling or to the movies with us. He was goofy, and the girls could joke around with him. Unlike in my relationship with Matthew, I wanted the girls to know P.J. Brian was in a relationship now and I wanted them to see that I had met someone who loved and respected me. Every time I saw the way P.J. interacted with my kids it made me fall in love with him again. He was giving and sweet, and a good cook, which was a relief because I still wasn't.

Despite his young age he wasn't upset when he learned that I couldn't have any more biological children. P.J. had had a close relationship with his stepmother and said that he had never imagined himself having his own kids. He enjoyed the nurturing relationship he had with Courtney and Marija but didn't have a macho desire to have kids of his own. It was as though he'd been waiting to meet someone exactly like me.

Though I was older than P.J., I frequently found myself learning social skills from him. "Not everyone needs to like you, Laura," he would say if I complained that a friend had snubbed me. "Why don't you decide whether you really care about her before you get all upset?" If we fought, he was quick to apologize. I called him my gentle giant. When we had a disagreement and I explained my side, he didn't interrupt me. He sat quietly, taking it all in, and then he responded. Whenever I got introspective and broody, he would say, "Time to get out of the deep end of the pool." It helped me worry less and keep things in perspective. I was finally in an adult relationship—and I loved it.

That winter, in January 2008, my divorce was finally settled. I was awarded sole custody of the children and slightly more than fifty-fifty visitation time. Though I would have preferred more time, I was relieved to have been granted sole custody. I would not have to consult with Brian about educational and medical decisions, travel, or extracurricular activities, which meant I could continue what I had been doing since they had been born. I knew that if we had gotten shared custody every minute decision involving the girls would have taken multiple rounds of negotiations.

I received ninety thousand dollars in the divorce settlement, and I paid my mother fifty thousand for the legal expenses that she had paid. I felt like a thousand-pound weight had been lifted from me. The decree based my spousal support on the assumption that I could earn forty thousand a year as a registered dietitian. I was going to have to work full-time.

The day I received the decree, I took it to the Social Security and DMV offices and filed to have my name changed to Laura Lynette Vikmanis. I was elated to get my old name back. It was like the home movie of my life was being played in reverse.

Every week in the fall and winter I checked the Bengals website for cheerleader tryout details. When I went to my daughters' cheerleading competitions, I watched closely, trying to learn things. By this time Courtney had started cheering, too. At the competitions some of the Cheer Moms looked at me curiously. I had been the mom who didn't stay for practices, and even organized a car pool so I wouldn't have to drive Courtney all the time. Now I was coming to every practice and studying the girls. The Cheer Moms didn't understand what had made me go from blasé to interested.

One snowy weekend morning when the kids were with Brian, I went downstairs to my computer, opened Bengals.com, and clicked on the CHEERLEADERS tab. "Click here for more information about Tryouts for the 2008 Ben-Gals and dates for the clinic and tryouts." I was shocked to find a live link. I leaned in close, wanting to absorb every piece of information.

The application was there and I read it three times over, like the instructions on Charlie's ticket in *Charlie and the Chocolate Factory*. I printed it out—even though I would not have to hand it in for months. If cheerleading was a class, I was going to be the star student.

Date of Birth. I wrote "9/10/1968," praying that whoever read it would misread it as 1986.

Age. I wrote "39" in the tiniest numbers you have ever seen.

Dance Experience. "One and a half years Dance Theater Dayton, four years aerobics instructor at Manhattan Club for Women, Manhattan Beach, CA." Both Dance Theater Dayton and Manhattan Club for Women no longer existed. I hoped no one would look into it too closely.

Requirements: 21 years of age by September 1, 2008. That would not be a problem.

From what I was reading there was no age maximum, or at least none that they publicized.

Attached to the application was a letter to prospective Ben-Gals with the basic information about the team. "Practices are twice a week June to December and three times a week in the month leading up to the pre-season." It was a grueling schedule but I was willing to put in the time for the thrill of cheering on an NFL field, just like the girls I had watched so admiringly at the games.

"Each cheerleader is paid $75 per game." I'd had no idea the pay was so low. I thought NFL cheerleaders made tens of thousands of dollars per year. But this wasn't about the money, and it wasn't about the pom-poms. It was about healing from Brian's abuse, recovering from my lifelong body-image problems, restoring my self-esteem, being unafraid to take a flying leap. I wanted to bounce back from the painful things that had been said to me, by my dad and Joel. Do something that everyone else thought I couldn't do. Prove to myself, not anyone else, that I could set a goal and attain it, no matter my age, no matter my background, no matter my history.

The letter said that outside paid appearances were possibilities. I wondered what "possibilities" meant. Were there a lot of them? That would create even more scheduling headaches with Marija and Courtney.

"Attire for both tryouts and clinic: spandex sports bra and spandex shorts, white bottom tennis shoes with small ankle golf socks, nude color or your own skin tone color panty hose. Glamour is important and will contribute towards your score. Full complete hair style and makeup is highly recommended." On the website there were photos of past auditions and the girls were all wearing glittery, trendy outfits that looked far more sexy than athletic.

Where was I going to buy clothes like that? The only short shorts I had said "PoleKittens" on the butt.

I decided to go to a mall in Cincinnati that had a Nordstrom and other high-end stores. I went inside a Bebe, which had stylish clothes for young women, but they didn't have anything sporty. I kept walking and saw a Bebe Sport. It had hip athletic and club-bing clothes targeted toward young women—tiny silver shorts, some with rhinestones, and sexy warm-up suits, just like the ones I had seen in the website pictures. All the other shoppers were in their twenties, but if I could shop at Hustler alone, I could shop at Bebe Sport alone.

I went into the dressing room and after trying on a bunch of sports bras and the skimpiest shorts I had ever seen, I selected a turquoise bra and black shorts with white-and-turquoise stripes. I picked a Large for the shorts because I was so self-conscious about my belly flesh protruding over the band. But when I looked at myself in the mirror, I didn't look too bad.

At the register, the checkout girl said, "This will look really cute. Are you going to wear this at the gym?"

I hesitated and said, "No. Actually, I'm going to the Cincinnati Ben-Gal clinic."

"Oh," she said. "We had another girl earlier today who bought an outfit for the Ben-Gal clinic, too."

Ding. I had come to the right place.

When I told Marija and Courtney that I was auditioning to be a Ben-Gal, their first reaction was confusion. "You're going to do tumbling?" Courtney asked. They didn't go to NFL football games and didn't know what professional cheerleading looked like.

"It's more dancing than tumbling."

"Aren't cheerleaders really young?" Courtney asked. "Like in their twenties?"

"Yes, but there's no age maximum. They just pick the best dancers."

"You're trying to be a teenager," Marija said.

"Maybe I am," I said. "I guess I could just go buy a sports car or dye my hair three shades lighter, but I don't want to do that. *This* is what I want to do."

Marija rolled her eyes. I could see that she was judging me, but not sure that she should. In many ways she is like her dad. She's strong and opinionated, she doesn't take any guff from anyone, and she often butts heads with me.

Since the separation, Brian had continued to denigrate me behind my back, saying things to them like, "Your mom only cares about herself. She doesn't care about you and Courtney at all." The stress of hearing these things was taking a toll on the girls, particularly Marija, who always had a closer bond to Brian than Courtney did.

Marija believed much of what Brian told her. She was trying to figure out which parent to be loyal to—as though it was a choice. She was also beginning her own adolescence, now eleven years old. So I understood why she was unsettled to learn that her middle-aged mother wanted to be on an NFL field cheering with a bunch of twentysomethings.

When I told P.J. that I was auditioning, he was encouraging but he didn't understand the many steps in the tryout process. I explained that it was only a clinic. "I'm going to get some information," I said, "and then I'll see if I want to try out."

"That's great, baby," he said, and gave me a kiss. He had no idea how far it would go.

BEING NIKKI MILLWOOD

I DROVE UP TO THE GATE OF PAUL BROWN STADIUM IN Cincinnati and pressed the button on the intercom. "I'm here for the Ben-Gals clinic," I said, feeling like Dorothy in *The Wizard of Oz*, going up to the door to Emerald City. The guard on the intercom told me where to park and the gate opened as though by magic. I passed Cadillac Escalades, a BMW, and a Lexus with the mysterious license plate 1CHEER. I squeezed my beige 1998 Buick Regal into a spot.

After going through security, I walked down a long hallway to the gym. I passed name plaques, photographs, and seats from the old Riverfront Stadium hung up high on the walls. I thought about Grandma Colleen and Grandpa Burch going to the Bengals games in the sixties and seventies. I passed the players' weight room, with its gleaming barbells and medicine balls, and then the players' locker room. I got a peek through the window at their cubbies, the uniforms hanging there, ready to be worn. (It was only April and players had not yet returned for scheduled training.)

I arrived at a basketball gym with white walls and a huge Bengals tiger on the floor. On the side were round tables with chairs set up around them. I wondered if actual Bengals played basketball here. I checked in at a table. A stern-looking but striking woman handed me a name tag sticker and safety pin. "Go to the bathroom down the hallway to your left, change into your outfit, and pin this to yourself."

I changed into my L'eggs panty hose, Bebe Sport outfit, and tennis shoes, and went back to the gym. Girls were streaming in. Some had their outfits on under their clothes and changed right there. As more girls came in, about eighty of them, it became apparent that I was the oldest by far. The girls had smooth, tan skin and no varicose veins. Their bellies had not carried babies. Though my abdominal muscles were well formed, my belly skin was like a balloon that's been blown up and deflated twenty times. When I did plank position I could look down and see my pooch hanging down. These girls had no cellulite and no idea that someday they would. Their faces were wrinkle free, their lips lustrous. And their hair—oh, their hair! My hair was dry and brittle and weakened by years in the sun. Theirs was long and big and thick. (It would be months before I realized that many of these girls were wearing extensions.)

Some of the girls already knew one another and came in together, in groups. As I chatted with the women at my table, I saw by the name tags that there were no Lauras among them. These were not the girls' names of the late sixties but the late eighties. Britney, Rachel, Alyson, Alison, Allison, Brooke, Erin, Heather, and Jade. They said "like" a lot and they all had sparkling mobile phones and PDAs. It turned out that many had done competitive cheerleading in college. When they asked about my background, I just said, "I was in a dance company." I couldn't tell them that when I was in college, competitive student cheerleading was just beginning to take off.

As I looked around at the army of Barbies I had a flash of panic and thought about walking out. Maybe this whole thing had been a stupid idea. I was too old to be here. I took a few breaths and tried to put things in perspective. *I am in the same gym that the Bengals work out in, inside Paul Brown Stadium. My mom has never been here, Lisa has never been here, Grandma and Grandpa were never here. This is not an audition. It's a clinic. I'm going to get some information and try to get through this and then I'll decide what to do.*

The only way to get ahold of my nerves was to develop an alter ego. I had heard a joke about how to find your stripper name: Take the name of your first pet and combine it with the name of a childhood street. That made me Nikki Millwood. *Just be Nikki Millwood*, I told myself. *Have the confidence of a stripper and not a middle-aged mother of two who drives a Buick and carpools her kids to cheerleading.*

A group of women came into the gym and a hush fell over the room. There was something special about this group. They had perfect hair and makeup and they wore Ben-Gals satin jackets, tiny black shorts, and matching tennis shoes. They reminded me of the Pink Ladies in *Grease*. One of them, a slim, pretty woman in her fifties with a Florence Henderson haircut said, "I'm Charlotte Jacobs, the director of the Ben-Gals and a former Ben-Gal. I began cheering in 1974, when I was seventeen years old." I did some quick math in my head. That made her in her early fifties. She was the only person in the gym older than me. "With a few breaks I cheered until 1989, and I came back as director in 1994, but I also have a full-time job outside of the Ben-Gals."

I couldn't believe she had devoted so many years to the Ben-Gals. I thought she was tough but sweet, and immediately I wanted her to like me. She introduced the sideline captains: Shannon, a knockout redhead with tiny teeth and thick, flowing locks who also worked as the team's glamour coach; Tara, an ivory-skinned brunette; Brooke, a fit woman with big breasts and incredible muscles; Aisha, a tiny girl with insane abdominals and a bright, energetic manner; and Deanna, a voluptuous woman with curly hair, high eyebrows, and incredible abs. Traci, the woman who had signed me in, was Charlotte's assistant and co-coach.

Current Ben-Gals director Charlotte (second from top) cheering on the team during the 1974–1975 season in Riverfront Stadium
PHOTO: Charlotte Jacobs

The captains started leading us in stretches. It had been so long since I had been in a dance class—what we did in PoleKittens wasn't anything like this. Here we did across-the-floor drills like leaps and kicks. The student in me took to it right away. As we leapt the captains yelled, "Higher! Higher! Not like you're going over a puddle! Pop your legs up! Go straight in the air." We stood near one another and kicked in unison. "Don't bend your shoulders! Kick that leg high but don't cheat. Keep your head and chest up!" I was having a ball. I imagined my feet inside a pair of white boots, kicking on that bright green field.

The captains started stretching and doing splits and all the girls followed. I had done a split maybe once on the Fairmont Firebirds but I pretended I knew what I was doing. Then they did turns. I had learned pirouettes in the dance company and my muscle memory came back. I was the little single mom that could.

They taught us a dance, a "filler," and Tara explained that fillers are the short dances cheerleaders do on the sidelines throughout the game, not the long ones that they do in the end zone before the game and between quarters. There were no mirrors in the gym so I had no way of knowing how I looked. We showcased the dance in small groups, one line at a time as we had at the L.A. Clippers Spirit tryouts. Shannon kept saying, "Big heads. Big heads. Cheerleaders have to move their heads a lot." My neck was starting to ache.

Afterward we had a water break, changed into street clothes, and moved into the Bengals conference room, the room where the players watch game footage and talk strategy. The seats were enormous and cushy to accommodate the players. I wiggled my butt around, wondering if Dhani Jones, Chad Ochocinco, or Carson Palmer had ever sat in the seat I was in.

Charlotte stood up in front of everyone and said, "I want to give you some basic information about being a Ben-Gal. If you make the team, your number one priority is to represent this organization with professionalism and a positive attitude. It is an extraordinarily demanding job and it is not about the money. Our practice schedule is extremely rigorous and we have a strict policy on tardiness and absences. We expect all Ben-Gals to keep their physique and appearance in line. You'll be hearing more about that in a moment. There are weekly weigh-ins and you'll also be hearing what we expect from Ben-Gals in terms of diet and exercise."

Everything Charlotte said only made me want to get on the team more. Promptness would not be an issue; I got everywhere fifteen minutes early. And even though I was far from the best dancer in the room, so far I had been able to keep up.

"Some of you may be here because you think that being a cheerleader allows you easy access to the players." You could have heard a pin drop. "That could not be further from the truth. If you go into the Bengals locker room for any reason at any time, you will be dismissed from the team. There is no fraternization with the Bengal players or personnel except at public events. If you have a problem with this policy, then being a Ben-Gal is not for you."

Girls looked at each other. Clearly this was news to some of them. I smiled. Beyond the fact that I was in love with P.J., I was too old to date a football player and I didn't have a wedding fantasy of marrying a successful man. I'd already tried that and it hadn't worked out so well.

Brooke stood up and gave a brief talk on fitness. A former University of Kentucky cheerleader, she would go on to become the 2009 Fitness Universe Pageant Champion. "As important as it is for Ben-Gals to be beautiful," she said, "it is also crucial that we be fit. On Game Day we are on the field for three hours, moving most of that time. We have to eat right, which means eat clean. That's lean proteins, chicken and vegetables, low carbs, no fast food. We have to keep our weight down, but we also need defined and toned abs, arms, and legs. When we're not at practice we do interval training because that's how the games are—high intensity and low."

Brooke sat down and Shannon stood up—the captain with long, gorgeous red hair. "First of all I want to thank all of you for being here today. We appreciate your interest in the team and we want you to dream big and try hard. I'm going to talk to you a little bit about our expectations for the tryouts in terms of personal appearance. When you come to the tryouts, we want to see you as you're going to look on the field. I'll explain what that means."

They dimmed the lights and she did a PowerPoint presentation showing photos of "appropriate" hair. The hair was always puffy and high in the back, like a bouffant. "We begin the games with very full hair. That's so fans can see us all the way up in the stands. Make your hair as big as possible so we can see it. Don't wear any jewelry except your wedding ring if you are married. That includes earrings other than studs, nose piercings, lip piercings, and tongue piercings. If you have tattoos, wear coverup to conceal them."

She clicked to a close-up of a Ben-Gal's face. "No frosted lipsticks or eyeshadows. No glasses, contacts only. Finally, if you are selected to be a Ben-Gal, you will need to wear Orange Flip." There was a slide of a Revlon lipstick. "That is the color the Ben-Gals have been wearing as long as anyone can remember." We winced. It was bright orange and ugly.

"If you are selected to be a Ben-Gal, you will be in the Ben-Gals calendar. We started our calendar in 2003. We shoot the photos in different locations around Cincinnati and we hire professional stylists and makeup artists." She picked up a calendar and thumbed through the pages. The girls leaned in with excitement. Clearly some of them had pinup fantasies. "Now I'd like to introduce you to Alyson."

A woman stood up. She was wearing a cute business outfit—a black-and-white-checkered skirt, a pink blouse, and a jacket. "This is me in the calendar," she said and showed a gorgeous picture of herself in a skimpy bikini. "I came to the clinic just like you guys here. I was only twenty years old, too young to audition, but I worked really hard, came back the next year, and made it on the team. I am now going into my second year as a Ben-Gal. I am pursuing a masters in early childhood education but no matter what I go on to do, I will always be proud of the friends I made and the experiences I had as a Cincinnati Ben-Gal." When she said that, I felt a jolt. Here was someone who had attended a clinic, just like I was doing right now, and eventually had made the team. Maybe someday I would be giving the same speech.

After Alyson finished, we had a question-and-answer period. "How many girls do you select?" someone asked.

"Thirty or thirty-two," Charlotte answered. We murmured. It wasn't a lot. "That number includes veterans. Veterans must try out again every year, and though some do not make it, most of them do." Another murmur. With that kind of competition it seemed outrageous to think any of us stood a chance. Even if only half the veterans came back, that meant there were just sixteen spots for rookies, and surely girls would come to the preliminaries who weren't here at this clinic.

"Do cheerleaders cheer away games?" someone else asked.

"No," Charlotte said. "Only home games. That's ten unless we make it to the playoffs." At seventy-five a game, that meant $750 a season. It wouldn't even cover the gas I would need for my twice-weekly, two-way, forty-five minute commute to the stadium, much less the foundation, hairspray, panty hose, eyeliners, curling iron, tanning sessions, hair color, manicures, tennis socks, and false eyelashes I did not yet know I would have to buy.

Someone asked what we should wear to the preliminaries. "Sports bras and gym shorts," Shannon said. "Some girls even wear boyshort bottoms. You can bling out your outfit with a bedazzler, but that's up to you. Being fancy won't win you more points."

"If you want to," added Tara, "you can come up at the end of this session and we'll give you a card for a woman who makes custom tryout uniforms. You can also ask us anything you want to about appearance and we'll try to give you some pointers."

I went up, nervous but encouraged that they were making themselves so approachable. "I was hoping I could get that card for the seamstress," I said to Shannon.

"Sure," she said, handing it to me.

"And I was also wondering if you had any advice about my appearance."

She squinted. "You need to make your hair bigger."

That's easy for you to say, I thought, looking at her Rapunzel hair.

"Make sure it's way fuller than you would wear it on the street," she said. "You can buy extensions, if that helps." I could read between the lines. "You're older than the others," she was saying, "and you need to work harder to look good."

The first Monday after the clinic I went to Kentucky to the seamstress's shop. It was in Ludlow, over the river from Ohio, a tiny little town out of a Western movie. In the shop I found a middle-aged woman named Karen. All over the walls were pictures of dance and competition cheerleading teams. I ogled the photos and sparkling uniforms, feeling like I was backstage at *Jubilee!* in Las Vegas. "I want to order an outfit for the Ben-Gals tryout," I said.

"Do you know what style you want?" she asked.

"I have no idea." I looked through one of her photo albums for inspiration. At home the kids and I designed different outfits. Courtney got really into it, sketching out different cuts and colors on her pad. I looked online at cheerleader pictures and picked a black, blue, and white outfit because those were Marija and Courtney's school colors.

When I returned to Karen on a different day, I had second

thoughts about the colors. "Should I do Bengals orange and black instead?" I asked.

"You might stand out more if you choose different colors," she said.

I came back a few weeks later to pick up my outfit. It was fancy and professional-looking and it made me feel almost like a real cheerleader.

My preliminary was the first one, in late April. After that would come the semifinals and finals, if I made it that far. The day of my preliminary, I was the very first to arrive. Because I was first, I was given "1" to pin to myself. The girls were coming in droves until there were about 120 of them. Half of me was thinking, *Just have fun and do the best you can, honey,* and the other half was thinking, *Why did you even bother coming?* It was my mother's voice warring with Brian's voice. The worst thing about my marriage was the way I had internalized that hateful, negating voice. But now I had another voice in my head that talked back. It was some combination of my mother, my PoleKittens teacher, Lisa, and P.J.—all these people who believed in me. The voice said, *You're here, you can't leave now. You might be older than these girls but you can dance fine and you can do the Fireman up and down a pole. What do you have to lose by trying?*

Just as I was regaining my confidence a girl came up to me and said, "Your outfit is the color of the Dallas Cowboys." In my excitement to choose Marija and Courtney's school colors, I had inadvertently picked Dallas Cowboys colors. I was mortified.

We stood in the middle of the gym in front of the captains to learn the dance. It was four eight-counts and we had to learn it in about five minutes. Though I was distracted by my outfit faux pas, somehow I got the basic steps. Thankfully the dance didn't have any kicks, turns, or splits.

Because I was assigned number one, I had to dance first with number two. I was shaking but I tried to hear that new voice in my head. *Just get through these five minutes with your cute Dallas Cowboys Cheerleader outfit and you'll be fine.*

At the end of the dance we all had to end in Ben-Gal Pose, head snapped, hands on hips, feet in fifth position, chest out and head high, smiling. My lips were so dry they stuck to my teeth. I thought I was going to pee. But I had done it. I had learned the dance. *Good for you, honey!*

I went to the back of the line and watched the other girls. Some had a lot of flair and I felt like I could predict which ones would make it to the semifinals. I noticed that the really good girls had relaxed hands instead of raised pinkies. Their dance style was hip-hoppy and sassy. Most of the girls were slender but some had a few more pounds on them and were better dancers. I began to see that not all cheerleaders had to look exactly alike. The women were becoming more beautiful to me as I saw their skill. I realized this wasn't only about outer beauty, but inner. Maybe I could make it on to the team despite my age.

When the last pair was done, Charlotte said, "Now everyone is going to do it again." I had forgotten the dance. My partner and I moved to the front. I tried to remember the sequence and somehow the moves came back. This time I acted like a Ben-Gal, really busting it out and getting in the moment.

The captains asked us to walk across the gym in groups of five and do Ben-Gal Pose so they could look at our figures. While we did this they were writing stuff down, glancing up and down at us, and whispering. It was nerve-wracking. I became extremely conscious of my legs being too short and my hair not being blond enough. My lips were shaking, my calves trembling. Surely they could see how over-the-hill I was. When I smiled, my wrinkles showed. Were they looking at my belly skin? Could they tell I'd had a kid? Could they tell I'd had two?

When all the girls were finished, Charlotte said, "If we call your number, we want you to stay for a meeting and we'll tell you about the next tryout. If we don't, you can pack up your things and go home."

I heard her call, "Number one."

Wait a minute. Did they say that if they call your number you should leave or you should stay? I looked at the other girls to gauge their reactions. The ones whose numbers were called were high-fiving each other. I became certain that I had misheard and Charlotte hadn't called my number. When she finished, I went over to her and asked, "Did you call my number? I'm number one."

She looked down at the sheet and said, "Yeah. Number one can stay."

I had made it through one round! I hadn't been cut. No matter what happened from here, I could tell anyone I met that I had made it through the first round of Ben-Gal auditions. I hadn't humiliated myself. I had done just fine, in fact, better than fine.

The rejects were pouting. Some were crying. They gathered their things quickly and left. The group thinned out until there were only about ninety of us left. There was a feeling of excitement and pride. We all sat down and Tara said, "You'll notice that we didn't test you on kicks, turns, or splits today. That's because we do them at the semifinals in three weeks." I felt like I was going to throw up. "The semis will begin with an interview. You should bring business attire for that. Then we'll do technique for the kicks, turns, and splits and score you on it." *Uh oh.* "It's a lot to get through so be ready for a really long day."

When the meeting was over, I went up to the captains and coaches. "Is there anything else I should know about the semifinals?" I asked Shannon.

"Your hair," she said.

"I made it bigger, like you said."

"It needs more volume. Maybe use a curling iron or curlers."

I went out and bought a curling iron. For the next two weeks I experimented with different hairstyles, trying to get it as big as I could.

I was nervous about doing splits, so I asked Courtney for help. "Can you teach me how to do a split? I'm not flexible enough but I have to learn them because they're really important to making the team." My quiet, introverted younger daughter suddenly lit up. She was incredibly flexible and splits came easily to her. She showed me how to stretch to get greater flexibility, and go down farther and farther into the straddle. "Don't lean on your butt," Courtney said. "You have to lean forward if you really want to get the biggest stretch." We practiced with my left leg in front because I remembered ending the kick sequence with the left leg and eventually I could get a foot off the floor. I saw the pride she was taking in being able to correct me. She knew more about something than I did, and this was important to her. Here was my nine-year-old teaching me something I really needed to learn. I could see her glowing as she coached me. We both enjoyed the role reversal.

The semifinals were held on the plaza level of the stadium. There was a big glass wall and you could see the city from it. I felt awed, looking out at the city, all of Cincinnati laid out before me.

This time a lot of other girls had come early, too, so I was number twelve. I had curled my hair and I was wearing my interview outfit: a pants suit and high platform heels. Because of the platforms, the pants were above my ankles. Despite my clam-digger look, the interview was the only part of the process that didn't intimidate me. A month before, I had left the hospital, because there were no full-time positions, and taken a job as a representative for a small pharmaceutical company. My new job forced me to talk to doctors all day long, selling Vitamin B_{12} nasal spray, a moisturizer, and a urinary tract infection medication. I was good at it. And even though Brian had robbed me of my self-confidence, I had started to get it back. Like my father, who had gone from engineering to business over the course of his career, I had a knack for interpersonal relations.

For the interviews, Deanna, Traci, and Charlotte sat on high barstools at a cocktail table. I walked up. "What do you think about the Bengals as a team?" Charlotte asked.

I hadn't been prepared to talk about football. "Actually I don't know a whole lot about the team," I said, figuring I would probably get into more trouble if I lied, "but my family has had season tickets since 1968 and Bengals games were on TV all the time at my grandparents' house." She smiled and nodded. As long as we weren't judged on football statistics, I had probably done all right.

Then I noticed Charlotte looking down at my application, pointing to something. She was going to tell me that there was an age limit. I had skipped something on the form, some crucial line that said, *Cheerleaders must be under thirty*. My kids were going to laugh at me when I came home. The other prospects would see my tears and realize I'd been rejected due to my age. It was all over.

She pointed to the paper and said, "I see . . ."

"Yes?" I said, swallowing hard.

"I see that you live really far," she said. "Are you aware that Ben-Gals cannot live more than fifty miles from the stadium?"

I giggled. "I live thirty-nine miles away," I said. I had read the rule in the information packet and Google-mapped the distance from my house.

"Do you think you're going to be able to drive this far all the time? Do you have a good car?"

"Absolutely."

My age never came up, not then or at any other point in the process. Years later, Charlotte told me after I made the cut that age was not at all important to her. All she cared about was picking the best dancers, the most professional girls, and the ones most likely to have positive attitudes. I do not know whether she felt a unique bond with me because I was close in age to her, but if she did, she won't admit it because she likes to be perceived as age-blind, able to see only talent and sparkle. The notion that age—or anything else—would bias her offends her belief that only the most deserving women are picked to be Cincinnati Ben-Gals.

For the technique portion of the semifinals we all changed into our outfits and stood on a black-and-white-checkered dance floor (there had been a prom there the night before). "Everyone will get points based on her technique," Charlotte said. "Those points will go toward your final score."

The elevator doors opened and about twenty women came out. They were laughing, easy and confident, all in chic-looking Bengal-colored orange-and-black outfits that looked far more professional than the homemade ones most of us were wearing. They were beautiful and comfortable and graceful. These were the Ben-Gal veterans.

The veterans stood to the side and practiced the turns—left single, right single, left double, right double, and the kick sequence, which ended with a split on the right leg. They got it in a snap. They even looked bored.

"Did she just do the split on her right leg?" I asked the girl next to me.

"Yeah," she answered.

I had been practicing on my left leg. How was I going to do it on my right leg with no practice?

After we warmed up, we walked to the end of the dance floor and lined up according to our numbers to perform for the captains and coaches. We started with the turns, which didn't seem too hard. I was fine on the singles but messed up on the doubles. I wanted to look like a ballerina, but instead I stepped out of the turn to catch my balance. That would surely count against my score.

I wasn't that bad on the kicks, but I still had no idea how I was going to do a right split at the end. I just went for it, and because I was so nervous I slid down like a deranged robot, farther and farther, until I hit the floor. My hamstrings were on fire. I was certain I'd ripped them, but I tried to make my wince come off as a smile.

During the leap portion I tripped on the raised floor, right in front of the captains and coaches. The room went silent. It was like the scene in *Flashdance* when Jeanie falls over on the ice to "Gloria." I had to walk back to my starting point. I was close to crying. Charlotte said, "You can do it again if you want." So I did it again and this time I didn't trip.

After what seemed like endless conferring between the captains and the coaches, we all lined up like we were in a beauty pageant to learn who could stay. "If I don't call your number," Charlotte said, "please come try out again. I can't tell you your scores but I can encourage you to come back. Please don't give up. We're so grateful to all of you for getting through this very long day."

I heard my number. I knew it hadn't been a mistake. We were down to about seventy girls. A few weeks earlier I had been happy simply to be at the clinic, gathering information. Now, assuming all the veterans made it, I had about a one in three chance of making it myself. They weren't great odds but I was proud to have come so far. I had proved to myself that I was among the best. That was the important thing, not necessarily getting on the team. But although I told myself this, I had to admit that what I really wanted more than anything else was to become a Ben-Gal.

By this point we had been at the stadium for five hours and I was completely exhausted, ready to go home. Deanna stood up and said, "Is everyone ready? I'm going to teach you the dance you'll perform at the finals." *More? We have to stay for more?*

It turned out to be thirteen eight-counts long—not a little two eight-count dance. It was fun and sexy and the music was "Shake Your Pom Pom" by Missy Elliott, a song I had never heard before. I loved the dance but I could not remember one eight-count of the choreography. I was frustrated and tired, trying to follow along. I had my camera with me so I could scrapbook the event, and as the girls began to walk out, I asked Deanna if I could video her doing it. She said yes and I taped her. If she hadn't, I would never have been able to learn the dance.

On the drive home I cried from exhaustion and elation. I called P.J. and said, "I made it to the finals."

"You mean there's another round?" he said.

"Yep."

"So after that are they going to pick the team?"

"Yeah," I said. "I probably have a one in three chance."

Throughout the whole process he had listened to my Ben-Gal chatter with only one ear. "Clinic." "Preliminary." "Semifinal." Now he was hearing "finals." As a sports fan he knew that was serious. "So what does this mean again? Are you going to be on the field if you get on?"

"Yeah," I said. "But I don't know if I will."

The finals were one week away. I knew it would be the most nerve-wracking portion of the process. Charlotte said there would be fifteen to twenty judges selected from the community, including local celebrities.

At home I watched the video of Deanna over and over again and practiced with Courtney and Marija two to three times a day, while Penny watched me, her tail wagging. "Tell me what I'm doing wrong," I said to the girls one night after school.

"You should use facials," Marija said. A "facial" was the cheerleading term for the mouthing of different vowels as the cheerleader goes into different positions. High school and college competitive cheerleaders use facials, but not NFL cheerleaders.

"They said at the clinic not to do facials," I said.

"I think you should do them anyway," Marija said. She did not yet understand that NFL cheerleading bears almost no resemblance to competitive cheerleading. The two are apples and oranges. In NFL cheerleading there are no stunts like pyramids or throws. It is almost entirely dance. Competitive cheerleading is like gymnastics, with back flips, roundoffs, and somersaults.

But the girls could see that my moves were too tentative. Cheerleaders had to be confident, they had to own the moves. Over the next week I practiced so much that they memorized the dance. "Be sharper," Courtney said. "More hip-hop."

"I don't know what hip-hop is!"

"Stronger gestures," she said. "Your hands look silly. You're not supposed to put your pinkies out. Relax them."

For three and a half years I had shuttled them back and forth to cheerleading, sitting around and watching the practices with

Cheer Moms, and now my daughters knew enough to coach me. At that moment I felt grateful to have daughters and not sons, and grateful to live in a part of the country where girls started cheering in third grade. Surely I would be the only one at the finals who had been able to ask her daughters for help. What was I thinking? I would be the only one at the finals with daughters.

The only thing that made me more anxious than the dance was the bathing suit walk. They had told us that we had to wear bikinis. We were not allowed to wear panty hose, just jewelry and heels. To me this was asking us to appear with no makeup, like in those scary "before" pictures you see on face-lift ads. At the audition and semifinals I had felt protected by the panty hose underneath my shorts, but in a bikini everyone would see my thick thighs, postpartum belly, and the varicose veins that remained even though I'd had surgery to repair them. The judges would rank me so low that I wouldn't make it.

I went to the Victoria's Secret site and began browsing bikinis until I found one I loved: a blue suit with a gold chain at the hip and gold chains around the neck. When it came in the mail, I tried it on.

"What do you think, P.J.?"

"You look hot," he said.

Even the girls liked it.

The night before the finals, I stayed at P.J.'s apartment in Cincinnati because it was closer to the stadium. He left early for work and I got ready by myself. The other times I had auditioned he had seen me beforehand; this time I was running blind. Remembering Shannon's hair advice I made it huge, curling it and then brushing out the curls and teasing it. On my drive to the stadium my hair was so high that it touched the ceiling of my car. People in other cars were staring. I thought it was because I was sexy but later I realized it was because of my enormous, Ivana Trump–like hair.

Check out the helmet hair.

At the finals the other girls weren't as friendly as they had been before. Everyone was in competition mode. They weren't going to tell me if my hair made me look deranged.

The judges included funk musician Bootsy Collins, local meteorologist Steve Raleigh, former Ben-Gals, and restaurant owner Jeff Ruby—all sitting at long tables at the back of the gym. Charlotte explained that the judges would tally us on several categories, including glamour, physique, showmanship, and skill set. "Each category will be worth five points," she said. "At the end we will tally all of the judges' scores. The bathing suit competition works differently, however. That is just a 'yes' or a 'no.'" I could see Bootsy Collins scrawling *No funking way!* when he got a load of me.

For the dance we went two by two, most of the rookies paired with veterans. My partner was Latasha, an African American woman who was much taller than me. Because the dance was hip-hoppy, I was intimidated. Everybody was watching—and there was a camera crew taping the whole thing, with bright lights.

But thanks to Marija and Courtney's help, I remembered the steps. When I finally finished I wanted to burst into tears out of relief.

For the bathing suit walk I put on my high heels, darkened my makeup, and sprayed my hair so it was even bigger. Everyone lubed up their legs and bellies with oil and put on jewelry. We went one by one past the judges.

There was so much to remember. *Chest up. Don't trip in your heels. Make sure your bathing suit isn't riding up your butt. Suck in your stomach.* I tried to move to the music but didn't want my flesh to jiggle. The judges were only a few feet from me, and I saw their eyebrows go up when they got a look at my hair. Some of them winced. I walked all the way down to the end of the room and noticed Charlotte standing there. She nodded just slightly. Even though I had helmet hair she thought I had done okay. My aging body had passed muster. As I turned around I saw a guy on the floor with a camera and realized he was filming me. My saggy thirty-nine-year-old butt had been right in the lens.

When each girl finished, we stood in rows of five while they stared at us. Then Charlotte said, "Turn around," and we all turned around. *Clench your cheeks but not too tight because if you do, your cellulite pops out. Arch your back. Don't tuck your butt under or it will sag.*

Twenty years ago I had been at Los Angeles Memorial Coliseum auditioning for the L.A. Clippers Spirit. I remembered the dreams I had had for myself at nineteen, the optimism I had felt about the future. I never imagined back then that I would marry a man who abused and belittled me. Some of my dreams for myself had come true—I had two amazing children—but most of the past twenty years had been a slow and steady shattering of my optimism. I had been emotionally battered to the point where I stopped allowing myself to dream. I didn't know what I wanted. I didn't know what I *could* want.

The first step of my recovery was allowing myself to dream, the way I did in my new empty house that day in June 2007. The second step was choosing a dream. Your dream might be to become a black belt in karate or running a marathon or becoming a master chef, or even losing your last five pounds of baby weight. Mine was to become a Ben-Gal and all that it represented about football and about my hometown. And I didn't care if other people thought it was stupid or naive. I wanted to be out on the field of Paul Brown Stadium doing a kick line for tens of thousands of fans.

I looked around at the girls to my left and right, at their shining but frightened eyes, and I realized with surprise that I had more confidence than they did. Even if I never made it on to the Ben-Gals, I had moved past where I was just two years before, when I told Brian I wanted a divorce. I had wisdom from age and the ability to appreciate moments like this. I hoped these girls would have joyful lives, get an education, and allow themselves to dream. I prayed that no man would ever harm them with words or hands.

After the bathing suit competition ended, Charlotte called us to the center of the gym. "Each of you will get a letter in the mail," she said, "letting you know whether you've been accepted on the team. We will tally the results over the next couple of days and the thirty-two top-scoring women will make the team. You should receive it by the end of the week, next Monday at the latest."

We took a group photo. I noticed a camera crew doing individual interviews with girls. One of the crew members, a fortyish woman with glasses and short brown hair, came up to me. "We're making a four-part series called *The Making of a Ben-Gal* for Fox

Sports Ohio," she said. "It's to show people what the process of getting on this team entails. Would it be okay if we interviewed you about your experiences?"

"Absolutely," I said. On camera she asked how I felt. "This is so great," I said. "I'm almost forty and being a Ben-Gal is something I really want to do." Afterward she asked if they could come to my house to interview me in a couple of days. I said sure, excited to go on TV.

When I got home, all I wanted to do was veg out with P.J. and not think about anything. We lay on the couch and he kept stroking my hair, pushing it down because it was so big. It made a crunching noise.

The whole week I had second thoughts about being a Ben-Gal. I had wanted it so badly but now that it was a real possibility I would make it I was scared. I told P.J., "I know I said I wanted it but holy crap, what if I actually do?"

"Why are you worrying about something that hasn't even happened yet?" he said.

On Thursday the TV producer, also named Laura, came to my house. I had told her to come at five so Marija and Courtney would be home and could get on camera with me. As soon as I got back from work I did my hair and makeup. The girls and I sat on the couch. With the camera rolling, Laura asked some questions about my auditioning and what the girls thought about it. Then the cameraman turned off the camera. I thought the interview was over.

"It turns out you're not going to get a letter in the mail," Laura said. "We actually have it right here." I thought she was kidding but then I saw an envelope in her hand. "Would you mind opening it on camera and reading it aloud?" she asked.

I had to have made it. She obviously knew I had and wanted

this exciting moment for her television show. I felt like Ed Mc-Mahon had just knocked on my door.

The lighting guy was flipping on his light and the camera went back on. The girls, who had worked so hard to help me prepare, were saying, "Mom! Mom! Oh my God!"

Laura gave me the envelope and I opened it and pulled out the letter. "Dear Ben-Gal Candidate, Your hard work at tryouts was very much appreciated as competition was at an 'all time high.' Unfortunately, your score did not make the final squad. We thank you for giving your best as well as your valuable time . . ." At the top Charlotte had hand-written, "Good tryout, Laura. I'm sorry it didn't work!"

My throat closed. I blinked back tears. The girls leaned in and hugged me. I could see Laura's face behind the camera. She was hunched down in her chair. "I'm so sorry," she mouthed.

When the camera went off again, she said how badly she felt. She said that all the other girls they had taped had been accepted. This made me feel worse. Brian's insults were rushing back to my head—"stupid," "dumb," "worthless," "ugly," "fat."

"It's fine," I lied. "I'm going to be okay."

"Are you going to try out again next year?" she asked.

"I don't know."

"You have to. You need to stick up for women our age."

The girls were hugging me and patting me on the back. "It's okay, Mom," Marija said. "You did great. You can try out again."

"We *want* you to," Courtney said. I wasn't sure. I didn't want to go through the excitement, only to be disappointed again. I sent the girls out to play. I just wanted everyone in my house to leave so I could go up to my bedroom and cry.

SMELLS LIKE TEAM SPIRIT

I CRIED FOR AN HOUR, SULKING. THEN I REMOVED MY TRYOUT outfit from my bedroom closet and put it downstairs in the standing closet in my office as though symbolically shelving my dream. P.J. came home and consoled me. "You came so far," he said. "You made it all the way to the finals on your first try. How many other women did that?"

"Not many," I said.

"You should focus on the good part, how far you got," he said, "not the fact that you didn't get on. Some of those girls have been cheering since they were kids. You stopped dancing for, like, twenty years before you started up again. You have to give yourself a break."

"I love you," I said.

That night I laid awake in bed. *I'll just sit with this and think about it for two weeks*, I told myself, *and then I'll see if I want to try out again.* By the time I woke up I knew the answer. I went from "I'm never auditioning for the Ben-Gals again" to "Maybe I should consider it" to "This is how I'm going to get on," in one night. I wanted to prove to myself that after everything I had been through—the numbness, the deadness, the soullessness that I had felt for so long—I could find my spirit again and get on the team.

"Girls," I announced the next morning at breakfast. "I'm going to try out for the team again next year. A lot of women don't make it till their second or third time trying out. I really want this and I'm going to do everything I can to get on, just like you guys work so hard to win your cheer competitions." I wanted them to see that when you don't get what you want, you shouldn't just give up. I wanted them to see that hard work could pay off—though I felt that if I got cut again, I was going to jump into the Ohio River.

I was convinced that one of the reasons I had been rejected was because my hip-hop dancing was so pathetic. That fall I signed up for a hip-hop class in a strip mall. Though billed as an adult class, it turned out to be all twelve-year-old girls and me. On the first day one of the kids came up to me and asked, "Are you our teacher?"

"No," I said. "I'm a student." She looked at me like I was crazy.

Another girl came up to me. She was a friend of Marija and when she saw me, she said, "Is Marija taking the class?"

"No, she's not," I said. "*I* am." She gave me the same look as the other girl: lip slightly curled up, bewildered. Why would an over-the-hill mom be in a class like this? I tried not to dwell on that critical look. I had whiled away hours chatting with jocks at the Porch of All Sorts. I had a stripper pole in my basement. I had done half-marathons. I had slept with a man on the first date. I had shopped at Hustler alone. What did I care what a twelve-year-old kid thought of my taking a hip-hop class?

Our instructor turned out to be about twenty-five, but I figured it was better to have a cool young teacher than an old one. After the first class, I took her aside. "I just want you to know why I'm here," I said. "I auditioned for the Ben-Gals and got cut at the very end. I want to try out again but I need practice doing hip-hop. I was trained in jazz and tap so this is all pretty new to me."

"That's awesome that you're trying out again," she said.

As ridiculous as I felt in the hip-hop classes, dancing next to one of Marija's friends, my confidence grew. I learned how to do the moves popular in cheerleader choreography: popping, the pony, glides, and head whips. Because the dance style was a bit sexy, a lot of twelve-year-olds struggled, but because of my pole-dancing class I didn't. I wasn't as bad at hip-hop dancing as I had thought.

Instead of a recital we had an observation day where parents could come in and watch. I asked Courtney and Marija to come but they were too embarrassed, so I had to dance in front of all the moms whose daughters were in the class. They were in street clothes and there I was doing the Crip walk in workout pants and a skintight top. They thought I was going through the biggest midlife crisis in Springboro.

Now that I was taking hip-hop with tweens I felt like I could do anything. In my sessions with Rose I had been talking about my shame of my flat chest. Half-jokingly I had said to her, "I've thought about getting a boob job."

"Why don't you, then?" she had said. I was pleasantly surprised that she wasn't judgmental. Since then I had been thinking more about whether implants would improve my self-esteem, or just make me feel worse. Later that fall, I decided to use some of the money from my settlement to finally have the surgery. I loved the idea of spending some of Brian's money on new breasts because he always said fake breasts looked stupid. P.J. was supportive, no pun intended.

At my consultation the plastic surgeon said, "Your assignment when you come back is to bring girly magazines with nude photos and good lighting. Bring me a picture that shows exactly the size you want." I went back to Hustler and ventured into the sex den part to buy girly magazines. Lisa and I looked through them at my house. I picked out a photo of a girl with really big boobs, double Ds, and brought it to the doctor. While some might judge these as too big, I felt I needed to make a change that was truly significant, having been self-conscious of my small chest my entire teen and adult life. This was the only size that could give me cleavage, and I had dreamed of having it since I was an adolescent girl. Molly Ringwald had put on lipstick with her cleavage in *The Breakfast Club.* My mother and Lisa could hide tissues, money, the *Oxford English Dictionary*, in the space between their breasts. I wanted cleavage like that and I was tired of wearing push-up bras to get only a hint of it.

As I was about to go under I realized that this physical transformation was only the latest step in a journey that had begun two years earlier when Brian moved out of the house. I wanted to gain the physical confidence I needed to accompany my newfound emotional confidence. When I woke up and saw the bandages crisscrossed on my chest and breasts rising from my chest, which they had never done before, I started to cry. I didn't know why I had waited so long. I felt like every woman with a boob inferiority complex should go out and get fake ones.

Once my scars healed and I was going outside again, I felt like a different person. These were the breasts I had always wanted. I loved my new body. I started talking more kindly to myself in the mirror. I would say things like, "Wow, you look great naked." I felt more sexual. I got more confidence in bed with P.J., who liked to say, "I've loved all your boobs."

But the implants looked fake—and people had strong reactions to them. Something changed as I began to walk around with a pair of double-D breasts. People stared at me and not always nicely. They would roll their eyes, sneer, or turn away and whisper. The nastiest looks came from women. They weren't that different from the looks that obese people get.

At first these looks bothered me. Women seemed to go through a mental calculus when they saw me. They clocked the boobs and then they decided: *She must be a porn star, a stripper, or a slut.* It was as though they felt my boobs told my entire story. Because the glances were so hurtful, I had a brief moment of regret about my decision. I worried that I had gone too big.

Over time I moved past it. I told myself that other people's opinions of my body didn't matter. I had gotten the surgery for myself and I didn't need to defend it or explain it to anyone. If people wanted to glare at me, I couldn't stop them, but I couldn't let it get to me.

Knowing that I would be trying out for the Ben-Gals again the following spring, I developed an intense exercise schedule to make sure that I didn't put on weight and that I was in great shape at the tryouts. Every Monday, Wednesday, and Friday I woke up at five in the morning, before the girls were up, drove to my gym, and did forty-five minutes of weight training, using free weights, machines, and medicine balls.

I didn't ask anyone for help because I had been a certified personal trainer at Manhattan Club for Women and had learned new exercises from training Donna. I wore my iPod and didn't talk to anyone, though I watched other people when they didn't know it and got ideas from their routines. I introduced plyometrics, a type of performance training that includes exercises with strange names such as mountain climbers, crabs, and crawl-outs, into my workout. Every Tuesday, Thursday, and one weekend day I ran three to five miles outside. On weekends when I didn't have my kids I did a longer run, six or seven miles.

One morning at the gym as I was lying on a bench doing triceps extensions, holding a twenty-pound medicine ball above my face, I lost my grip. The ball landed on my face and dropped onto the floor. I looked around quickly, hoping no one had noticed, and put my hand to my nose in agony. "Are you okay?" a guy near me said. He was buff and he appeared to be about my age. I nodded, embarrassed. "Those are called nose breakers," he said.

As I waited for the tryouts to roll around again I spent a lot more time watching the Bengals on TV with P.J. I asked him questions about the rules, expanding on my previous knowledge: the plane trip to L.A. and *The Complete Idiot's Guide to Football*. He was patient, and because he was a diehard fan himself he didn't mind me asking all the questions. I was the dream girlfriend of a thirty-year-old guy: a hot older woman who loves sex, can't get pregnant, wants to be a cheerleader, and is obsessed with football.

We went to games and I watched the cheerleaders closely, recognizing girls from the tryouts, but I also watched the players. Unfortunately, the Bengals 2008 season was abysmal. The team ended the season at four, eleven, and one, and many of their most famous players, like Carson Palmer, were barely present. There had been a lot of injuries and fans were down on owner Mike Brown (Paul Brown's son), who had never hired a general manager. Others blamed coach Marvin Lewis.

I didn't care how bad the Bengals were. They were my team and I wanted to cheer for them. I wanted to be a part of something bigger than myself.

Finally the Super Bowl came and I knew it would be only a

matter of weeks before Ben-Gals tryout information went online. One day I went to Bengals.com and saw a link that said a former Ben-Gal named Nikki VordemEsche was teaching classes in Cincinnati, open to the public, to help prospective Ben-Gals prepare for the tryouts. These classes would no doubt be more useful than my hip-hop class with twelve-year-olds.

There were about twenty women in Nikki's class, all in their twenties, some of whom I recognized from the 2008 clinic and tryouts. Almost everyone would be auditioning for the Ben-Gals. Nikki had been a Ben-Gal for seven years and taught the class in a tumbling gym that she owned. If I didn't know she had been a cheerleader, I never would have guessed. She was a married mother in her midthirties who wore no makeup, had a blunt, unflappable manner, and was a phenomenal dancer.

At the first class I told her that I had auditioned for the 2008 Ben-Gals but had been cut at the finals. She said she had been there, running the sound cues. She squinted at me as though trying to remember which one I was, and finally she snapped her fingers and said, "You're the one with the hair."

"Yes!" I cried. "That's me! The big hair!"

"How come no one told you it was too big?"

"I don't know. Shannon kept telling me bigger and bigger, and I just did it the way I thought she would like it."

"Okay, here's your first tip," Nikki said. "Don't do that again. Wear your hair exactly the way it is right now."

From that moment on I knew she could help me. In her class I learned kicks, splits, turns, and former Ben-Gals dances. "This is the dance we did at kickoff," she would say. I felt like I was getting the inside scoop. It was like PoleKittens and hip-hop put together. She gave us pointers like, "At the auditions, and even at the clinics, the coaches are always watching you, even when you think they're not. Make sure you show up dressed to the nines. Never let them see you in sweats."

She taught us how to walk and how to hold our heads. She said we had to be on time and have a positive attitude at tryouts. We did a mock bathing suit walk. All the challenges that had filled me with dread the first year now felt familiar, if not easy. It was like having a spy on the Ben-Gals.

One of my classmates was a low-key woman who was slightly older than the other girls. Her name was Brandy Sanchez and she was from Kentucky. She was twenty-nine and tall, with brandy-colored hair. She worked in paper-supply sales and she was married, which made me think she might be more mature than some of the single girls. We started talking and soon became close. I told her about my age and kids and divorce. Brandy told me that she had auditioned twice before, and then taken two years off, and now she was auditioning for the third time. She had cheered in college at the University of Louisville and desperately wanted to be a Ben-Gal. She said, "If I don't make it on this time, I'm not trying out again." I felt we were similar because we both had so much at stake.

When I went to the stadium for each round of auditions I had new friends, Brandy, my classmates, and some other women I had gotten to know at the clinic. One of them, Elizabeth, had kinky blond hair and looked like Elizabeth Berkley. She was a chemical engineer and I was in awe that she was pursuing such divergent interests at the same time.

We didn't have the veterans' level of confidence, but we were unified, like sisters. I decided that if I didn't make it, I would be proud to sit in the stands and watch any of these women cheer.

Nikki's class had allowed me to bond with a fun, smart, confident, and sweet group of women. It was the most important gift she had given me. I wasn't yet a Ben-Gal but I felt Ben-Gally.

During the tryouts Nikki put us in touch with a veteran Ben-Gal named Jade. She had a dance studio in her basement and to get extra pointers, we practiced the tryout dance in front of her and her mirrors so she could coach us on technique. One day she let us put on her white Ben-Gal boots and dance in them one by one. They were too big but I didn't care. Brandy and I called them "magic boots," because when you're in them, you dance like a Ben-Gal. When it was time to take them off, I felt like I was taking off my prom dress.

By the time the finals came, six of the women in Nikki's class were still in contention, including Brandy and me. That year the finals were held in a Kentucky reception hall and open to the public for twenty-five dollars a ticket. These ticket fees were one of many ways that Charlotte—and other cheerleading directors around the country—were bringing in extra money for their teams. If the public liked cheerleaders, then cheerleading teams were going to make some money off of them.

I invited P.J., Lisa, her husband Jim, my mom, and the kids. Jim had a car lift in his garage and, like my father and Lisa, he loved to work on cars. "You know, Laura," he joked as the finals were beginning, "if you get to be a Ben-Gal, I'm going to hang the Ben-Gals swimsuit calendar in my garage."

"Oh God," I said. "Let's just take it one day at a time."

At the reception hall there was a dance floor, a DJ, and professional lighting—like a wedding party but with a local news crew. The judges sat at a big, long table, and the celebrities were drinking the entire time, which would either help me or hurt me, I wasn't sure. Clearly these finals were as much about publicity for

Auditioning in 2009 (the second time's the charm)

the Ben-Gals as anything else. This time I did my dance, which included double turns, splits, and leaps, perfectly.

A few days later I got a call from a Ben-Gal named Lindsay C., whom I had gotten to know at the tryouts the year before. She made the team, while I didn't. Lindsay was a quick-witted girl with a short, blond bob and a pert smile, and she looked like Cameron Diaz. "I'm going on the radio with another veteran to talk about the tryouts," she said. "Since you went through them twice as a rookie, we were wondering if you could come on the radio with us and talk about your experiences."

I said, "Yes, totally!" I had never been on the radio. I told my entire family what time I would be on, so everyone was listening. I arrived at the station, 700 WLW and in the studio, I saw Lindsay C. and another veteran named Lindsey H., who had huge sexual energy, brown hair, brown eyes, and a tattoo of a fairy on her lower back.

The radio host was Bill Cunningham, a goofy middle-aged guy known for his quick wit. The microphones went on and Lindsay, Lindsey, and I talked about the auditions. I saw Bill squint at me. "Laura," he said, "you look a little more mature than the other girls. How old are you?"

"Forty."

"No way!" Lindsay's and Lindsey's jaws dropped.

The studio door opened. Charlotte came in. I thought it was strange that she was coming in during the middle of our interview. She took a seat behind a microphone and handed Bill a sheet of paper. "Charlotte Jacobs, the Cincinnati Ben-Gal director, has just joined us," Bill said. "She has given me a list of the girls who have made it on the 2009 squad. She also has the notification letters for the three girls here in our studio. We are going to have them read the letters on air and then we'll read the complete list of 2009 Cincinnati Ben-Gals."

I flashed back to the *Making of a Ben-Gal* program the year before. The Ben-Gals couldn't possibly do this to me again: reject me in front of the whole city, on the air. I had gotten to know Charlotte from having gone through the process twice and I knew she wasn't cruel. Maybe I had made it. Bill held up the sheet in his hand. I could see a narrow column of names printed on it and tried to see if there was a long one, near the bottom. But there were three of us waiting to hear and it wouldn't be very dramatic if all of us got on. Neither Lindsay nor Lindsey would be cut. I had seen them at finals and they were both fantastic dancers. I was the odd one out.

"You know what?" Bill said. "Laura, since you're the rookie, you're going to open your letter first."

"No," I said. "I don't want to."

"I want you to open it."

He passed me the envelope. I ran my finger under the seal and pulled out the letter. I had double vision but I spotted the word

"Congratulations." There was some writing and beneath it a list of names. I scanned the list and then there it was—the V with all those letters after it. Never had I felt so happy to have a long Latvian last name. I read the letter aloud on the air, my voice quivering.

Charlotte, Lindsay, and Lindsey were cheering and clapping. The other girls opened their letters and then Bill read off the names of all the girls who had been accepted. I heard Elizabeth's name and Brandy's, and two women from Nikki's class. I felt like I was Julia Roberts getting cast in *Pretty Woman*.

I drove home from the radio studio, crying. My cell phone rang and rang with congratulations—Lisa, Jim, P.J., my mom, and friends from Kettering who hadn't spoken to me in years but had heard the segment.

After I stopped crying and the phone was quiet, I had a moment to think about what had happened. Now it was real. The first team meeting was on Tuesday. How was I going to juggle being a Ben-Gal with the reality of my life?

THE GAZER, THE GUMBYS, AND ME

THE FIRST BEN-GALS MEETING WAS HELD IN THE BENGALS TEAM conference room. Before I was on the team, I had felt like a guest in those big cushy seats. Now I felt like I belonged. One of the best things about making the team was that now I would see my new friends twice a week.

Brandy and I watched the veterans saunter in together, about a dozen of them. They sat together and talked loudly about their summer vacations. All the rookies listened closely, wanting to hear how they interacted so we could imitate them. (Later I would learn that veterans meet in the Ben-Gals locker room before each practice to gab and get ready. How the veterans always managed to arrive together was one of many mysteries I would not solve until I became a veteran myself the following year.)

I noticed that the veterans' slang was different from the slang Marija and Courtney used. It was twentysomething slang. They said things like, "I'm a hot mess," "It's all good," "We got this," and "No worries." They were also fond of acronyms. If a girl said something funny, another girl would slap her right thigh rhythmically and say, "O.M.G. That. Is. Hilarious." But she wouldn't laugh. If a veteran was talking about a woman she didn't like, she would say, "She is such a B-I-T-C-H." Maybe they used acronyms because they were used to spelling "B-E-N-G-A-L-S" in cheers.

At seven P.M., Charlotte, Deanna, and Traci (who were co-coaches this year); Tara (the captain and a corner captain); and the other corner captains came in. They were Sarah J., a tall, slender brunette with waist-length hair who would later become captain; Rachel, a sandy-haired, cat-eyed flexible dancer; and Latasha, who had been my dance partner at the 2008 tryouts.

We went down the line saying our names and talking a little about ourselves. Two things surprised me. The first was that I was not the only mother on the team. There was another girl, Heather, and she had a toddler.

I was delighted and impressed to discover that many of the girls had highly ambitious careers. In addition to Elizabeth, the chemical engineer, Tara was pursuing a PhD in cancer and cell biology, Jade was an attorney who had come to the finals the same day she took her bar exam, Andrea a nurse, Lindsay a pharmaceutical rep, and Jessie a medical student. Sunny, a gorgeous Korean American woman who would also become captain, ran her own dance studio. But there were also a bartender and a girl who waitressed at Hooters.

I myself had been laid off from my pharmaceutical-rep job and had taken a position running a weight-loss program at the office of my family physician. I counseled patients who wanted to lose weight, talking with them about their behavioral problems—the young mom who binges on Ben & Jerry's for comfort, just like I used to do, or the husband who gets a soda and a candy bar every time he fills up the car with gas for the company it provides when he's alone. I helped them notice the way they used food to fill emotional holes, as a drug, a source of friendship, or a source of punishment. It was a strange juxtaposition: by day I helped obese or food-addicted people and now, at night, I was at a cheerleading practice with a bunch of tiny, skinny girls, most of whom probably needed to eat more.

When it was my turn to introduce myself, I said, "I'm Laura Vikmanis. I'm a dietitian, I live in Springboro, and I have two daughters." I was very careful not to say my age. I didn't want to be known as the Ben-Gal-who-was-so-old-she-needed-Ben-Gay.

Tara welcomed us and explained that although thirty-two girls had been selected, only twenty-four would cheer at any given game once the football season started. The four six-girl "corners" (the groups of girls that would cheer on the four corners of the field) would be determined in July. But any girl who didn't make weight, arrived late, didn't do enough charity events, or danced poorly could be removed from her corner at any time. That meant she would not cheer the upcoming game. Instead another girl would be swapped in. The message was clear: We were a team but we were also in constant competition.

Sarah J. passed out the rulebook and said we were not to show it to anyone. (Shhh.) It included the pass code that opened the Emerald City–style gate at the stadium that I had gone through at the clinic the year before. I felt like my boyfriend just handed me the key to his apartment. She proceeded to go through all nine single-spaced pages of the handbook. If you missed a mandatory practice, you couldn't cheer the next game. And if you missed a game for any reason, you couldn't cheer the one after that. The only acceptable absence was for your wedding, when you could miss one week's worth of practice without penalty. I gave Brandy a look. Some of the Ben-Gal rules were stuck squarely in 1970.

Our goal weights would be set over the first month of practice. Once they were, we would weigh in at every practice. If a girl was more than three pounds above her goal weight, she would be pulled, which meant that she wouldn't cheer the next game. (The buffer was for menstrual fluctuations.) I was anxious about keeping within the weight constraints, but confident I could pull it off with hard work because I was a dietitian.

The 2009 Ben-Gals—my rookie season. (I'm second row from the bottom, center.)
PHOTO: Paula Norton

Sarah J. said we were expected to look professional at all times, even away from the stadium. No T-shirts that showed belly. (Too trashy.) No belly button rings, body piercings, or glitter. I laughed at the glitter part. I had never worn glitter. "Professional attire and glamour is expected at *all times*," she read, "and you may be sent home and/or benched before any game, practice, job, team function, charity event, etc. Well-groomed hair and makeup is expected at all times. You are a Ben-Gal at all times." Glamour meant tan skin (whether bed-darkened or tanner-darkened), foundation and blush, neat hair, neat ponytails, form-fitting clothes, high platform heels, modest jewelry, and no colored nail polish.

We would pay a refundable deposit of one hundred dollars for our standard Ben-Gal uniforms, the halters and miniskirts, and we had to launder them with Dreft—which I hadn't used since I had babies.

For practices we were expected to wear the same type of outfit that we had all worn to the clinics and auditions: sports bras and short shorts, with panty hose underneath, and sneakers with white ankle socks. "No panties are to be worn under practice clothes or uniform, not even thong panties," Sarah J. read. The panty hose had a built-in cotton crotch, and if we wore underwear beneath them, there would be panty lines. Panty lines to cheerleading coaches were like garlic to vampires. (Later we would learn that one of the girls openly flouted the no-underwear rule by wearing a G-string under her L'eggs.)

Despite all of the rules, Sarah J. also talked about the rewards of being a Ben-Gal. One of them was Pro Bowl. Pro Bowl was the greatest honor an NFL cheerleader could receive. Only one girl was selected from each NFL team. Because the other cheerleaders voted on who should go, if you were selected it meant you were well-liked by your teammates, not just the coaches. Pro Bowl girls, Sarah J. explained, were put up in a hotel in Honolulu or Florida for a week and did lots of media. It was a cheerleader's wet dream. I knew I wasn't nearly a good enough dancer to make it to Pro Bowl, but maybe someday if I worked really hard. . . .

I had to get a grip. I didn't even know if I would "make corner." That was the first goal. Then I could decide whether to audition again. And if I got on for another season or two, then maybe I could think about the bells and whistles like being a page of the calendar or going to Pro Bowl.

After the Ben-Gal meeting, we all went to Mainstay Rock Bar in Cincinnati, where our boyfriends and husbands joined us. P.J.

came and met some of the other boyfriends, who were all talking about tailgating. Thus, the Ben-Guys were born. Some Ben-Guys refer to themselves as "cheerleader widowers" because they don't see a lot of their girlfriends during football season. (One of the veterans said to me that night, "You know your Ben-Guy is supportive when he walks around for two weeks with orange hands from applying your tan gel before a game.") The veteran Ben-Guys told the rookie Ben-Guys what to expect: a lot of lonely nights, but also a lot of fun and some perks. Because each Ben-Gal received one free ticket per game, the guys now had a way to see every home game of their favorite team. And at seventy-seven bucks for a full-priced ticket that was good swag.

That night, surrounded by Brandy, Elizabeth, and the rest of the team and meeting the boyfriends and husbands of my teammates, I felt like I was becoming part of something bigger than me. I was a member of a community. I started to kick back and enjoy myself. A lot of people were taking pictures and I noticed that every time a camera came out to take a shot of a veteran, she would hide her beer or cocktail behind her back before she posed. It was my first social event as a Ben-Gal but I was already learning one of the rules: Never drink while being photographed.

My closest friend on the team was Brandy, the married girl from Kentucky. We shared the same attitude about cheering, and because we were among the oldest, we weren't interested in partying like some of the younger girls. Our nickname for ourselves was the Recruits. Our strategy was to "ride stealth," which meant: follow the rules, avoid gossiping, don't seek out attention, and run away from drama.

One of my other buddies was Sarah G., who we called Southern Sarah. She was from deep Kentucky and her accent made everything she said sound sweet, even when she told a raunchy joke. She was tall and pale with red hair, and laughed at us whenever we tried to imitate the way she talked.

I was also close with Kimberly, the team joker. In her early twenties, she was a second-generation Ben-Gal who still lived with her parents. She didn't drink and didn't go out much but she was a cutup. She could do perfect imitations of every girl on the squad.

As we got to know the other girls Brandy and I developed our own nicknames for them. One striking brunette, Lauren, had the nickname "Abs" because she had incredible six-pack abdominal muscles. You could bounce a quarter off her abs. Abs was a natural dancer. She remembered choreography immediately and always asked overly detailed questions like, "Is my toe up or down?" "Where's my knee on this?" "Which shoulder am I cocking?" I liked her because she helped me learn the dances.

Tess was the Negative. She was very small with naturally thick, long brown hair and a face so friendly it caught me off guard—I never would have guessed that behind that smiling face was such a negative personality. Tess spread toxic energy like it was swine flu. She had something nasty to say about everyone behind their backs. She cheered because she loved being out on the field, but everything else she had to do—like events and appearances—she considered a pain in the butt.

Tess was also an oversharer. Brandy and I would be sitting at one of the tables before practice, talking about something personal, and Tess would walk over and say, "What are you guys talking about?" and then chime in with a way-too-personal story. She worked as a bartender and was always saying things like, "So Dhani and Rey were in the bar last night," referring to Bengals players Dhani Jones and Rey Maualuga, as though they were personal friends. We suspected she exaggerated her proximity to fame.

Sunny was the Deadly Serious. She was hands down the Ben-Gals' best dancer, and had a lot of style. She rarely smiled, except when she was dancing, but once in a while, joking around on a break, she would flash a megawatt grin and make you feel like you'd won a prize. Despite her deadpan style, she always gave me special help on complicated dances and reassured me when she could see that I was struggling.

Sarah J. was the Praiser. She always told each girl what she was doing right. When she had a criticism she Oreo-ed it—sandwiched it between two cookies of praise. Just as she did at the high school where she taught she played a teacherlike role with us, supportive and encouraging. She was rumored to have dated a Cincinnati Reds guy but she didn't talk about it, which made us certain it was true. (Her positive attitude became even more inspiring when in early 2010, an anonymous commenter on a gossip website wrote that she was having an affair with the Bengals kicker Shayne Graham. Soon another post appeared, claiming that she had sexually transmitted diseases and had had sex with students in her classroom. She had to stand in front of her students and tell them that everything was untrue. She wound up suing the site's CEO for defamation of character and was awarded $11 million in a default judgment, though as of this writing she hasn't seen a dime of it.)

There were other archetypes on the team, and though the girls changed from year to year I noticed that the types stayed the same. Naked Girl was the one who was always naked in the locker room. She came up and prattled on casually, as though she was wearing clothes. It made for an awkward exchange, and we responded to her while carefully averting our eyes. The Gumbys were cousins of Naked Girl. They were the super limber girls who could do perfect splits and bend their bodies in strange, yogalike contortions. They acted like they weren't proud of it but it was obvious they were because limber girls are assumed to be better in bed. They enjoyed this perception.

The Social Butterflies arrived at practice an hour before everyone else just to chat and hang out, and then stayed an hour later, until the stadium closed and the guards kicked them out. The Eater was the slender girl with the trim, toned body who ate constantly—fast food, chips, pasta, Cheetos. We stared at her, transfixed, wondering where all those calories were going. Candy Girl, friends with the Eater, was the one who ate only sweets but was among the skinniest girls and just happened to have beautiful white teeth.

The Grinds were the ones who were always doing dance moves during downtime, on water breaks, before practice, and after. They could not stop running through the choreography, and they made every girl around them think that she should be practicing harder, too.

The Gazer stood in the back, looked off into space, and didn't pay attention to the coaches. She had wide Bambi eyes, acted like she was stoned, and always said, "Whaaaat?" when a coach announced what we were doing next.

The Extensions were the girls who had semipermanent hair extensions that cost a few hundred dollars at the salon. They could not stop flipping their fake long hair, like teenage boys who finally grew their hair long enough for a ponytail and marveled at it, day after day.

The Brainiac was the girl with the highest level of education or the most highly intellectual career. She didn't joke around, had a dry sense of humor, and rarely smiled. For the life of us we could not figure out why she was a cheerleader.

The Models—well, they were models. They seemed to view cheering as a step down.

And then there was Quiet Girl. She was the one who never spoke the entire year and we wondered how on earth she made it through her interview.

Do cheerleaders get along? Mostly. As with any group of co-workers, most are easygoing, but there are always a few you don't like. The most prominent division on the Ben-Gals is not between the young girls and the older girls but between the Real Boobs and the Fake Boobs. This is true despite the fact that at any given time, a third of the Real Boobs are considering implants. Real Boobs say things to the Fake Boobs like, "I just want to look better in a bathing suit, but I don't want my boobs to look huge and fake. Boobs like that are really stupid." We Fake Boobs nod slowly, unsure whether the Real Boob is saying this to hurt us or because she is an idiot. Secretly we count the days till the insensitive Real Boob changes her opinion and buys herself a set.

But the Fake Boobs can be competitive, too. Lindsay, the girl from the WLW radio show, was a Fake Boob and seemed unnerved by the prospect that any girl on the team might someday get implants and look as good as she did. When Brandy mentioned at one practice that she was considering implants, Lindsay told her, "Oh, you definitely don't want them. My recovery hurt so much. If I had the choice, I would not do it again." I had to take Brandy aside and tell her that my own recovery had taken just a few days and if she ever chose to get implants, her pain threshold might be different from Lindsay's.

As much as I wanted to blend in with the team and not be known as the geriatric cheerleader, there were times when the age difference felt glaringly obvious. Some of the younger girls came from wealthy families and still lived with their parents. At practice they sat around the gym complaining, "Oh, I was up so late last night studying for a final" or, "This was such a stressful weekend. I had to go to my girlfriend's bachelorette party and I didn't get home until four." I smiled quietly to myself or exchanged a look with Brandy, thinking about everything I had had to coordinate—P.J.'s work schedule, Marija and Courtney's after-school activities, car pools, and my own client schedule—just to make it to practice on time.

The "Ben-Girls" were always talking about Facebook and up-loading pictures. I did not have a Facebook account, and I never got to see any of the photos because no one emailed them. I didn't get a Facebook account until fall of 2010. Once I did, it took me months to figure out how to use it, though now I'm on it daily.

Because the Ben-Gals were young, beautiful, small-town girls, many were in the midst of wedding planning while they were on the team. The single ones moaned about their commitment-phobic boyfriends while the engaged ones flashed their humongous rocks. When the Negative and her boyfriend got engaged, she began planning her wedding obsessively. At every practice she went on about the floral arrangements, goodie bags, and rehearsal dinner. I remembered how I had done the same thing with my own wed-ding, paying less attention to my future husband than to the table settings. Secretly I thought, *You are so caught up in the wedding, honey, you are going to end up just like me.* Within a few months of the Negative's wedding, things didn't work out, and they eventu-ally separated. I wasn't surprised.

When a girl would muse about marriage or children, I wouldn't volunteer advice because I had learned from being a mother to two daughters that unwanted advice could be read as criticism. But when a Ben-Gal approached and said, "Laura, are you glad you got married young?" I had to open my mouth.

"Definitely not," I would say. "And not only because I'm divorced. I missed out on so much fun when I was married. Being married to someone takes work, and kids are a strain on the relationship, especially when they're small. Finish your education. Go out and live your life. Get a masters, and then get married."

"If I have kids late, my body won't bounce back," the Ben-Gal would say.

"You are twenty-three years old," I would answer. "You can wait till your late twenties to have a baby. I promise, you'll still be fertile. Madonna was 38."

Some Ben-Gals were kinder about my age than others. Abs often arrived at practice talking about her boyfriend, Tyler, who didn't like her being a Ben-Gal. "Tyler would be so glad if I said good-bye to all of this," she said one night. "He thinks I'm too old to cheer." She was thirty.

"What does he think about me?" I asked carefully.

"He thinks you're way too old to cheer."

I turned away, hurt, but then I thought about it. What did it matter what someone else's boyfriend thought of my cheering? Brandy thought it was amazing what I had been through and overcome. P.J., my kids, my mom, and Lisa were proud of me. Just as it was nobody's business why I had gotten implants, it was nobody's business why I was cheering. I had to stop listening to negative voices. I had to be my own cheerleader.

I DID IT MY WEIGH

DURING THE FIRST MONTH OF PRACTICE THE FOCUS WAS ON getting our weight down and learning dances. I knew that my goal weight, once set, would be incredibly important because I would have to maintain it all season. My teacher Nikki had given us an important pointer. She suggested that throughout June, the weight-setting month, we eat and hydrate *before* weigh-in. That way we would come in heavy. Once the individual weights were set, we wouldn't eat beforehand and then we would always be under. I followed her strategy and my weight was set at 123 pounds, up to 126 after the three-pound buffer.

As a dietitian I was encouraged to see that there was some variety in the goal weights, according to body types and muscle composition. Though Sarah J. was extremely tall, five-eight, she was also naturally thin, so her weight was set at 114. Sarah G., who was five-eleven, got her weight set at 146.

I was nervous that the weigh-ins would make me revert to extreme eating and exercise, but I had learned that balance was the only way to lose weight—not extremes. To get myself from the low 130s down to 123 the first thing I did was buy the same digital scale that was used in practice so my weights would be consistent. Then I did exactly what I recommend to my clients, work on the three areas that lead to weight loss: better food choices, behavior modification, and exercise. All three don't need to be working at the same time, but if none of them are you won't see any progress. It's certainly not easy but it's not rocket science. To lose weight you have to eat less, eat smartly, and move.

The first phase of my new regimen was what I called "fasting," eating six small meals per day with limited calories, including protein bars and shakes if my schedule was tight (the same physician-approved ones my clients use at the beginning of their programs). The purpose of this was to decondition myself from poor behavior like eating mindlessly in the car or in front of the TV. I didn't do that stuff often anymore but I wanted to become more aware of when I did.

Then I moved into the second phase, which was to eat food only, no bars or shakes, but carefully regulated meals—oatmeal for breakfast, a hard-boiled egg for snack, yogurt or salad with chicken for lunch, fruit or cold vegetables for a snack, meat and cooked vegetables for dinner, and maybe a low-calorie pudding or a little bit of chocolate or ice cream if I could afford the calories. My philosophy was: You can have what you want, just not as much as you want. At the same time I cranked up my outside-of-practice exercise, the weight training and runs. I stuck to 1200 calories per day, journaling everything I ate and using a calorie counter. Any time I ordered a salad I got the dressing on the side and then dipped the tip of my fork into it before each bite. Overall the principle was to do high protein (chicken, lean beef, eggs, and egg whites), good carbs (apples, strawberries, cucumbers, carrots, whole-wheat bread), high fiber (bran flakes, more fruit), and low fat.

I kept a strict food diary to to become fully aware of my habits.

Sometimes I raised my calorie limit to fuel my increased activity, but not so high that it prevented me from losing weight. I paid a lot of attention to sodium and allowed myself snacks, but healthy ones like whole-wheat crackers, Greek yogurt, and fruit bars that I kept, along with my not-so-healthy diet sodas, in a black freezer pack that I called my "feed bag." (My dirty little secret is that I drink way too many diet sodas. I am trying to wean myself off but it's hard to break a twenty-five-year love affair with artificial sweeteners.) If P.J. and I went to a restaurant for dinner, I usually stuck to meat, fish, chicken, and cauliflower, squash, or green beans on the side. When I was craving fries I made the waiter bring me exactly five fries. It took a lot of willpower but allowed me to satisfy my craving without making all my hard work go to waste. I always said no to "free dessert" or "large salad for the price of a small" or all the other things restaurants to do entice people to eat more. Perhaps hardest of all, I learned to stop eating when I was satisfied, a moment that often came before my plate was clean.

P.J. was an amazing cook and often, despite my best efforts, I took in most of my calories at night—though it was the exact opposite of my advice to my clients. (To lose weight it's always better to spread your calories out through the day or get most of them at lunch, not dinner.) He would prepare roast chicken, pasta, burgers, grilled vegetables, and burritos, and everything tasted so good I couldn't resist.

Sometimes Marija and Courtney made fun of my eating habits. "Oh, Mom," they would say at dinner, dangling their forks in front of me. "This spaghetti is *so good*. How come you're not having seconds?"

"I'm full, it's okay," I would say. Though I was watching my own food intake very carefully, I encouraged healthy habits in the girls. I didn't want them to feel that they had to deprive themselves. They were both athletic—with cheer and track—and understood that to perform well as an athlete, you had to take in protein and healthy carbs.

There were days when it was difficult to switch gears from weight-loss counseling at work to being at practice. I'd show up to practice and Abs would say, "Oh my God, do I look fat today?" as I shook my head.

"Do you understand how ridiculous you sound?" I would answer. "I work with people all day long who would die for your body."

At work, some clients had trouble seeing me as a real person once they learned that I was an NFL cheerleader. "It's easy for you," they would say. "You're naturally skinny and you dance so much you'll never gain weight."

"I'm actually not naturally skinny," I would say. "I have to eat very carefully to maintain my figure. I may not be overweight but that doesn't mean I don't struggle just like you do. I love food. And I have to limit my calories and be on top of my behaviors."

By the end of June I was a couple of pounds under 123. I would make my buffer weight of 126 every practice for the next three years. I didn't like the weigh-ins, but my increased focus on food intake helped me understand my own clients better. On days when I felt powerless over food, and grabbed an extra slice of pizza or ate too many chips, I asked myself what had made me feel that way. Usually it wasn't about hunger but my emotional state—stress, loneliness, exhaustion. The next time I noticed those feelings, I tried to satisfy myself with something other than food: I called Brandy to talk or told P.J. I needed a hug or sat on the bed to have a good cry. This helped me deal with my feelings in a healthier way.

As I got my weight down I started to appreciate in a personal way the connection between nutrition and wellness. I noticed that if I went a week skipping exercise or eating foods like high-calorie fried chicken, or too many cookies, I felt exhausted and depleted. When I ate well and took care of my body, I didn't just look better, I felt better.

Officially, cheerleading practice was from seven to nine-thirty, but in reality they often went later. The most dramatic part of every practice was weigh-in. Weigh-ins have long been an NFL cheerleader institution. In their book *Deep in the Heart of Texas: Reflections of Former Dallas Cowboys Cheerleaders*, sisters Suzette, Stephanie, and Sheri Scholz outlined the many abuses the DCCs put themselves through to make weight: starvation, diet pills, chain-smoking, iced coffee, rubber pants, dehydration, laxatives, dexies, diuretics, black mollies (speed), sugar, and even cocaine. "Everybody knew who was snorting cocaine because they were so skinny," they wrote. "Nobody could dance that much and lose weight. Fuel was needed for all that exercise. It's not possible to be that emaciated and still work that hard. Without 'the little helper' they just didn't have enough energy."

Ben-Gals director Shirley Bird used weigh-ins from the very beginning of the Ben-Gals in 1970. Her own daughter Christy went over her weight for one game and Bird would not let her cheer, but Christy was friends with Charlotte, who was also on the team, and Charlotte convinced Ms. Bird to make an exception.

From six to six-thirty at every practice, we gathered in the gym, socializing, texting, doing anything we could to keep our minds off food. Many of us had not eaten in four or five hours. (I myself did not eat after two on a weigh-in day though, like my team-mates, I had dinner at six thirty, immediately after weighing in.)

Weigh-in affected every aspect of our lives, including romance. Girls often said, "He asked me out for Wednesday, but I put it off till Friday because of Thursday weigh-in. Now I can eat as much as I want and I'll have three and a half days before the next weigh-in." Others said they had gone to tanning beds and saunas to sweat off water weight. (I am ashamed to say I go to tanning beds, though I have never done it to lose weight.)

At six-thirty on the dot, girls started lining up at Traci's table, all wanting to be weighed early so they could eat immediately afterward. Traci would saunter in with her digital bathroom scale and put it on the floor. One by one each girl got on, and Traci recorded the weights in her attendance book. She remained poker-faced about the weigh-ins, but when a girl didn't make her weight, I could always tell just by watching the way she acted. First the girl would lean forward on the scale to see if it changed the weight. When that didn't work, she would remove her chicken cutlets, shorts, socks, hair rubber bands, bracelet, or tank top. "Just wait!" she would tell Traci desperately. "Let me just take off this necklace and step on the scale one more time!" Sometimes this striptease continued until she was naked.

On one occasion a girl said, "I have a tampon in. I'm going to take it out." She went to the bathroom, came running back in, got weighed, and raced back to the bathroom.

The Bengals gym was next to the kitchen, and depending when in our season it was, often while girls were removing bras or shorts, the football coaches and players were sitting at the other end of the gym at the round tables, eating dinner. Traci would say to a half-naked Ben-Gal, "Do you see those guys over there? Would you please put your clothes back on?" The girls didn't care. All they cared about was making weight.

As soon as girls were weighed they sat down and gobbled salads, sandwiches, or chips so they would have the energy to cheer for practice. I would eat a protein bar, a few pretzels, or a veggie patty I had heated at home (no bun). Some of the younger girls would eat French fries, McDonald's burgers, chocolates, and little-kid candy such as Sour Patch Kids or Nerds. I was not a fast-food junkie (even though I enjoyed it on occasion) because I was too old and I knew too much. I had learned long ago that you gain more weight if you starve and binge than if you eat moderately every few hours. How could these girls eat like that and stay slim? Maybe some of them would purge when they got home from practice. Or maybe they were just hungry from depriving themselves all day, and this meal was their reward.

Inevitably some girls had trouble making weight. My rookie season only two girls out of thirty-two regularly made their weight without going to any extremes. For them it was effortless. For the rest of us it was a constant struggle.

Sometimes a girl got off the scale, frowning, and said, "I just can't seem to get these last two pounds off. Maybe I should try Hoodia, that herbal appetite suppressant." I'd notice her searching my face for a reaction, trying to see if I approved.

"Do you want my opinion?" I would ask.

"Yes."

"If you want to lose weight, it's better to choose your foods carefully and count calories than to put anything else into your body."

Other girls said things like, "I made weight today—but not the right way."

"Do you remember that you're talking to a dietitian?" I would ask.

"I know, I know," she would say. "I promise I'll talk to you if I need your help." I didn't pry because I believed firmly that some-one needs to ask you for help before you can help, but I would spend the rest of the practice feeling worried.

· In my second and third seasons on the team, I found a way to mesh my work as a dietitian with my commitment to the Ben-Gals. The coaches asked me to give a talk about diet and exercise at the clinics before tryouts. In my talk, I was careful to emphasize balanced, mindful eating, and avoiding extreme deprivation. I could see the girls nodding as I talked. I wished that, back in 1986 when I was in the dance company, there had been a voice of sanity. It might have stopped some of the girls from becoming bulimic.

In addition to the Ben-Gals clinics, over the years I have also spoken at occasional practices about the importance of nutrition and fitness. Individual girls have approached me for help and I've worked with them on food diaries, exercise regime, and behavior modification. Once they could see results, they thanked me. I am gratified that I am helping young women eat more wisely—teaching them that they have to fuel their bodies with the right kinds of nutrients in order to perform. I hope the information I give them stops them from developing the kind of poor eating habits I had as a teenager. I want them to develop a healthy relationship with food, one they can carry with them into the rest of their lives.

I wish the NFL, and its cheerleading directors, would embrace and see the beauty in healthier, curvier body types. NFL cheerleaders are expected to have a figure that rarely exists in nature: super slim with big boobs. Because very few women are blessed with this figure naturally—I know I'm not—it can be almost impossible to attain it without using drastic and dangerous measures, just like I did as a teenager in the dance company when I eliminated food groups. As a dietitian and a mother of adolescent girls I find this troubling. But I'm not the one who makes the rules, and I don't think weigh-ins will go away in my cheering years. They are the Pap smear of cheerleading.

Traci, who was on the University of Cincinnati Dance Team before she got on the Ben-Gals, told me that when she was in college, girls on her team used colon cleansers, laxatives, and diet pills to keep their weight down. She said one cheerleader from her college now has a spastic colon because of what she did to herself. Deanna, who cheered on the Ben-Gals from 1999 to 2008, said that girls took whatever they could to keep their weight down, like Hydroxycut, Slim-Fast, and Slimquick.

Because of what she witnessed at UC, Traci said she now tries to insure that Ben-Gals pursue healthy eating habits. "I've told women they weigh too little and need to gain weight," she said. "We don't want people ruining their bodies by taking laxatives or diet pills. We don't want anyone hurting themselves."

At around seven o'clock, after our weigh-ins and "dinner," our practice began. The captains stood up in the front to watch as we arranged ourselves in long lines to rehearse dances and fillers. I struggled with two aspects of dance practice: remembering my choreography and making my style cooler. Though the competitive cheer girls picked up the moves within minutes, my forty-year-old brain often took days to remember even a few minutes of choreography. Just as I had a dance down pat, the captains would decide to change it and I'd have to start from scratch. Because it took me so long to remember dances, I often pleaded with the captains to go through them one more time.

For one summertime practice, we were out on the field in very hot weather. It must have been a hundred and five degrees. We were sweating our butts off doing a long routine and afterward Sarah J. said, "Okay, does everyone feel good about it?" All the other girls nodded overeagerly, desperate to go inside.

"Can we run through it one more time?" I asked. There were death looks like I had never seen.

At home I enlisted Marija and Courtney's help. I stood in the living room with the music, doing dances over and over again: bare bones until I got the sequence, then with very slow music to make sure each portion was right, then faster music. They would tell me what looked good and what didn't. There were advantages to being the oldest Ben-Gal: I had a built-in focus group at home.

When I was between clients at work I would stand up and run through my fillers. I practiced in my car, in my mirror at home, in the kitchen fixing breakfast, and at the grocery store. I practiced cheerleading moves the way some women do Kegels.

I was relieved in mid-July when we received our practice poms because they hid my jazz hands. But they smelled. Practice poms are game poms that have been retired, which means that by the time a girl gets them, some other girl has been cheering with them for a full season. They make your hands sweat, and if you don't leave them out to dry when you come home from a game, they reek. Brandy's practice poms had lost so much tinsel over time that we called them dog tails.

Soon after I received my practice poms, I got the white Ben-Gal boots that I had been coveting since I was on drill team my senior year of high school. That night at home I walked around in them to break them in, while P.J. and the girls mocked me. I didn't care. I felt like the Velveteen Rabbit starting to become real.

As the dances became more familiar, we spent more time at practice showcasing them: performing them in small formations for the coaches and captains. I hated this because I felt like I was under a microscope. The coaches would whisper in low tones, and then arrange and rearrange us so they could begin to design the corners. Showcasing was a difficult and excruciating process that pitted us all against one another. The idea was to make sure not only that every corner danced well but that it had an attractive variety of girls. Coaches would switch two of us, a tall girl for a short girl, a brunette for a blonde, and then, a few minutes later, cry, "Undo!" The girls would scamper back to their original spots. If you have ever watched a florist create a floral arrangement, you know what showcasing looks like.

Once the corners were set, it meant that any girls who did not make corner (often as a result of being overweight, by four pounds or much more) would not be on the field during games. Instead they had to go to the private suites to hang out with rich fans.

After the showcasing portion of practice came conditioning. This was any form of exercise, like Zumba, yoga, Pilates, plyometrics, or drills. We ran up and down the stairs of the stadium, or went on the field to do "suicides" (sprinting across the field and back) or "burpees," where you go into a squat, thrust your legs behind you into plank position, jump back into a squat and jump into the air. I discovered that despite my age, I was in much better shape than the younger girls. Because I worked out so much, my cardiovascular health was good, while the younger girls didn't need to work out to stay slim. "Let's do one more set," I often said, as the young girls screamed in fury.

Sometimes we were out on the field until dark. The stadium staff rarely turned on the floodlights for us, so we had to practice in the pitch black, unable to see our own feet. Paul Brown Stadium is in the heart of downtown Cincinnati, next to the Cincinnati Reds stadium, so if there was a baseball game we could get a few rays of secondary light.

Often after an outside practice, pieces of our poms wound up littered all over the field. "Okay, everyone!" one of the captains would shout. "Time to pick up pom poop!" We lined up and went down the field, picking up the tinsel. What's it like being an NFL cheerleader? You cheer in the dark and clean up your own mess.

At the end of each practice, around nine-thirty, as we would be packing our things and saying goodbye, Deanna would say, "Okay, raise your hand if you didn't make weight today." A few sheepish hands would go up. Lindsay was often one of the girls raising her hand because her boyfriend was a millionaire and she liked to go out for fine wine and meals, so her weight fluctuated.

"You guys are going to have to stay," Deanna would say.

That meant Fat Camp, though only the cheerleaders, not the coaches, called it that. Fat Camp was an extra half-hour of high-intensity conditioning, like ab exercises, jump squats, and squat thrusts, usually out on the field. On occasion it also included a full review of every dance. I never had to stay for Fat Camp because I made weight. I was motivated by the horror stories that I heard from Fat Camp survivors. The punishment was so humiliating that it served its purpose beautifully: Usually after one Fat Camp, the girl made her weight the next time.

WHAT EVER HAPPENED TO BEN-GAL JANE?

THROUGHOUT THE SUMMER LEADING UP TO THE FOOTBALL season, girls received personalized Glamour Evaluations from Shannon, where we learned what we needed to change about our appearance. We felt about the Glamour Evaluations the way you feel about an annual physical: you want to get information but you're terrified that something really bad will turn up. As preparation for the evaluations the coaches took full-body shots of each girl in her practice uniform, frontal and rear, and a closeup of her face. Over the course of the next month each Ben-Gal was pulled out of practice for twenty minutes to sit with Shannon at a table in the back of the gym and get a no-holds-barred critique. (Shannon, the former glamour coach, was no longer on the team but had come in just to help us out with appearance.)

As practice after practice passed and I had yet to receive my evaluation, I got more nervous. After every Ben-Gal finished her conference with Shannon, she would return to practice looking wounded, like she had just been dumped by her fiancé. I would notice her fiddling nervously with her hair or looking anxiously over her shoulder at her butt. At the end of practice, I would approach the girl. "So what did she say?"

"My makeup looks whorish and I need to tone it down."

"My hair is cheap and strawlike. I can't cut it more than twice a year or else I have to buy extensions."

"I cut my panty hose too low and she says I have plumber's crack above my shorts. Let me die."

"I have batwings. When I stop waving, my arm keeps on waving."

"My thighs are too fat. It makes me look short. I have to walk two miles a day."

"I have cankles. I need to do calf exercises so I have a better silhouette."

"My skin is too pale. I look like Morticia Addams. I have to wear self-tanner."

"I need to use more foundation to cover my pimples."

"My bra straps are coming out over my shoulders. I have to pin them with a safety pin or get a crisscross bra because the Ben-Gals don't 'support' visible bra straps."

"My face is too round. I have to lose my baby fat."

"I have a potbelly and I need to stop drinking beer."

"I'm skinny fat. From a distance I look skinny but up close there are rolls on the sides of my back."

If this was what girls half my age were hearing, what was I going to hear? "You need Botox." "You look like a grandma." "I can see your crow's-feet." "Your butt sags." I already worked out six times a week. I did three different glute exercises but now I was going to have to add a fourth. What if she said I had to tease my hair more? Shannon was the one who had admonished me to wear bigger hair at my first tryouts—when I didn't make the team. I was going to have to cheer football games looking like a Southern beauty pageant contestant beyond her prime. Fans would point at me and say, "There's the old haggish one that looks like Tammy Faye."

After the Glamour Evaluations, we would notice girls' looks start to transform. A girl would come into the next practice with her hair in a new style because Shannon had given her instructions to change it. She would keep this new look until the coaches decided that it no longer worked and gave the girl a new Glamour Evaluation with different instructions. No one complained about the cost or the inconvenience. Though we each had to look our best, we knew that in the end what mattered was how we looked together.

Finally my turn came. I was standing in a line, learning a filler called "Bounce," when Shannon came up to me and tapped me on the shoulder. She led me to a table in the back and laid out my photos. I didn't like seeing my body up close. It was like seeing your face in one of those magnifying mirrors without realizing it's a magnifier. For a second you think you look like a scary witch all the time.

"Overall you're doing a good job with your makeup, Laura," she said, "but it's not dark enough. You have pretty eyes and I want them to pop. Darken the black line above your lashes. I'm not thrilled with the false lashes that you're wearing. See if you can find thicker, fuller lashes, okay?" I had already gone through three different brands.

"Your eyebrows are pale," she went on. "You're going to have to use a brow pencil. And your foundation needs to be heavier, with darker blush for contrast. As for your hair, I like it curled, the way you're wearing it. Keep doing that this season and we'll let you know if we want you to change it. The color is too light, though. Have your colorist bring it down a tone." My hair was highlighted with blond but the rays from the tanning bed turned it yellow.

She flipped to the full-body shot. "I'm pleased with your muscles," she said. "You're in much better shape than a lot of these younger girls and it shows. I like your abs and your arms. This is exactly the look we want."

After practice, Brandy came up to me. "Well?" she said.

"My hair is trashy but she likes my tone!"

As I drove home that night I realized that I had the ideal personality for cheerleading. I wasn't afraid of being told what to do with my body, my face, and my hair. I enjoyed it. I wanted to please the coaches and captains. Maybe that interest inventory in tenth grade had been right about me when it said I was suited for the military. NFL cheerleading was a lot like the army. It had camaraderie, a hierarchy, and a lot of rules but you were rewarded if you excelled and because of this, you wanted to do whatever you could to stay in the good graces of your superiors. We weren't that unlike football players in the preseason who fear but love their coach, and do everything they can at training camp to stay on the roster so they have a chance of playing games. Cheerleading was strict but fair. And while Brian had been a malevolent dictator, Deanna, Traci, and Charlotte were benevolent ones. They could be a pain in the butt but it was because they wanted the best for our team and for us.

One of the oddest things about practice was that we were dancing for two and a half hours in *full hair, mandatory false eyelashes, and makeup.* The idea was to show the coaches what we would look like on the field. There is nothing like the sight of cheerleaders sweating their butts off in heavy caked-on foundation and smoky eye shadow. Over the course of the long practices our hair got wet with sweat. At water breaks we frantically retouched our foundation. By the time practice was over, we looked like thirty-two Bette Davises in *What Ever Happened to Baby Jane?*

During my rookie season, Ben-Gals makeup included the notorious Revlon Orange Flip. It was Bozo orange and I had one tube in my practice bag, one hidden in case I lost it, and a few at home. Every time I passed a drugstore I would pop in to buy three at a time, thinking, *The Cincinnati–Dayton region must be responsible for 90 percent of national Orange Flip sales because no woman but a Ben-Gal would choose to wear this color.* Sometimes I forgot to remove it after practice and if I had to run into a convenience store on the way home, the clerk would stare at me like I had escaped from an insane asylum.

In my second season, before we cheered our first game, Charlotte announced that after much consideration, the coaches and captains had decided that we would switch from Orange Flip to Cherry Pop, a warm and classy-looking red. Sarah J. had lobbied her and convinced her that it was time for a change. You could hear the cheers all the way out in the streets of Cincinnati.

My first year it took me almost forty-five minutes at home to get ready for practice. First I sprayed my hair and teased it. While the hairspray was drying, I did my makeup, much more than I wore to work: foundation, powder, eye shadow, eyeliner on the lower and upper lids, mascara, blush, and lipstick. After makeup, I put on my fake lashes. I separated the lashes using the sharp part of a safety pin and pushed the lashes onto my real lashes with the safety pin to make sure they were flush against my eyelids. Yes, I have pricked my eyeball—and had tears running down my face for an hour. Some days lashes were easy. Other days they were hard. Just like there are good hair days and bad hair days, there are good lash days and bad lash days.

When I was done with my makeup, Courtney helped me brush down my hair in front of the mirror and smooth the teasing, making sure there were no spots in the back where you could see through the hair to the scalp.

I often arrived at the stadium in my work outfit and saw the other Ben-Gals emerging from their cars dressed in Stadium Cute: slinky dresses, platform heels, scoop necks, and low-rise jeans. They wore Victoria's Secret PINK, BCBG, and Forever 21. One girl came into a practice wearing a shirt that said, "French Me." I couldn't—and didn't want to—wear something like that, but I did want to look a little cooler. One weekend I took Marija, who was twelve, shopping with me to an upscale jeans store, bribing her with the promise of jeans for herself. Excitedly, she picked out different jeans for me, with rhinestones or flap pockets, but not too low-riding. We picked a very tight pair and she loved them. "You're wearing Ben-Gal jeans now," she said. "You finally look young again." I bought the pair she liked, but every time I wear them I feel like a sausage.

The reason our everyday glamour was so important was because we were supposed to represent the team wherever we went, near the stadium or away from it. We always ran the risk that we would see Charlotte or someone else affiliated with the team when we didn't look Ben-Gally and get chewed out. We believed that Charlotte could see us from above, like a hovercraft. I was outed only once when I was not Charlotte-ready. I was at my favorite market early in the morning. I had just rolled out of bed and I was in sweatpants, a hoodie, a baseball cap to cover my bed head, and no makeup. A woman my age approached, with a knowing look in her eye. She looked at my blond hair and my baseball cap, and the necklace around my neck that read BEN-GAL.

"Are you a Ben-Gal?" she asked.

I realized, embarrassed, that my baseball cap had a Bengal tiger head on it. "Yes, I am, but I don't look like one right now," I said, hurrying for the checkout.

Brandy got it worse. One weekend morning she was dressed in sweats with no makeup and ran into Charlotte at the grocery store. The look in Charlotte's eye showed that she wasn't happy with how Brandy looked. Brandy said hi and scurried to another aisle. Now, whenever she goes back to that store, she always looks for Charlotte's car in the parking lot before she goes in.

Though I was expected to look like a Ben-Gal all the time, I soon realized it was not good for my relationship to act like one all the time. One of the great ironies of my good fortune to get on to the Ben-Gals at age forty was that I had a rigorous evening schedule at a point in my life when I was just beginning to appreciate time to myself. Unlike most married women with children, I didn't have my kids every night, and because they were school-aged they were getting more independent. I also had a boyfriend I was crazy about. When I wasn't with the girls, P.J. and I could go to dinner and to movies and have sex as often as we wanted.

Now that many of my nights were taken up with practice, that changed, and P.J. missed me. "I hate it when I go to bed and you're not there, and when I wake up, you're not there because you're working out," he said. On nights that he *was* awake when I came home, I returned from practice wanting to tell him gossip about my teammates. Sometimes he indulged me. Other times I could tell by the look on his face that he didn't want to hear it. It grounded me and made me realize that at home I had to switch from Laura the Ben-Gal to just plain Laura. I stopped myself in the middle, peeled off my lashes, got into my jammies, and got into bed with him so he could tell me about his day, too. There were times when I didn't mind going from Ben-Gal to galfriend.

In July, both Brandy and I learned that we had "made corner"— the same corner. We were thrilled. We felt like the work we had done in Nikki's class had paid off. I was put in the second of two rows, in the middle, and was relieved because I could look around me at the other girls in case I forgot a piece of choreography. My corner captain would be Latasha. She was tough and didn't smile very often but I knew she would make our corner look good.

As excited and relieved as Brandy and I were we learned quickly not to rest on our laurels. Every practice the captains and coaches would rotate new girls in or out of the corners to keep us on our toes. In this way cheering was like the first year of law school. You snooze, you lose. This was so ingrained in us, that we showed up to practice ill, grieving, PMSing, or depressed because we knew that if we missed a mandatory practice, we would have to miss two games.

I myself realized what I was willing to sacrifice after a bonding weekend for the Ben-Gals at a downtown hotel. Brandy and Kimberly were my roommates. The plan was that we would have a big party, spend the night at the hotel, and then go to the stadium the next day for a practice. The party was at a sports bar called Bulldog's Roadhouse. I drank light beer continuously over a couple of hours. Then we went to another bar called FB's. I didn't feel drunk when I went to sleep that night, but in the morning I looked at myself in the mirror and I was green. "I think I'm sick," I told Brandy.

I stood over the toilet, heaving. I didn't understand how I could be so hungover. Our practice that morning was a full two hours. I wanted to skip it but I couldn't tell Charlotte, *I can't make practice, I'm hungover.* On the way to the gym through the stadium I had to stop and throw up in a trash can. Several times during practice I had to run to the bathroom to throw up more. But I never once considered going home.

Girls who had legitimate excuses for missing practice were sometimes penalized. One girl did not appear at practice during a game week. She had not been put in a corner in July but she had been working hard and the coaches had just decided to swap her in a corner for another girl. She had been really excited and happy, and we knew that she would never be absent without calling.

Worried, we called her cell phone. Her mother answered. It turned out that the Ben-Gal had gotten into a car accident. She wasn't seriously injured but she was shaken up and had turned around and gone home. Even though she had been in an accident, she was not allowed to cheer that week due to her absence.

Another girl was grief-stricken because her dog had been run over that day, but she came to practice that night anyway. The coaches were not trying to be cruel; they couldn't always tell the real emergencies from the invented ones, and strict enforcement was the only way they could ensure that girls weren't trying to trick them. Still, I thought it was unfair that bereavement was not considered a valid excuse for missing practice, but a girl's wedding was. I was never going to get married again and would have preferred exceptions for funerals or family emergencies. Cheerleading had not yet caught up with other American workplaces in terms of sensitivity to work-life balance.

But the rules were the rules and we got the message. It was spelled out in the rulebook very clearly. "Insubordination. Webster defines this word as 'not submitting to authority; disobedient.' Synonyms—rebellious, mutinous, defiant. Insubordination to even the slightest degree *IS ABSOLUTELY NOT TOLERATED!!!!!! You will be benched or dismissed!!*"

Because our mandatory practices were so long and exhausting, the captains and coaches tried to mix things up every once in a while so we didn't burn out. One practice a yoga instructor might come in, another practice a Zumba teacher. One night Charlotte told us that two choreographer friends of hers and a belly dancer would be teaching. The belly dancer could make her abdominal muscles roll. The choreographers, both men, were athletic and flexible, and after leading us through a typical stretching routine, they started doing moves that reminded me of tai chi. They made cat noises and hissing sounds and put their hands up like clawing paws. "You must be a tiger," one guy said. "A Bengal tiger." We were convinced there were hidden cameras, but it wasn't a joke. Charlotte was doing the exercises very earnestly, hissing and growling, and we kept peeking over at her, trying not to laugh.

For another practice Charlotte announced that a former Ben-Gals choreographer named Jayson would be coming. He had danced in one of the Jackson sisters' videos and ran dance camps for kids. There were rumors that he had worked with Britney Spears.

Jayson turned out to be very snippy. He had us do a four-minute kick line, which exhausted us because we never do kick lines for that long. We do not have the stamina of the Rockettes. Though he came to a few practices he never learned anyone's name and never tried to. He would say, "Hey you! Blond girl in the back! Sharper!" If girls were whispering, he would shout, "You gals are so chatty! Be quiet when I talk! My preschoolers don't do this!"

At one practice one of the girls asked him, "Did you really choreograph Britney's videos?"

"Google me!" he said. We later learned that he had been her dance teacher in Louisiana.

Despite the countless hours we spent in the stadium, we rarely saw any football players—even just passing by or poking their heads into the gym. It was like there were two single-sex colleges inside Paul Brown Stadium: the Bengals and the Ben-Gals. Once in a while if I arrived very early, I might see Dhani Jones or Chad Ochocinco on a bike in the weight room or out on the field, and I got a rush as if I had spotted a movie star. But during the early summer, for the most part it was as though the players didn't exist. (This was especially true in 2011, when we started practicing in mid-May and the NFL was in the middle of a lockout. It was bizarre—all that cheerleading practice without even knowing whether we would have a football season.)

As players returned from training camp toward the end of the summer, we began to see more of them. During one practice on the Tuesday before a Thursday game, the players were in the gym eating pasta. We came in for weigh-in, our mouths watering from the smell of their food, and lined up at the scale. As the girls ripped off their clothing, the players' mouths started watering for a different reason. We noticed the cornerback Adam Jones in the gym, eating. The next day he wrote on Twitter, "Man I got to see all the cheerleaders weight in LMAO it was great and they was really cool." Grammar is not Mr. Jones's forte.

I Tweeted back, "Wanna come in and weigh in with us next time?" He said he would, but I'm still waiting.

The most common interaction between players and Ben-Gals

involved items that had been lost on the field, which we shared. At training camp one year, kicker Shayne Graham found a bra pad on the field. He gave it to coach Marvin Lewis, who put it in Charlotte's mailbox, in typical understated Marvin style.

At times we found something on the field, like a sparkly stud earring, and couldn't tell if it belonged to a Ben-Gal or a Bengal. (When it comes to jewelry, white girls and black guys have a very similar sense of fashion.) Whoever found it would ask around whether anyone had lost it. Girls would joke, "If it's a player earring, it's mine," because players wore many more carats than we did.

Though the Ben-Gals and Bengals traveled in different circles and income brackets, inevitably some of the guys got curious about the cheerleaders. During one season a Bengal seemed to develop a particular interest in Chelsey, a beautiful girl with raven black hair whose sister was also on the team. He would drift onto the field during practices and we all knew it was so he could watch her. One day Charlotte pulled Chelsey aside and told her that the player wanted to be set up with her and she had told him "No way." He had given Charlotte his game glove to give to Chelsey and Charlotte showed it to Chelsey. A week later the player got engaged and we joked that secretly he was pining for Chelsey.

Despite the rule prohibiting fraternization, inevitably some girls "fraternized" anyway. One season a Ben-Gal who had been on the team for several years before I got on abruptly decided not to re-audition. I had gotten to know her at the 2008 tryouts. She was a petite brunette and a highly skilled dancer and I was surprised to learn of her decision. After asking around, I learned that she had started dating one of the Bengals. Charlotte had told the girl she had a choice to make—and she chose the guy. Apparently the relationship had been serious and the two had been planning to get married, but then the girl found out that he was seeing other women on the side. She never came back to cheer. I always wondered whether she felt the tradeoff was worth it.

WELCOME TO THE JUNGLE

AS SUMMER ENDED AND COURTNEY AND MARIJA HEADED BACK to school, they realized the extent of my new time commitment. I felt guilty but on my off nights and weekends, I made a special effort for the three of us to eat together, go to the movies, or go bowling. It helped that they were at an age where their social lives were in overdrive and they were busy with school activities like cheer and track. Something strange had happened as I had become a Ben-Gal: After those early years of being a stay-at-home mom and micromanaging my kids, I had stopped seeing myself as the only person who could nurture them. I recognized that I was no longer the center of their universe—and I knew that I shouldn't be. I wanted them to have rich social lives and I was particularly grateful that my busy schedule allowed Lisa, Jim, my mother, and P.J., who stayed at my house some of the time, to develop warm relationships with them.

Though the kids were understanding about my Ben-Gal duties, Brian continued to make negative comments to them about my cheerleading. The restraining order had diffused some of his anger, but he seemed to have lingering resentment toward me and no compunction about sharing it with the girls. "Dad says you're acting inappropriately," Marija said one day after a weekend visit with him. "He says a woman your age shouldn't do that."

"Why not?" I said. "It makes me happy and I'm as good a dancer as the other girls. What's wrong with it?"

"He says the outfits are too skimpy and you shouldn't be wearing them."

"I don't pick the outfits, honey." I told the kids about the little girls who love the Ben-Gals, and how we run a camp for kids called Junior Ben-Gals and make charity appearances for the community throughout the year. "Cheerleaders are entertainers," I said. "Our uniforms are costumes. We wear them because they make us fun to watch out there on the field. Yeah, the skirts are pretty short and our bellies show, but I don't dress like that at work or at home with you guys."

"Dad says cheerleaders are selfish and shallow," Courtney said.

"Did you remind him that *you're* a cheerleader?" I asked.

"He says it's different in the NFL," Marija chimed in. "He says NFL cheerleaders are sluts who only cheer to get close to football players."

I wanted to scream. "Actually," I said, "cheerleaders aren't even allowed to talk to players except for events. And just because I want to dance on a football field it doesn't make me shallow. Is it shallow for a woman to want to dance in a Broadway play? You like to dance."

"I guess not," Marija said. But her brow furrowed just like her father's. She was trying to make sense of what both her parents were saying.

What was it about cheerleading that set off such rage in Brian? Was he trying to poison the kids because I had discovered something I loved? Would he have been as angry if I had started running triathlons or gone back to school to be a pastry chef?

I had no idea of the extent of his rage until two months after I made the Ben-Gals, when I was served with court papers from Brian. The papers stated that he wanted to increase his time with the girls and end his spousal support because, according to him, I was living with P.J. (In truth P.J. only stayed at my house some of the time.)

"[The Mother] recently became a member of the Cincinnati Bengals Cheerleading & Practice Squad," read Brian's memorandum. "As such, she commits much of her time to training, practicing, team social events and commitments, and travels to Cincinnati. When the Mother is away, the minor children are most often with Mother's significant other . . . or home by themselves. While Father encourages a healthy relationship between his children and their Mother's significant other, he would like additional time with his children when their Mother is unavailable."

I felt like I was being punished—not only for cheerleading, but for finding something I loved to do. Brian was using my cheerleading to try to take the girls away from me. I knew that the part about additional parenting time was really about money. If he spent more time with them, his spousal support would go down.

I went to Stevenson's office, panicked. He said that Brian was probably trying to build a case to get full custody in the future, even if this visitation request was denied. "Do you think he could get it?" I asked.

"It's extremely unlikely," he said, "but you have to consider the possibility that the magistrate will decide to grant him more visitation. We're going to argue that much of your cheerleading practice takes place when the kids are busy with their own activities or at Brian's anyway, but I don't know how she is going to see it."

I hoped that she would be on our side. I was facing a much bigger battle than the one I had fought to make it on the Ben-

Gals. This was a battle over the morality of cheerleading. I was going to have to convince my kids, and the court, that I was on the right side of it.

One day in early August, in the midst of my stress about the court papers, Charlotte and the coaches handed out our uniforms. Though their attitude was matter-of-fact as they gave them out, Brandy and I were trembling. I felt like Cinderella about to try on her ball gown.

The uniforms were in special garment bags that said, BEN-GALS CHEERLEADING, and each one had our first name embroidered on it. The uniform was an off-the-shoulder, white halter top with a rhinestone B over the cleavage and a miniskirt. I was given a Large for the halter, and because the captains had told us to, I wore a pushup bra underneath. Not smart. I looked like Anna Nicole Smith on steroids. It is criminal for a woman with size DD implants to wear a pushup bra. When I got my halter on, Heather, the one other mom on the team, looked at me and said, "Your boobs are hum*on*gous." I had hoped we could be friends but the look on her face was not kind.

It turned out that Heather was right. After that, I wore only regular bras under my halter top. She wound up leaving the team before the first game and I didn't have to worry about what she thought anymore.

As soon as I got home I tried on the uniform again, jumping around in front of P.J., doing my dances. I didn't yet know that I would be wearing this same uniform for the next two years, one that would start to show lipstick, sweat, and other stains, and look far more beautiful from a distance than up close. I was over the moon. I had my game poms, my white boots, my uniform, and my own black garment bag. It was really happening. It wasn't a dream. I was the forty-year-old cheerleader.

A few weeks after we got our uniforms we were invited to cheer at the Bengals Training Camp at Georgetown College near Lexington, Kentucky. It would be our first chance to interact with the players in public, and my first chance to cheer in front of an audience. The Bengals would be playing their annual mock game. Carson Palmer and Chad Ochocinco would be there, and HBO, too, filming *Hard Knocks,* which followed the Bengals that year.

Shortly before the trip, I went up to Charlotte at practice. "Are we spending the night at training camp?" I asked.

She and Traci burst out laughing. "Are you kidding?" Charlotte said. "By the time you girls get there, the players will not have seen their wives or girlfriends for two weeks. We're not spending the night. If you spent the night there, they would find you."

Though training camp was only an hour's drive, I decided to bring P.J., Marija, Courtney, and my mother and have us all stay in a hotel after the game was over, so no one had to worry about driving home late. I wanted the girls to see what I was doing so they could be supportive. With the court date to decide visitation most likely months away, I needed them to see how much joy cheerleading brought me. I also wanted them to evaluate for themselves the things that Brian was telling them about cheerleaders.

The football field at training camp was grass, unlike the Field-Turf at Paul Brown Stadium. I felt like I was on the drill team again, seventeen years old. My mom, P.J., and the girls were in the stands and I smiled at them, knowing that they could see me. I

had bought two jerseys, Palmer's and Maualuga's, with my 30 percent discount at the stadium's Pro Shop, and the girls were wearing them. The Ben-Gals wandered around the field and fans got
signatures and snapped pictures. Courtney and Marija could see
that it wasn't just me wearing that microscopic uniform. I was part
of a group, there was nothing wrong with it, and we were getting
positive attention.

Halfway through the game we did our dance in the middle of
the field. I felt a rush of energy cheering for a live audience, knowing my family was there to support me. Afterward they came
down from the stands to greet me. "You were so great, Mom!" the
girls shouted. My mother was glowing, but P.J. was silent. I worried that he thought I was a bad dancer.

"So, P.J.," I said. "What did you think?" He got a sheepish look
on his face. "What is it? Did I mess up?"

"I went out for a smoke in the middle," he said, "and when I
came back, you were done. I'm so sorry." He looked crestfallen. I
was hurt and disappointed. (A few weeks later he quit smoking
cold turkey. That was the silver lining to his missing my very first
public dance as a cheerleader.)

After the game, Courtney and Marija had the players and the
Ben-Gals sign their jerseys. I introduced them to the other
Ben-Gals. I could see the wheels beginning to turn in their heads.
If you want to impress tween girls, you have to give them a little
access to fame.

Some of the Ben-Gals at training camp were shocked to learn
that I had school-age daughters. Marija was almost as tall as some
of the girls on the team. One Ben-Gal looked in awe from my
daughters to me and said, "These are your daughters? How old are
you, Laura?"

"Forty," I said.

"Oh my God, are you kidding?"

"Nope."

"I had no idea you were a mother."

My first game as a Cincinnati Ben-Gal was on Thursday, August 27, 2009. My whole family was coming, and because of Marija and Courtney's cheerleading and visitation schedule with their dad, it was one of the few games that season that they would be able to attend.

The game had been scheduled for seven-thirty P.M., which meant that the Ben-Gals had to arrive at the stadium a little past three. I worked a half-day and went home. I went through my pack checklist to make sure I had everything I needed: diamond stud earrings, two bras, clean white boots, white socks, panty hose, game poms, skirt, halter top, B insignia for the cleavage, photo ID, extra hose, extra socks, curling iron, hairspray, white towels, deodorant, face wash, fake lashes, bobby pins, makeup, Shout wipes, wrinkle spray, Advil, tampons, baby wipes, mints for fan deck appearances, a marker for signing autographs, comfy clothes for down time, safety pins, and, my favorite item of all, "panties for after game." Because we didn't wear panties under our hose, if we didn't bring panties, we had to go home from the game commando. Despite the fact that we knew this, girls repeatedly forgot their underwear. If you ever meet an NFL cheerleader after a game, consider this: There is a good chance that she is not wearing any underwear.

I spent an hour getting ready for the game in full hair, full makeup, and my cute, arrive-at-the-stadium outfit: tight sausage jeans, BCBG top, and black, shiny, strappy platform heels. I went through my bag three times to make sure I had everything. Finally my suitcase and my garment bag were by the kitchen table ready to go. But I was rushing so much that I loaded my car with my suitcase—and forgot the garment bag containing my uniform.

Halfway to the stadium, in the midst of early rush hour traffic, I realized what I had done. My pulse raced. If I arrived at the game without my uniform, I would not be allowed to cheer. There were no concessions made for girls who forgot their uniforms, no extras at the stadium for us to wear in situations like this. If I turned around to get it and arrived late, I would not be allowed to cheer. My entire family would be at the game and I would not be on the field. The regular season hadn't even started yet and I had blown it already.

I called P.J., weeping and hysterical. "I forgot my uniform," I said. "Oh my God, oh my God. Are you home yet? Can you bring it to me? Can you meet me halfway there?"

"I'm not home yet," he said. "Call your corner captain and say you're running late."

"You don't understand! She won't care! If I'm late, she won't let me cheer!" The reason we had alternates, those eight extra girls, was for situations like this. I knew that any of them would be thrilled to take my spot instead of having to entertain rich guys in the private suites.

My dilemma was complicated by the fact that Ben-Gals do not just drive up to the stadium for games the way we do for practices. The thirty-two of us are given only five parking passes for each game. So we all park our cars at a TV station about a mile away from the stadium, pile into five cars, and then carpool to Player Parking. I was supposed to go in Brandy's SUV, but if I wasn't at the TV station by three o'clock, her car would leave without me.

I had left only fifteen minutes of buffer time and by the time I realized I'd forgotten my uniform, I was already halfway to the stadium. There was no way I could make it home and back in time, but I had to try. I got off the highway, turned the car around, and drove toward Springboro at a hundred miles an hour. I was convinced I would get pulled over by a cop but if I didn't go a hundred, I had no chance of making it.

I called Brandy and told her what happened. I was shifting gears, talking on my cell phone, and speeding. If I got pulled over, the officer wouldn't even begin to know what to cite me for. "Well, just go as fast as you can," she said.

"I don't think I'll make it," I said, beginning to cry again. Now the makeup I had worked so hard to apply was going to wind up smudged all over my face.

"I'm going to call Latasha," she said, "and tell her you had car trouble. I'll call you back. Just try to make it, hon."

At home I grabbed my bag and threw it into the car. On the way back to Cincinnati the traffic was even thicker. I was weaving in and out of cars. The phone rang. "Here's the plan," Brandy said. "We're going to squeeze into four cars instead of five. We'll leave you a parking pass at the gate. So just try to get here." She had told Latasha I had a flat tire—knowing that if Latasha knew the real reason, she wouldn't be able to bend the rules for me.

The fifty-minute drive to the stadium took thirty-five. I arrived at 3:20, drove up to the security guard, and said, "I'm one of the Ben-Gals, you have a pass for me?" When he handed me the pass, I couldn't believe the plan had worked. I hooked it on my mirror, pulled in, and parked. In front of me the girls were lining up to have their bags sniffed by the security dogs. I ran up and got in back of the line. Brandy turned around and mouthed, "I can't believe it." I was teary but blotting my eyes so I didn't mess up my makeup even more. I was so worked up, mentally and physically, that I could not conceive of how I was going to cheer a three-hour football game.

What Brandy did for me that day typifies what it means to be a Ben-Gal. She went to bat for me but did it shrewdly because she knew that the truth would not win me an exception to the rules. I will never forget the way she saved me the day of my first game—Laura Vikmanis, the flying pig of Cincinnati.

Before the game we had a full practice on the field. We ran through all of our dances and then the captain, Tara, gave us a pep talk that I imagined was similar to the one that Marvin Lewis would give his players in their locker room a few hours later. "You have to remember the changes we've made to the dances," Tara said. "You have got to be adaptable and incorporate fixes, and everyone's energy level has to come up ten notches at least. Act snotty. You need to be more prissy! Noses in the air, smile, and be supersharp. We're going to have fun today. You girls look great! Just have fun, have fun!"

We filed off the field to the Ben-Gals locker room to change for the game. It was the first time I had seen the locker room. It was brightly colored, with a black-and-orange carpet, a Bengal B in the middle, and BEN-GALS painted on the walls. The locker room was our special place—but unlike the players' locker room, it did not belong to us exclusively. It was used for special events on nongame days, for bands or children's charities. The bathroom had urinals in it. Just like the uniforms, the locker room was ours and yet it wasn't.

The room was bordered by a few dozen cubbies. Though there were small lockers on the bottom and top of each cubby, no Ben-Gals left personal items in the lockers overnight, for fear that something might get stolen. Instead we lugged everything we could possibly need to the stadium for every game, not just the standard uniform but anything we could possibly wear to cheer in.

This meant that we were carting around thirty extra pounds to every game. It was not until my second season that we were issued official Ben-Gals rolling suitcases. Before then we looked like a team of crazy ladies going to a bachelorette party in Vegas, our eclectic assortment of bags and suitcases bursting at the seams with rollers and push-up bras.

As I walked into the locker room I could smell food. One of the few perks of game days was a catered meal paid for by the Bengals organization. A table was laden with salad, lasagna, veggies, rolls, and dessert—five-inch chocolate chip cookies, cheesecake, blondies, and brownies. We dove into the food because there was no weigh-in on Game Day and, even better, we wouldn't have to weigh in again till Tuesday, five long days away, since this was a Thursday game.

After we ate dinner that night, we all changed from our practice outfits—now sweaty and disgusting—into our uniforms. The smell of hairspray, deodorant, eyelash glue, and baby powder mixed with the aroma of lasagna. We checked one another's appearances, helping apply eyelashes or pointing out panty hose runs. The Grinds practiced. The Negative complained. The Models vamped. Everyone snapped cell-phone photos. Charlotte came in and gave a little pep talk.

When everyone was ready, we went out on the fan deck, the JungleZone, and signed team photos. It was a big, busy scene with games for kids and a contest in which people sang George Bird's Bengals fight song, the "Bengal Growl," on camera. I watched the stadium fill up with fans and signed my autograph hundreds of times. How had I gone from a woman filled with self-hatred to a cheerleader signing her autograph for little girls?

We went back to the locker room to freshen up, the rookies the most excited of all. The corner captains put on their wristbands, the same ones the quarterbacks use, with the order and names of our dances printed on paper tucked inside. We did our long walk through the underbelly of the stadium toward the tunnel, and Tara led us in her prayer.

On the field we did our intro dance. I remembered everything that came before this moment, from my ballet dances as a child to Brian locking me in the bedroom to my divorce and recovery.

We lined up in two rows, making an aisle. The Bengals mascot was coming out onto the field—Who Dey, the Bengal tiger. (Who Dey is named for a 1980s cheer that goes, "Who Dey? Who Dey? Who Dey think gonna beat dem Bengals?" The response is supposed to be "Nobody!" but today a few frustrated fans answer, "Everybody!") Fireworks were going off as announcer Bob Kinder introduced the players. I was unprepared for the deafening sound. The ashes looked like enormous bugs wafting down from the sky. And then the players were running between us, so close, so big, smelling of fear and power and ruthlessness. I could see that they were charged up, but I could also see that they were boys, in their early twenties, their lives ahead of them.

We lined up in the end zone for the national anthem, standing in Ben-Gal Pose. The American flag was carried out. The crowd got quiet and a high school girls ensemble sang the anthem.

We broke up into our four groups and cheer-walked to our corners, long strides, heads high, chests out. It wasn't until I got to my corner that I realized how close the fans were—right in front of us, some almost close enough to touch. I tried not to look anyone in the eye so I wouldn't get distracted and forget my choreography, but some of the other girls gave Cheer Sex. That's when you find a guy to look at and make eyes at him for the whole dance.

Guns N' Roses' "Welcome to the Jungle" came on. Some fans were yelling at us, though I couldn't hear what they were saying.

Nothing had prepared me for the reality of a stadium packed with fans. I heard the opening chords on the electric guitar but I was so emotional that I forgot the choreography. Axl Rose was singing "Welcome to the jungle/We got fun and games." I pretended that the music wasn't blasting through the stadium sound system but coming from Tara's tiny stereo in the gym at practice. I told myself that we weren't in front of all these cameras and fans but inside the Bengals gym, just us girls.

It worked. The moves came back. I started to dance. So *this* was why I had practiced for hundreds of hours. This was why I had worked so hard for a year and auditioned again after being rejected. This was why I put up with the coaches' sometimes domineering style. It was so I could be here, in Paul Brown Stadium, continuing a tradition that had begun in the nineteenth century and been carried on by everyone from *Desperate Housewives* star Teri Hatcher, who cheered for the San Francisco 49ers, to George W. Bush, who was head cheerleader at his boarding school, Phillips Academy.

On the sidelines, dozens of people I had never seen before scurried back and forth doing their jobs: cameramen, sound guys, security staff, journalists, referees, and Who Dey. There was also an enormous camera on a blue dolly and I had to make sure it wasn't rolling right at me. There were handlers whose job was to clear a path for the camera and make sure it didn't injure anyone. I was terrified of it anyway.

Most of the fans seemed to enjoy the cheerleaders, but the corner near the visitors' tunnel, ironically enough, was the most enthusiastic. Later in the season many of them would do our cheers right along with us. There are few things funnier than drunk, burly men doing cheers.

Each of our four corners of cheerleaders had its own "mom,"

a coach or helper who was there to give us whatever we needed. They got our water ready for the two on-field water breaks we got per game. They let us know if a bra was peeking out from a halter top or if hair needed to be fixed. They also served as our unofficial stage managers. Each one was on a walkie-talkie. The music producer up in the booth would radio the name of the next song to Traci, she would announce the filler title into her walkie-talkie, and all the moms would cue us in sync. The fillers had titles like Peaches, Old School, Throw, Snap, Windup, Hippie Chick, Bounce, Hair, and Shake. They read like a catalogue of obscure sexual positions.

The twenty-second fillers we did at practice turned out to be much more tiring when we had to repeat them many times based on the length of the time-out, the commercial on the video screens, or the song. Like little Energizer bunnies, we had to keep going and going until our corner captains told us to stop. Often this went on until we were ready to fall down.

There were times during that August game when it seemed that the producer had it in for us. Sometimes he would play the music too slowly and we couldn't find our rhythm. On some occasions music did not start, and when it did, it turned out to be the wrong song. Most fans probably had no idea, but we did and it was frustrating. Other times he played music too fast, and we had to go into double time to keep up.

But not everything was the producer's fault. One corner captain frequently got confused by all the commercials that played on the screens. She would begin dancing any time the "I'm lovin' it" McDonald's ad came on because the music sounded like one of our dances.

Every time we stopped a dance, we went into Ben-Gal Pose. The head snap was just like in *Legally Blonde* and after doing it a couple of dozen times over three hours, I would need a chiropractor. Everything that cheerleaders do to be sexy—snap their heads, flip their hair, stick out their chests, engage the abdominal and glute muscles, pull their shoulders back—wreaks havoc on the body. We aren't in as much pain as the players by the end of a game, but we are sore. You can always tell how tired a Ben-Gal is by the way she shakes her poms. If she shakes with a lot of energy, she's doing all right. If it looks like she is holding two wet Angora sweaters, then you know she needs help.

Over the course of that first game, I discovered that about half of the Ben-Gals did not understand the rules of football. The crowd would go crazy at a play and one of us would say to the other, "What just happened?"

"It was fourth down and they got an interception."

"What's an interception?"

The reason for the hard work, the self-tanner, and the nose breakers

My own understanding of the rules fell somewhere in the middle. Sometimes the terminology eluded me. I would say, "The quarterback is trying to make a connection" instead of "The quarterback is trying to complete the pass." I called the receiver the catcher. And even though P.J. had explained it to me half a dozen times, I still wasn't entirely clear on the definition of a punt.

Because so many cheerleaders were shaky on the rules, we preferred our dances to our cheers, which correlated with game action. My rookie season, any girl in any corner could start a cheer, and then the rest of her corner would join in.

I was very careful not to initiate cheers because whoever started the cheer had to remember which team we were playing, if we were on offense or defense, and whether the action had stopped due to an injury, because we never cheer during injuries. And sometimes I worried that I would start the cheer at the same time as another girl—which often happened.

In my second season, the rule was changed so that one designated girl per corner got to lead cheers. During my third season I was that girl. It's still scary every time I do it but I like the extra attention. I feel like I'm coming full circle, from my seventh-grade sideline cheering to doing it on an NFL football field, thirty years later.

In the future, cheerleader training should most certainly include a crash course in the rules of the game with one of the Bengals assistant coaches. It would be a win-win situation. We would get to ask all the questions we're afraid to ask one another, and the coach would get to spend a couple of hours with thirty-two of the most beautiful women in Cincinnati.

At seventeen seconds before halftime during that Bengals-Rams game, we paraded back into the locker room for a break. (Ben-Gal cheerleaders don't do halftime shows at games. Those are allotted to local bands or charities. We do halftime shows only at Halloween if there is a game on October 31, Christmas, and sometimes for the Junior Ben-Gals game.) In the locker room we freshened up, talked about the game, scarfed cookies, and drank lots of water. Anything that had been bothering us the first half—snags in hose, falling fake eyelashes, bad hair, errant bra pads—got fixed. A few minutes before the third quarter began we went back onto the field.

Nothing prepared me for the intensity of cheering with an actual football game going on behind us. At practices we were all that existed. Now there were these three-hundred-pound guys behind us, tackling the hell out of one another.

During one time-out per quarter, we ran from our corners out to the center of the field and did a feature dance. Some of the players would still be standing there. Ochocinco would be glancing at us, half-interested. Others looked bored or flashed a smile. Then the time-out would end, our song would stop, and we would race back to our corners before the next play.

I wondered if the players had any idea how early in the season we started practicing and how little we were paid in comparison to them. In 2009 the minimum salary for rookie NFL players was $300,000. The same year, a Ben-Gal cheerleader earned $750—and that was only if she cheered ten games.

When the players interacted with us on the field, it was usually for show, a way of getting the fans revved up. They understood the symbolic power of cheerleaders. At one game in 2005 after a touchdown, Chad Ochocinco (then Chad Johnson) mock-proposed to a cheerleader named Daphne, and the fans went crazy. In a 2010 game he handed Sarah J. the football after a great catch and the clip was played on TV.

Though the Bengals lost to the Rams, 24 to 21, that August

night, it was only the preseason and even they didn't seem to care. The Ben-Gals walked back to our locker room down the Bengal brick road, congratulating one another for getting through the first game. I was drenched. We all were. Cheerleaders do not *take* off their uniforms after a game; they *peel* them off. We chugged diet soda and water. We blotted our faces and reapplied foundation and makeup, because how we looked after the game was as important as how we looked before it.

It was ten-thirty at night by this time. In order to avoid stadium traffic and get to sleep before the sun rose, we changed back as fast as we could into Stadium Cute, our pretty dresses and heels, to head home. We walked down the long, winding hallway and just before the exit, we passed a holding area for fans seeking player autographs. There were barriers holding them back. I felt like a Hollywood celebrity walking the red carpet. "Can I get your autograph?" a cute male fan shouted. Just as I was signing it, quarterback Jordan Palmer (Carson's brother) came out behind me and it was like I had disappeared. The fan leaned over me to get to Jordan. I finished with my Sharpie and slipped him back his program. No matter how famous cheerleaders felt, compared to players we didn't exist.

After the game, P.J., Lisa, my mom, Marija, and Courtney and I went to a restaurant and talked about the game. "I couldn't believe that was you out there," Marija said. "I had to keep reminding myself that it was you."

"I had to keep reminding myself, too!" I said.

My mom said she hadn't realized how much we danced over the course of a game. The girls had had fun and I felt that they were beginning to reach their own conclusions about cheerleading, different from the ones that Brian wanted them to make. I wished that *they* would be the ones deciding whether to change the visitation.

Games were the payoff for the hard work we did all season. They were exhilarating, intoxicating, and exciting. But what we went through on Game Day could be torturous. Football season went from August to January. We cheered in crushing heat and freezing cold. In summer we dealt with sweat, heat, body odor, and fans that were drunker than usual. Bugs flew into our mouths or eyes and we had to keep cheering, swallowing them or blinking them out. On really hot days when I looked out and saw fans drinking those cold, sweating beers, I wanted to run up into the stands and grab one.

When it rained we wore waterproof eyeliner and mascara, but for one game a girl forgot them. She used a Sharpie on her upper lid and no one was the wiser.

My least favorite time to cheer was winter. We wore big winter jackets so we were like little kids in snowsuits who can't move their arms around. We came in with hacking coughs, strep throat, and horrible colds—every girl afraid to miss a game no matter what the cost to her health.

When it was really cold, we had mucus running down our faces, and our hair lodged in the mucus and stayed there. We had to wipe it off subtly with the backs of our hands. For one game in November a bunch of kids joined us on the field. They stared at the snot running down into our mouths, incredulous that the cheerleaders who looked so hot from afar looked so gross up close. *I know I have snot,* I wanted to tell them. *I would like to do something about it as much as you would like me to, but unfortunately I am not allowed.*

In winter we did anything we could to stay warm. Our uniforms transformed—we wore shorts, little jackets, heavier coats, and long black pants or catsuits. No one liked the catsuits because the crotch area showed camel-toe and we worried that it would show up in a fan photo. I worried about that, too, but I liked that they felt like Spanx. Sometimes, no matter what we wore, we were freezing anyway. We wore heat packs inside our shorts. During one game my pack migrated down into my hose, so I had this big white thing bulging out until I dashed over to the wall to fish it out.

One Ben-Gals winter uniform was a Santa outfit: a red-and-white miniskirt with a black Santa belt, which was cute, and a white fur jacket with a pleather inside, which wasn't. It made us look like the Michelin Man. I felt like I was dancing in a garbage bag, but I loved the Santa outfit because it kept me warm. You can take the girl out of California but you can't take the California out of the girl.

In the 1970s, conditions for NFL cheerleaders were even less forgiving. Cheerleaders had to bare their skin no matter how cold it was. As the Scholz sisters of the Dallas Cowboys Cheerleaders recalled,

> When we performed at games, rarely were we allowed to wear anything but the uniform, no matter what the weather. During the first half of the game we had to be in the shorts and halter top. We'd walk out of the dressing room and that icy wind would come whipping down the tunnel and we'd freeze on the spot.
>
> Everybody in the stands would have blankets, arctic jackets, portable heaters, ear muffs, fur coats. And we'd

be pleading, "Suzanne, can we at least wear our warm-ups?"

"Absolutely not! The fans pay to see you in your uniforms," she'd say while bundled in a caramel-colored fox jacket.

One year, just before Christmas, Charlotte gave us imitation Uggs to wear with sparkly Bengal Bs on them and a captain suggested that we wear them on the field. A Ben-Gal named Carla was given boots that were a little too big and during the game she sprained her ankle. She was carried off the field but none of the fans cheered or even noticed, the way they do for the players. Because she couldn't exercise in the off-season due to her injury, she gained a bit of weight, enough for the judges to notice at tryouts the following spring. She didn't make the squad. She was devastated and so were we. We felt she was being penalized for something that happened through no fault of her own. Flat-soled boots look great on the street, but are not ideal for dancing.

Weather was not the only job hazard of cheering. Eyelashes, hands, and poms whipped our eyes, scraping them, causing us to tear up for the next three hours. Sometimes contact lenses fell out (eyeglasses were not permitted on the field) and girls cheered the rest of the game with only one in, half blind. I had eyelashes drop halfway off. Clip-on extensions often came out—the reason I am not a fan of them. I am nervous enough trying to remember my choreography that I don't need to worry about falling chunks of hair, too. The girls who wear chicken cutlets in their bras oftentimes lose them and then have to pick them up and stick them back in without anyone noticing.

It was always disappointing that we didn't get to travel for away games. We performed only for home games. The advantage of bye weeks, when there were no games, was that we didn't practice and didn't have to weigh in, so we could all go crazy with our eating. But we more than made up for them with strict diets during the days before the weigh-ins.

The few times we did get to travel with the boys to special games, we were surprised to discover that the accommodations were not exactly four-star. One season we cheered a Hall of Fame game at a high school stadium in Canton, Ohio. The Bengals were playing the Dallas Cowboys. It was a four-hour bus trip and we were really excited to meet the Dallas Cowboys Cheerleaders. When we got to the high school, it turned out that our locker room was dingy and hot. There were no stalls in the bathroom, just two toilets with a wall between them and an open shower. There were a few packaged snacks and we were afraid to drink the water. When we found out that the Dallas Cowboys Cheerleaders had elected not to come, we weren't surprised.

All bodily functions of cheerleaders came second to cheering. Girls got their periods in the middle of games and couldn't deal with it until halftime break. During one summer game it was so hot that Abs got sun poisoning and had to walk over to a trash can to vomit. Sometimes I have to pee and have to hold it in for an hour or more, even if I went before the game. My teacher, Nikki, had told us that one Ben-Gal peed down her leg during a game. Kimberly has had irritable bowel syndrome since she was a child and always worried that she would have an accident during the game. Before we went out to the field, she would be in the bathroom in the locker room, trying to go. She would come out with a big, relieved smile on her face, and say, "I did it!" We would all cheer for her like she was a two-year-old who had just gone potty.

Cheerleaders hate football coach's challenges (that's when the coaches challenge a call and the referees review the play on a video), especially in hot weather, because they go on for two or three minutes and the producer keeps playing music, and we have to keep dancing the whole time. If the head ref can't determine the result, sometimes he'll call in another ref and it takes even longer.

The irony of these grueling conditions is that unlike cheerleaders during the 1970s and 1980s, we are not rewarded by a lot of television time. Cheerleaders are barely shown in football games anymore. These days advertising revenue trumps entertainment value. A shot of a cheerleader doesn't earn a network money, it's just pleasurable. Today, even when a network *does* air a "honey shot," the cheerleader's face is often covered by advertising logos. We wish we could peek over them. I have told friends and family in other cities to watch me on TV, only to have them say, "I thought I saw you for a second but it said CHEVROLET across your face and I wasn't sure it was you."

Nor are we rewarded for our efforts with very good money. If you add up the time we spend practicing and cheering those three-hour-plus football games in a typical season, we make about two dollars and fifty cents an hour—sweatshop wages. We are like a one-ring traveling circus within a nine-billion-dollar corporation. Paid events may bring in five or six hundred dollars more per season—and that would be a very good year.

The history of professional cheerleading goes back to an era when cheerleaders were high school or college students and volunteers, so any game pay was considered symbolic. Cheerleaders did it out of love for their home team and love for their community. But today's NFL cheerleaders, even if some are high school students, are not doing it for a lark. We are doing it to have a stepping-stone to have a future in dance. We deserve to be paid like adults.

There is only one NFL cheerleading team that receives minimum wage: the Seattle Sea Gals. After Microsoft cofounder Paul Allen bought the Seattle Seahawks in 1997, the team instituted minimum wage for the Sea Gals and a fifty cent raise per season. In 2011 a first-year Sea Gal made $8.67 per hour. The Sea Gals get paid for events at the same rate, at a four-hour minimum, and, most important, they get paid for their weekly practices. For 350 hours of practice and 50 hours of events a veteran could make four thousand dollars a year. It's still not enough to live on, but it's a nice supplementary income.

During the 2011 NFL lockout, one of the key issues between players and management was revenue sharing. Players wanted a bigger piece of the NFL's nine-billion-dollar pie. Instead the player revenue share was reduced a few percentage points—*to 48 percent of all revenue*. I am not saying that cheerleaders should get a percentage of team revenue, but I do think we should be paid salaries that reflect our value to the teams.

A 2003 *Forbes* magazine article estimated that NFL teams with cheerleaders bring in an extra $1 million in revenue per team in calendar sales, appearances, sponsorships, and clothing lines. Cheerleaders also bring traffic to team websites with cheerleader blogs, photos, and contests. Our public events and Web traffic can lead to increased ticket sales to games and a better profile for team sponsors, which means we are providing real economic value while still being paid less than teenage babysitters.

There have been several attempts by cheerleaders to organize themselves in the past—but they have failed. In 1992 a group of Washington Redskinette veterans resigned from the team, claiming nepotism, favoritism, insensitive racial attitudes, intimidation, harassment, and verbal abuse. The team went on without them. In 1995 the Buffalo Jills, who were not owned by the Buffalo Bills but an independent company called Buffalo Jills Cheerleaders Inc., won a ruling to form a union, the National Football League Cheerleaders Association, but in response to the newly formed union's new demands, the team's management company wound up going out of business. A few years later the girls got a new sponsor, an Italian restaurant owner, but their union disbanded. Today the Jills are sponsored by Cumulus Media, a broadcasting company, and are not unionized.

For treatment of NFL cheerleaders to change, cheerleaders would have to argue for better working conditions. But because we are a transient workforce, it's hard to imagine any of us caring enough to fight. By the time we were able to get any traction we would be past the cheerleader phase of our lives. Because most cheerleaders would rather keep cheering than take on management and risk being booted, aggrieved cheerleaders just wind up quitting. Others channel their grievances by working harder within the system so they can become captains or coaches, who can receive double to triple the per-game pay and have a higher profile.

Poor pay and hard work aside, there is nothing like the thrill of being on an NFL field when your team wins. The 2009 season turned out to be a good one for the Bengals—we swept the AFC North for the first time in team history and made the playoffs for the first time since the 2005 season. Our record was ten and six. Because we made the playoffs, the Ben-Gals got to cheer an extra game. It was extra exposure, extra excitement, and seventy-five extra dollars for each girl who cheered the playoff game. At the end of the season the Associated Press voted Marvin Lewis NFL Coach of the Year. We were excited to be cheering for a team that seemed to be turning itself around. We fantasized about going to the Super Bowl. Sarah J. said that if we won the Super Bowl, Mike Brown might choose to distribute the highly coveted gold-and-diamond Super Bowl rings to us.

After a winning game, we lined up in two rows as the jubilant players funneled through us on their way into the tunnel. The energy was incredible. With their helmets off, we could see their smiling faces. Everyone gave each other high-fives. Fans begged for gloves and towels to keep as mementos. Like 2009, 2011 turned out to be a record-breaking season. In October 2011, after the team's sixty-fifth win, Marvin Lewis became the Bengals coach with the most wins in history, surpassing Sam Wyche's 1991 record.

In December 2011, wide receiver Jerome Simpson scored a touchdown in a Cardinals game by flipping over a defender's head into the end zone. And on New Year's Day 2012, though we lost to Baltimore, we made it into the playoffs as a wild card.

But the 2010 season was not as bright as the two on either side of it. That year, the Bengals won only three home games in the regular season. Attendance was so low that several games were blacked out from local TV. It was demoralizing. Before a game, Tara would remind us, "If we wind up winning, you're going to make a tunnel for the guys at the end."

"I don't think we have to worry about winning," a Ben-Gal would mutter.

After a losing game, fans got to go home and talk about the many reasons the Bengals lost and everything they should have done differently to win. We, on the other hand, had to walk back to the tunnel with the losing players. The mood was radically different from after a win. The players hurried back to the locker room, either cursing or else completely silent. We scampered past them, trying our best to stay out of their way.

When the Bengals are losing really badly, it is not fun to be out on that field. The fans get drunker and nastier. They yell out, "Nice tits!" When we lost our round of the playoffs in January 2010 to the Jets, fans were furious. They threw their plastic beer bottles onto the field and some landed right next to me. "Get off the field!" a woman in a Bengals jersey shouted right at us. "You guys suck! Learn to dance!" Her makeup was smudged and it was obvious that she'd had ten too many sixteen-ounce beers.

I stared up at her, wanting to tell her, "You have no idea how hard we work." The Cincinnati Ben-Gals are not the Dallas Cowboys Cheerleaders, but we put thousands of hours into our practice, and here this woman was denigrating us. Maybe she felt sexually competitive or maybe she thought we detracted from the game, but most likely she was just angry with the Bengals and taking it out on us.

When I walked back to the locker room, I could hear her insults ringing in my head. But I reminded myself I wasn't cheering for the approval of a drunk Bengals fan. I was doing it for myself. I had to ignore the haters and focus on all the fans, like Lisa, who adored us and who couldn't imagine the Bengals without the cheerleaders. I had to be an entertainer until the moment I walked off the field. Chest up, big smile, and no matter what, never touch your hair.

THE BOOB HUG

MANY PEOPLE THINK AN NFL CHEERLEADER'S ONLY JOB IS TO cheer. That is not the case. Games comprise only about 10 percent of our time commitment. Seventy percent is practice and the other 20 percent is public appearances. The most important part of our jobs as Ben-Gals is to represent the team positively. The players are also supposed to project a good image, but by the time I became a Ben-Gal in 2009, they were not succeeding. From 2006 to 2007 nine Bengals had been arrested in nine months—for marijuana possession, driving while intoxicated, resisting arrest, drunk boating, spousal battery, and grand theft. Wide receiver Chris Henry was in the news constantly for his various problems with the law and died tragically in 2009 in a domestic dispute after falling off a moving truck in Charlotte, North Carolina. In 2010 linebacker Rey Maualuga was arrested for driving under the influence; he struck a parking meter and two parked cars. Running back Cedric Benson was arrested in 2010 for allegedly punching a bar employee in Austin, Texas. In 2011 police confiscated a package containing two and a half pounds of marijuana that had been shipped from California to wide receiver Jerome Simpson in Kentucky. Some Cincinnatians say that the Bengals are the last stop before rehab. To be fair, the Bengals are by no means the only NFL players who have had trouble with the law.

We Ben-Gals carried none of the baggage that some of the boys carried. (Or if we did, we made sure that no one found out about it.) Our job was to be low maintenance, cheerful, wholesome, and, above all, lawful. The Ben-Gals are like a smart, great woman married to a guy who just can't get his act together.

Events are the primary way we project a good image of the team and we are paid for doing some of them. Event sign-up happens at the beginning of practice. Girls cluster around the coaches' table and Traci calls out, "Anyone want to do a charity golf outing on Sunday?" Everyone checks their calendars to see if they are free.

Charlotte uses the event sign-up to play us off one another because she knows the income is important to us. She says something like, "This Friday from six to eight I need one girl to do a calendar signing at Kroger"—a major grocery chain headquartered in Cincinnati. There is grumbling. No one raises her hand. Then I raise mine, because my daughters are with their father that night and I don't sign up for events when I have the girls. "Thank you, Laura," Charlotte says. "You just made two hundred fifty dollars." The other girls groan. At times it is an advantage to be a suburban mom without a social life.

My very first Ben-Gal event was in June 2009. It was the Taste of the NFL, a big restaurant fair at the stadium that raises money to fight hunger. Cheerleaders had to walk around and pose for pictures with fans. I was very excited to see the players up close, for once, and to get to chat with them without risking being kicked off the Ben-Gals. At one point a bunch of the Ben-Gals, including Sarah J. and Sarah G., were standing in a circle with a cute man who seemed to know them. Next to these two extremely tall women, both wearing four-inch platform heels, he looked short. He was easygoing and a redhead just like Sarah G., so I said, "Are you guys related or something?"

"No, I'm the kicker," he said. "Shayne Graham."

Sarah J., one of the few genuine football fans on the Ben-Gals, shook her head slowly and started to laugh. Shayne had a reputation for having a healthy ego and she thought it was funny that I cut him down. I was so embarrassed that right after the event I went online to the Bengals site and studied the players' faces so it wouldn't happen again.

A big part of Ben-Gals events is posing for photographs with fans. Early on, Tara coached us on what to expect. "Always put your Sharpie in your boot for signing autographs," she said. "If you have a drink in your hand, even if it's water or pop, put it behind your back. Always smile. If a guy grabs you too tightly, take his hand off you and put *your* arm around *him* instead. When the picture goes off, don't forget to pop your knee in Ben-Gal Pose. That way you have a curvy outline."

I quickly learned other tips. If I was in standard uniform with pom-poms, I held them over my stomach pooch when I posed. If I didn't have poms, I posed with one hand on my hip but I didn't really hold the hip, I just rested the hand very lightly on it, so the skin didn't pooch out above my hand. (You can always pick a professional cheerleader out of a photo because she will be the one whose hand is resting oddly on her hip.)

If it seems like I am a control freak about how I pose for pictures, it's because in the age of modern technology I have to be. After a game or event, hundreds of people tag me on Facebook in pictures ranging from great to embarrassingly awful. Fans can post their photos wherever they want, with nasty comments and last names of cheerleaders appended. This was a problem that the Dallas Cowboys Cheerleaders never had to contend with in their heyday because there was no Internet.

Some male fans at events were downright rude. They leered, stared at our breasts, and tried to grab us in photos. Bar events were particularly unpleasant because the men had been drinking a lot. When we posed with them, they would try to do a "boob hug," where they reach their hand around you, raise it slowly, and try to touch the side of your boob. I would move the hand down to my waist or arrange myself far enough away that a man couldn't touch my boob if he tried.

While one guy was trying to get the shot, another would make a comment like, "I bet he's focusing in on her boobs." When I heard that, my first thought was, *What a jerk.* My second was, *This guy has no social skills with women and that's sad.* Or, *He's really drunk and he has no idea what he's saying.*

I understood why men objectified cheerleaders. When a guy is staring at a beautiful woman who is wearing a halter top, a miniskirt that barely covers her crotch, her belly and thighs exposed, her cleavage practically up to her chin, of course he sees her as an object. But I wished they had a little more class, wished they knew how little we were making.

My least favorite events were the ones where we had to appear in uniform. From a distance, on the field, I felt confident in my uniform but up close I felt naked. Whenever I heard that we were allowed to wear a shirt to an event, I was relieved.

After a rough event with too many obnoxious men, I told myself that I didn't sign up for events for those guys. I did it for the guys who were mature enough to talk politely with us, like the Bengal Twins. Steve and Jeff were middle-aged twins who went to every game together, had been Bengals fans since they were kids, and followed both the players and the cheerleaders, filling their cameras with action shots and giving us CDs with hundreds of photos on them. I made event appearances for the Bengal Twins, and the women who told me they were once cheerleaders, and the little girls who did cheering at school.

I even went for the kooky male fans. I preferred fans like that—the ones with big Bengal tiger heads or bizarre makeup and getups—because they were respectful. I'll take one helping of crazy when it comes with a helping of respect.

Often when a guy was really obnoxious, the Ben-Gals bonded about it. As he walked away, one of us would say, "Wow, he was creepy." Or, "That guy smelled." We laughed and felt closer to each other. It was a way of taking back the power the guy tried to take from us.

As the football season went on we started getting fan mail. Some of it came from prisons. The prisoners went online, looked at pictures of us, and then printed them out and requested autographs. My rookie season I didn't get one piece of mail, and when it was handed out to the other girls, I felt a little disappointed. Then I asked myself whether I really needed a fan who was serving a life sentence for murder.

Some male fans were obsessed with us. We called those guys the Creepy Stalkers or the Ben-Gal Creepies. They were middle-aged men and they knew our names, came to every event, took their own pictures, and brought them to the next event for us to sign.

It turns out that there have been Ben-Gal Creepies as long as there have been Ben-Gals. In a 1978 *Cincinnati* magazine article, a Ben-Gal named Vicki Woods told a reporter that she knew she was a sex object when "I got a call from a guy in Zanesville, Ohio.

He said, 'You know, I was at the game and of course there I was with my binoculars and I've been trying to get your number ever since. I've spent $20 on calls to various "Woods" in the book.' "

Today only our first names are on the Ben-Gal website, with a second initial if two girls share a name. Charlotte instructs us never to give out our last names and we are all grateful for that.

For some events we were instructed to come in street clothes. A few of the girls liked them because they had an excuse to dress provocatively. One year at a dreaded street-clothes event, a Ben-Gal wore hot-pant shorts with six-inch platform stripper heels. I would have looked ridiculous in that outfit because of my age. I wished Charlotte had told the girl that street clothes didn't mean streetwalker clothes.

There were times it was tough to go from Mom Laura or Dietitian Laura to Event Laura. I felt like Clark Kent turning into Superman. My phone booth was my car. One late-spring day I had to go right from the office to a golf event. In my office, I changed into a Ben-Gals jacket and dashed out as fast as I could, and in my car I switched from work pants to jeans. When the event was over, I changed back into my work clothes in the car, removed my red lipstick but not my lashes because I was running late, and went back to the office.

An hour later my cell phone rang. I had to go to Marija's school to talk to the counselor because Marija was having some troubles with her dad. In the counselor's office I noticed Marija staring at me with a funny look on her face. When we left together, she said, "Why did you have all that makeup on and your eyelashes?"

"I had a golf appearance," I said.

"Oh."

"Does that bother you?"

"No, but next time you come to school, try not to look like that, Mom."

Though the events created new stresses for my kids, they gave me unintended social benefits among the Cheer Moms. Now that I was a professional cheerleader, I appeared at some of the cheerleading competitions in heavy makeup and Bengal attire, having come from events. I noticed some of the Cheer Moms sneering, maybe because they were jealous or because they had never liked me in the first place. But others warmed up to me. "So when's your first game?" they asked, suddenly interested. "Do you practice a lot? Have you met any players?" It had taken me five years and a job as an NFL cheerleader to accomplish it, but I had finally won over the alpha moms. Victory was mine.

MISS NOVEMBER

WHILE WE'RE ATTENDING OUR FIRST EVENTS AND GETTING OUR weights set, we are all looking ahead to the most exciting event of the season for a cheerleader: the swimsuit calendar shoot. Beginning at our very first practice, the coaches ask us to bring in sample bathing suits and Charlotte or Deanna pulls a girl off the floor to model a suit, with different jewelry and shoes. They make notes, trying to figure out how they will mix and match us for the photos.

At one practice Charlotte announced that the 2009–2010 calendar would include double shots. In past years only some of the girls had gotten their own pages and the rest had tiny photos on the back. Charlotte said that I would be partnered with Elizabeth, and I suspected that because we were a double, we would get a full page. I was not only a Ben-Gal; there was a good chance I would get to be a month.

My shoot date was set for mid-June, at nine A.M., in an empty spec condo in a high-rise building across the river from Cincinnati in Kentucky. The coaches had selected one of my own bikinis, a Victoria's Secret black triangle-cut style that Courtney and Marija had picked out for me in the store.

The moment I got my shoot date I was in a mad rush to get in top shape. I had already been watching my food intake to make weight but now I had motivation to look even better. I minimized my sodium and alcohol intake for the weeks leading up to the shoot and the morning of my shoot I did not have a single drop of water or food in hope that my abs would appear firm and tight.

I showered so every part of me was squeaky clean. I kept my hair natural and for once in my life as a Ben-Gal, I didn't have to apply makeup because a stylist and makeup artist would be provided for us. The rest of the season we are our own stylists but on calendar shoots we are treated like celebrities. I was completely waxed (now that I knew what a Brazilian was) so not one errant hair would protrude from my bikini bottom, and my underarms and legs were freshly waxed, too. I had gotten my eyebrows threaded and had gone to the tanning salon to make sure my skin was bronze.

When I got there I saw the photographer, an affable-looking guy my age, shooting Lindsay in the dining room of the condo. Everything looked professional—the hot lights, the expensive camera, and the makeup and hair. Lindsay was straddling the dining room table on top of a furry rug, holding a football. I thought, *If they make me pose in a position that provocative, I hope I look as hot as she does.*

The stylist did my hair and then the makeup artist did my whole face, even heavier than what I usually wore to practice. Charlotte, Deanna, and Traci were there, along with two men: the photographer, Jim, and Charlotte's boyfriend, Dave, who was our unofficial production coordinator. Elizabeth, the Elizabeth Berkley lookalike, and I were supposed to look like we were in a bar, so we shot inside an empty walk-in closet in the apartment and sat on a freestanding bar that Dave had moved from the dining room.

At the advice of the veterans, I had brought a huge bag of tricks. I lubed up my legs with almond oil and put body tape over my nipples so they didn't look erect under my bikini.

Though the tension runs high during calendar shoots, Charlotte tries to make it fun by goofing around and putting us at ease. For rookies the shoot is the first time you really get to see the coaches' personality. You've gone through all those rounds of tryouts and now, at this intimate photo shoot where you are virtually naked, you finally see your coaches and director having fun. They'll come over and yank your bathing suit or give you a "butt chop," a karate chop to the butt so the suit rides up and makes the contours of your glutes come out. Elizabeth was in a corset and it wasn't hugging her the way Charlotte wanted it to, so Deanna sat on the floor, hidden by the bar, holding it tightly behind her.

The posing itself turned out to be much harder than I thought. I had imagined it like a *Sports Illustrated* swimsuit shoot, where the models move around a lot and the shots are meant to seem sporty. Instead, I had to be as still as an art-class model. Jim kept adjusting me and calling out directions: "Hold it right there." "Relax your wrist." "Don't put your hand there because it will look like you only have half an arm." "Turn your head. No, more to the right." "Suck in your stomach." The idea was to get the best body lines—the boobs big, the belly thin, no suits fitting too tight, and no fat hanging over anything, or whatever fat remained after eating so little in preparation for the shoot. By the end of my forty-five-minute shoot I was starting to shake. I was relieved to be done and I hoped the pictures would come out smokin' hot, even if it took a little help from Photoshop.

As soon as the calendar shoot is over, almost every Ben-Gal goes to her fast-food drive-through of choice and eats a huge meal. Instead of pigging out like the younger girls, I had packed some peanuts and chocolates in the car and nibbled on them on my drive home. I saved my real celebration for that night, when I went out for pizza with P.J., Courtney, and Marija. As a special treat I got ice cream for dessert. It's sad that a cheerleader feels like she is really going all out when she eats an appetizer, main course, and dessert, but that is the state of modern NFL cheerleading. A three-course meal is an indulgence, not an everyday occurrence (and more likely to happen during the off-season).

The Ben-Gals had no input into where we were placed in the calendar and which shot was selected. This was up to Charlotte. While the shoots were going on, she would come in to practice and try to amp up the suspense. "Oh, the shoot we just had was so wonderful," she would say. "You girls are getting more beautiful each year." Or, "I finally picked the month of July and I think it's the most gorgeous picture we've had in any calendar."

Am I July? we all wondered. *Who's July? Maybe she hasn't said anything to me because my month came out badly.*

The calendar release party was on September 11, 2009, on the top floor of a hotel in downtown Cincinnati. The day before, I had turned forty-one. I had brought almond sugar cookies from my favorite bakery to practice. They had footballs on them and the number 41. As I passed out the cookies the girls asked, "Who's number forty-one?" thinking that it was my favorite Bengal player.

"Me," I said. "*I'm* forty-one. It's my birthday."

I loved going into the calendar release party with all of my teammates knowing my age. I had come out to them about my age and now my swimsuit photo was going to be revealed for all to see.

At the party everyone was having cocktails and it was very hot. P.J., Lisa, and her husband Jim were there. "I'm definitely putting this on the wall of the garage now," Jim said to me.

Five Ben-Gals did a performance in top hats, fishnets, and canes, and then Charlotte presented the calendar. This seemed to be her favorite part of being director. She stood on a riser and the audience went quiet. She gave a little information about the girls on each page, like, "This Southern belle enjoys horseback riding and NASCAR. She's five-eleven, hails from the hills of Kentucky, and she is drop-dead gorgeous." We whispered back and forth about who we thought it was and then she said, "Miss January is so-and-so" and we clapped and cheered. The girl (or girls, if it was a double) went up on the riser and Charlotte presented a big blowup of the calendar photo. We hugged Charlotte and wiped away our happy tears as camera flashes went off all around.

When I saw that big cardboard blowup of Elizabeth and me looking so sexy and pretty and fit, I felt proud of who I was, both inside and outside. Who knew, back at Gold's Gym in Roswell in my baggy tee and big shorts, with Marija in the child care room, that I would someday be the month of November in a swimsuit calendar, wearing a triangle string bikini, with windblown (okay, fan-blown) hair? The photo was about something greater than my appearance. It was about moving from the past to the present, from mouse to tiger, from shy to outgoing. It was a visual manifestation of my dream.

Our calendar was so provocative that inevitably it got some of the girls into trouble with men. One Friday morning, Elizabeth and I were guests on a morning radio show at our local rock station, WEBN. That weekend the B-list eighties and nineties comedian Pauly Shore had come to Cincinnati to do a gig at a comedy club. He was in the radio studio promoting his gig and during breaks he flipped through the Ben-Gals swimsuit calendar. He zeroed in on Chelsey and said he wanted to go out with her.

The DJs got the idea for us to call her on the air. It was very early in the morning and she was barely awake. I said, "Chelsey, Pauly Shore is here in town doing a comedy set tonight. He looked through our calendar and fell in love with you. He'll give you and some friends free tickets to his show tonight and afterward he wants you to have drinks."

Here I am with P.J. as my first Ben-Gal calendar page makes its debut.

Pauly chatted with her for a few minutes on the air. I could see his anticipation rising. Surprisingly, Chelsey agreed to go. Maybe she was a fan of *Encino Man*. That night she and her friends went backstage before the show. As soon as they saw Pauly she realized she had been confused. She had thought he was Pauly D, the buff young star of MTV's *Jersey Shore*. She had never even heard of over-the-hill Pauly Shore. (Okay, I admit it, Pauly and I were born the same year.) But it was too late, they were already at the club and to be polite she stayed to watch the set.

Despite the fans' (and Pauly Shore's) enthusiasm for our calendar, the NFL has an extremely ambivalent attitude toward cheerleader calendars. "NFL" does not appear on our calendar, it's not sold on NFLShop.com, and it's not an official NFL product—though it is sold in the Bengals Pro Shop at the stadium, which means that the team makes money off it. My guess is that the League doesn't want to be associated with something so sexualized, or does not want to be seen as endorsing a product that six NFL teams don't have (since six NFL teams don't have cheerleaders).

No matter what the NFL thinks of cheerleader calendars, from a business standpoint they are a boon to us. We buy them from Charlotte and then sell them to fans for as much as we want. All summer we get advance orders from friends and family and we sign one another's calendars to make them more appealing to fans. They are like Tupperware or Girl Scout cookies for us. One season I made almost twice my game pay in calendars. I figure we deserved a little cash with everything we put ourselves through to pose.

A month and a half after the 2009 swimsuit calendar was released, Brian and I were deposed in Stevenson's office as preparation for our visitation and spousal support hearing. Because I didn't come into contact with Brian on a day-to-day basis due to the restraining order, these exhausting, stressful depositions were the only time I was forced to be in the same room with him. Stevenson and I walked into the conference room and I found Brian sitting at a long table with his attorney, Mindy Adair, a tough-looking woman in her thirties. Brian glared at me. I averted my eyes but I didn't want to let him intimidate me. Though I was deeply afraid that his plot would work, I didn't want him to know it. I had to be as confident in this room as I had been at the Ben-Gal tryouts, back when I had no idea I would make it.

A stenographer sat at the end of the table. Brian was deposed first. Adair got him to state that P.J. was watching the girls much of the time I was away at practice.

> Q. What occasions or times did you say [P.J.] baby-sat the children?
>
> A. Very often. Laura, in addition to her regular job, she's a Bengals cheerleader, and she has lots of schedules and demands because of that job, and there's a Tuesday and a Thursday practice from, I believe, 6:30 to 9:30, which for her driving time makes it 5:30 to 10:30, and he watches them during that time, both Tuesday and Thursday. There's a Friday thing on the square. There's a Saturday thing before the game on Sunday and the game itself and he's the one babysitting for that.

As I sat there listening I felt like I was standing in a bikini in front of those judges at the finals—but this time there was no excitement, only dread. Then I was being judged for my figure. Now I was being judged for who I was. Brian's answer omitted something important. Though P.J. sometimes cared for the girls during games, it was *at the games*. The girls were in the stands cheering

me on, having a great time. And for eight of the ten games that
season, they would be with their father anyway, which meant they
would not attend. I couldn't wait to give my side of the story.

When it was my turn to be deposed, Adair quickly got around
to my cheerleading schedule. It was clear what this was about. I
was being put on the stand for being a cheerleader.

Q. Do you intend on trying out next year?

A. Yes.

Q. Something that you like and enjoy?

A. Yes.

Q. Would it be a problem for [Brian] to care for the
children, the girls, while you are trying out?

A. We have scheduled time that they are supposed
to be with him and when they are not with him
they are either with me or with their grandmother.

Q. So your testimony is, it would be a problem for
them to be with [Brian], even though he's their
father?

A. I believe that the time they spend with their
grandmother is important as well.

Q. Well, you understand that courts view parenting
time as paramount to grandparenting time?

A. I believe that any involvement with the family
and the children is beneficial.

Though Adair had done her best to make me seem neglectful
by going to practice twice a week, I explained that the girls had
many after-school activities of their own. They were eleven and

twelve. There were cheerleading competitions and homework and social outings with friends. On many nights that I was at practice, the girls were out much of the evening, too.

I explained that Marija had taken a babysitting course and could take care of Courtney just as she took care of kids in the neighborhood. I said that I valued their bond with P.J.

> Q. How many [Ben-Gal events] would you say you volunteered for this year?
>
> A. Twenty.
>
> Q. Have you completed all twenty [events] or do you still have some upcoming?
>
> A. I have one on Friday.
>
> Q. What time on Friday, ma'am?
>
> A. It is at 6:00.
>
> Q. Is it your weekend or [Brian]'s weekend?
>
> A. It's my weekend, and the girls will be attending it.
>
> Q. Where is that located?
>
> A. Down in Cincinnati. It's a fashion show.
>
> Q. Okay. Do they attend all of the events?
>
> A. Not all, but some, yes.
>
> Q. And again, never the invitation for Father to have extra time during these events?
>
> A. They enjoy coming to the events when they come. Otherwise, I don't volunteer for them when I am with the children.

I think the lawyer was surprised to learn that not all cheerleader events were inappropriate for kids. She had been trying to make it sound as though I was a hooker who brought her children to work.

I was forced to describe my exact commute time to the stadium, the length of practices, and every component of my Ben-Gals commitment—including my personal workout schedule. She was trying to make the case that because I was gone early in the morning, even when the girls were sleeping, Brian should be able to have them one additional night per week, even though he would most likely have been sleeping at the same time that I was at the gym.

The way it was playing out in the deposition, it was as though my desire to stay fit—which filled both a personal and professional need—somehow made me a bad mother. I wondered what all the fitness-conscious moms around the country would think if they could be in this conference room with me. On paper this was about time management, but the subtext was the cheerleading itself. Everyone in America had an association when you said "NFL cheerleader." A bimbo who liked to party and only cared about herself. In the views of many, a cheerleader wasn't a good role model and she certainly wasn't a mother.

Adair and Stevenson asked detailed questions about my relationship with P.J. and I made it clear that though we had a romantic relationship, we didn't share bills or bank accounts and he wasn't there every night. We were not living as a married couple.

At the end of my deposition, I took an opportunity to defend my way of parenting the kids. I wanted the record to state that I wasn't embarrassed about anything I had done as a mother. When Adair asked me if I felt the girls should be spending time with P.J. when they weren't spending time with me, I answered:

> It should be anybody who's involved in their life, whether it's P.J., any other friends of mine that are significant or their grandmother, absolutely. I think the more people involved in their life, the better . . . I en-

courage relationships between my children with other people.

As I walked out of the office I was spent, worried for the girls' future. "Do you think he's going to win?" I asked Stevenson. "Do you think I answered the questions okay? Will the magistrate understand my side of this?"

He reassured me that I had done nothing wrong as a mother and that Brian was going to have a very hard time convincing Magistrate Wilson that I was an unfit parent. "In my experience it is extremely hard to argue for a reduction in visitation," he said, "unless one parent has been severely negligent. That means taking drugs or not feeding the kids or engaging in illegal or inappropriate activity in front of them. You're not doing any of that. You're a great mom, Laura. You're devoted to your daughters and you're not neglecting them and you're doing a good job juggling everything. In a lot of ways you're an even better role model to them now that you're doing something so exciting and positive for the community. The magistrate is going to see all of that."

I hoped she would be able to discern the truth like he said. But if she was a Bengals fan, she might have already seen the calendar—a calendar that showed me oily, glistening, and in the skimpiest bikini you could imagine. I didn't want her to view the photo through Brian's eyes. I wanted her to view it through mine. But I was worried. A picture was worth a thousand words, after all.

Because of what was going on with their father and the court case, Marija and Courtney had a tough adjustment to the calendar. It was a shock for them to go over to friends' houses and see it on teenage boys' walls. "It's so sexual, Mom," Marija said one night at dinner. "It's hard to look at you that way."

I suspected she was parroting Brian's words, but I didn't want to ask. "It is sexual," I said. "I can't pretend it's not. But I'm an adult woman. One day I'm going to be proud I looked like this. I want you two to be responsible about your own sexuality but I don't want you to be afraid of sex when you're older and the time is right."

"You're my mom," Marija said. "And you're practically naked. Dad says a good mom doesn't pose like that." Courtney was just listening, absorbing.

"Look," I said. "Some people like these pictures and some people don't, but it doesn't make me a bad mom. This photo has nothing to do with how I am with you girls or how much I love you. And it's not like you haven't seen me in a bikini. You guys bought the suit with me—and you see me in it every time we go to the pool."

That night I laid awake in bed for a long time. In an ideal world, they wouldn't have had to see the calendar. But it didn't work out that way. I couldn't shield them from it. And I was proud of the photo. It represented how far I had come since my marriage. It was hard for anyone who hadn't walked a mile in my white boots to understand the pride I felt in that photo of myself.

It had taken me almost twenty years to be able to pass a mirror and not see someone fat and ugly, as Brian used to call me. I was strong and beautiful, inside and out, words I never would have used to describe myself before. When a fifteen-year-old boy in Cincinnati looked at Miss November on his wall he had no idea of all I had overcome, but I did.

The calendar was harder on P.J. than I expected it to be. He thought I looked great but when he realized how many people were buying them and where they would go—in gas station garages and on teenage boys' walls—he didn't like it. "I bet guys take home your calendar and beat off to it," he said.

It was something I had thought about but it bothered me that he was saying it aloud. "I don't care," I said. "That's not why I pose in a swimsuit. This picture makes me feel really good about myself. This is our version of a trophy. And if some guy ruins his calendar doing what you just said, well . . . I just hope he buys another one."

It was true. I was proud of our calendar yet realistic enough to know that I was not attractive enough or young enough to be in the *Sports Illustrated* swimsuit edition. (But in case you're reading this *Sports Illustrated*, and think I'm wrong, please get in touch with me. I have two kids with braces.) Ninety-nine percent of NFL cheerleaders were never going to appear in the *Sports Illustrated* swimsuit edition. NFL cheerleaders are mostly small-town girls. We're pretty but we're not supermodel-pretty like Gisele Bündchen, and unlike Gisele we're not allowed to marry the quarterback. If we were as gorgeous as Gisele, we wouldn't be living in Cincinnati or Kansas City or Atlanta; a scout would have spotted us long ago and we would be in New York walking the runways, making tens of thousands of dollars a day. Our Ben-Gals calendar was our version of the swimsuit edition. It validated what we did and made up a little for our low pay.

Unlike the girls and P.J., Lisa and my mother were over the moon about the swimsuit calendar. As promised, Lisa and Jim hung it in their garage, and my mother bought dozens of them for her friends, male and female. I hadn't been sure how she would feel about it and I was relieved. "Laura," she told me, "if I had a body like yours, I would parade it down the street."

She had the 2009–2010 calendar hanging in her home office

open to my page. The thermostat was right outside the door to her home office and one day a man came to repair her furnace. As he was looking at it he noticed the calendar. His eyebrows went up.

"You're probably wondering why I have this on the wall," my mother said. She pointed to me in the photo. "That's my daughter."

"What?" the guy said in shock.

"Yep, that's my daughter."

"Oh my gosh, she's beautiful."

"She's forty-one years old."

From time to time I'll ask my mother, who is now seventy-one, how she feels having two daughters in their forties, one a licensed fireworks exhibitor and the other a professional cheerleader. She is proud of both of us. She remembers how confident I had been as a little girl, prancing around like Lady Godiva. During my marriage she saw me lose that spark. "All of a sudden I have a sexy little daughter," she likes to tell me. "Before, you were always hiding yourself. Now you're wearing tighter clothes, high heels, and skirts. It's like you've come back."

The first visitation hearing was scheduled for after the football season ended, in April 2010. The hearing would be an opportunity for Magistrate Wilson to ask follow-up questions of both Brian and me. Even though Stevenson had reassured me that nothing was going to change, I was relieved because this meant that I would get to spend Christmas with the girls.

We ran out of time that day and had to have another court date that June, when I had already auditioned for and been accepted onto the Ben-Gals for a second season. Brian had not scared me into quitting the team, even if he had tried to.

In the courtroom in June, Brian's lawyer Adair said that they were calling a witness to the stand, which was a shock to me because I hadn't been told there would be a witness. The courtroom door opened and to my surprise the witness turned out to be Marija, wearing a blue dress I had never seen her wear before. Later I learned that Brian's girlfriend had picked her up from school, had her change into the dress, and driven her to court. Marija hadn't wanted to testify because she felt caught in the middle—but was afraid she would go to jail if she didn't.

I wanted to leap across the room and scream at Brian, "Why are you bringing her into this? Don't make her take sides!" but of course I had to sit there quietly.

On the stand, Adair asked Marija a lot of questions about P.J. and our relationship, in an attempt to prove cohabitation and commingling of finances. Was he there every night? Did I pay him to take care of the kids? Was his car always in the garage? Did he do the grocery shopping? Marija told the truth, that he didn't always stay there and that his car wasn't always there.

The next few weeks, I checked the mail every day as soon as I got home from work to see if the court decision had come through. I had nightmares of not being allowed to see the girls again. I talked constantly to P.J. about my worries, and though he was as reassuring as Stevenson had been, I could tell I was exhausting him. My old insecurities were getting the best of me even though I knew I was a responsible, loving, committed mother.

In July I walked down the driveway to the mailbox and found an envelope with a return address from the WARREN COUNTY CLERK of COURTS. Inside lay my future with my daughters. I would find out whether Magistrate Wilson thought a cheerleader was an unfit mother. Even though Stevenson had reassured me, I was terrified.

I waited a few hours until P.J. came back from work to open the envelope. The girls were at their dad's. I held Penny in my lap for comfort, and sat down next to P.J. on the couch, the same cozy leather couch where I had first asked myself, *What do you like to do?* I had come so far since that moment but I was afraid I would be punished for it. The most dangerous thing a mother can do, as far as most of the world is concerned, is to do something for herself.

I ran my finger under the flap and pulled out the sheet of paper inside. Magistrate Wilson granted no changes to the visitation agreement or the spousal support payments. I started to cry. I put my head against P.J.'s shoulder. "He tried to change it but nothing's going to change."

"Of course nothing's changing," he said. "You're a great mom and it was obvious. He's not going to take them away."

The entire process, from Brian's motion to the decision, had gone on almost exactly a year, encompassing all of my rookie season. I felt vindicated that Brian hadn't succeeded in using my Ben-Gal status against me. I felt relieved that our magistrate was a woman. Maybe she had granddaughters who did competitive cheerleading and she knew that the old stereotypes just weren't true. I had cheered my children back to me.

SECOND DOWN
AND GOAL

THE VISITATION DECISION VALIDATED MY BELIEF THAT MY CHEER-
ing was setting a positive, and not a negative, example for the girls.
But I had no idea that in living out my own dream I would go on
to inspire other men and women to live out theirs. I was astounded
by the support I got from people all over the country and world
when it came out in a Yahoo.com minidocumentary that I was the
oldest cheerleader in the NFL.

In November of my second season, I got an email from a young
producer at Yahoo's "Second Act" series, which profiles people
who have made a big change in midlife. Her name was Kristen
Beissel. She had discovered that I was the oldest NFL cheerleader
after reading it in a local paper that had done a story on me, and
she wanted to do a story of her own. Her crew wound up filming
me at a game the following month. I was so nervous about the
camera crew that I messed up my kick line, even though I had
done it hundreds of times. Afterward I went to the cameraman
and said, "I hope you don't show that! I totally messed that up!"

I didn't know when the video would be uploaded, but one cold
Saturday morning I woke up and went to check my email. There
were hundreds of messages, forwarded from my only recently

opened Facebook account—wall posts and friend requests. It took me ten pages to go through them. I thought I had been hacked.

Then it occurred to me that maybe the "Second Act" had gone live. I went to Yahoo.com and watched the video. And then I started opening up the messages, afraid some of them would be nasty. As I read them I started to cry:

I read your story back in June 2010 and it has changed my life. I am a cheer coach for two squads and a school bus driver . . . I have let myself go for over nine years now because I have always put everything in my life before my health. I gained a whole mess of weight and was getting sick all the time. We ate out almost every day and I was setting a bad example for my kids. I have been working out and eating healthy since I read your story and I now have lost 43 lbs. I just wanted to say thank you for inspiring me and every Ben-Gal hopeful to follow their dreams no matter how old and out of shape we are!

—J.

I'm a mom of 3 boys and I'm 42. I recently decided to go back to school and get my degree. I was really nervous about it and I became a little doubtful of my ability to go to school at 42. Today I was accepted at school! And today I saw your story on Yahoo! I thought, "Well, if she's brave enough to be a cheerleader, I guess I can try for my doctorate!"

—F.

I felt compelled to write you to tell you what an inspiration you are! I have met a lot of inspiring women in my life, most recently as a breast cancer survivor. Since my treatment completion I am on the road to rebuilding myself physically with fitness and look forward to the next chapter in my life. Oh, and I'm also 42. Kudos to you, you're a fighter as well!

—D.

Though I used to dance every chance I had, I have not danced since the beginning of an abusive relationship I had during college. Unfortunately I have been gripped by fear and anger and my personality has not re-blossomed since ending the relationship. You have inspired me to take back the joy that is mine and reconnect with myself through the love of dance and movement. Thank you for reminding me that we are all beautiful and that our beauty shines most when we are doing something we love and working towards our dreams.

—K.

I can't believe that in five and a half years I have gone from hating everything about myself to inspiring strangers. If I can use my story to encourage people to get off the couch, to be less afraid, to love who they want to love, to leave an abusive marriage, even to try pole-dancing, then I have done something right. That is far more important an accomplishment to me than cheering football games on television.

As I write this book I am on the Ben-Gals for my third season and I am forty-three. Every conceivable aspect of my life has changed, from my body to my self-esteem to my relationships. The most gratifying change has been the way Marija and Courtney see me. Thirteen and fifteen now, they have come far from the days when they couldn't help but put stock in the hateful things their father told them. That first preseason Bengals-Rams game in 2009 was the start of a long process for them to begin to understand and support what I do.

Unlike a few years ago, they don't always feel the need to agree with their father out of loyalty. They are older and more independent. They are also extremely conscious of "dorkiness," and think that I am "cool" because I am a Ben-Gal.

Some of Marija's friends call me a MILF, which embarrasses her but makes me secretly smile. It can be weird to have a mom who is in Ben-Gal attire and full hair and makeup, driving you and your friends around town. One afternoon I picked up Marija at an ice cream store in the mall when I was dressed up, on the way to an event. She ran into the car and screamed, "Just drive, Mom! Drive!" like it was a getaway car, so her friends wouldn't see me.

Still, there are perks to having an NFL cheerleader as a mom. Last winter the girls went to Panama City, Florida, with their father and on the beach they met two boys from Kentucky. They were chatting and Marija mentioned that her mother was a Cincinnati Ben-Gal. The boys didn't believe it. I got a text from Marija saying, "This guy won't believe that you're an NFL cheerleader. Send him a picture!" I knew it would make her happy for me to send it, so I texted her a photo of me in uniform and the boys were extremely impressed.

Because they are cheerleaders, Courtney's girlfriends are impressed that I'm on the Ben-Gals. I came to one of Courtney's cheerleading events directly from a Ben-Gal affair, so I was wearing a Bengals issued top and a lot of makeup. Her girlfriends crowded around me, posing for photos and asked me a bunch of questions.

One day recently as I was getting ready for practice Courtney said she wanted to be a Ben-Gal when she got older. I was shocked. She had never said this before. "Why?" I asked her.

"Because you've made so many friends," she said.

I was glad to be wearing waterproof mascara.

The hardest part of my cheering for the girls has been the time commitment—and it's the hardest part for me, too. I would never be able to do what I do if they were younger and more dependent on me. It has gotten easier as they have gotten older. It's sad but true: a teenage girl wants to spend as little time with her mother as possible.

As the girls have become busier with their own commitments they no longer attend all of my games. At first I was hurt by this but now I have accepted it. I can't make all of their cheer and track competitions; there is no reason they should attend every football game. The first game of the 2011 preseason was Marija's second day of high school. She was going to come with my mother but she ended up staying home to do her schoolwork, which I understood.

When the girls miss a game, I come home with P.J., sit on the living room couch, and give them the dish. "Oh my God, the players came to our corner on a tackle and I had to back up ten feet!" Or, "We had a drunk jumper tonight and he got tackled by security!"

If they say they miss me, I say what any busy, working parent would say: "It won't always be like this. Just bear with me and we'll get through it." I remind them that football season isn't year-round, only until January. In the spring and summer, between seasons, I'm home more. As each season passes, my life as a cheerleader has become more normal to them.

My role as a Ben-Gal has been the biggest challenge that P.J. and I have encountered as a couple, aside from dealing with my divorce. He is often coming home exactly when I'm getting ready to go out for practice. Though he sometimes gripes about my insane schedule, he is the most supportive Ben-Guy of them all. He comes to every game, waits for me to get changed, and drives home with me. And he is 100 percent behind me, despite all of the added stresses the cheering puts on our relationship. After a game, he'll say with a wink, "Your kick line was really tight tonight." Before a game, as I'm getting ready, he'll say, "Be sure you don't forget your after-game panties."

Now that I am surrounded by engaged and married girls on the team I am more aware of the fact that I'm not married. That's not always a good thing. "What about you, Laura?" the girls ask me when they get engaged. "Are you and P.J. ever going to tie the knot?"

"Probably not," I say. "But you never know."

As much joy as it would bring me to make my commitment to P.J. legal, we have no plans to marry. I love being in a committed relationship, but my divorce taught me that you never know when someone's feelings for you might change. I am still not over the fact that my divorce cost me fifty thousand dollars and I never want to go through that again, or put P.J. through that, if he someday fell out of love with me.

Ironically, not being married makes me work harder at being a good partner to P.J. It keeps a frisson between us, keeps me wanting to be kind to him. Thankfully he understands my resistance to marriage and doesn't pressure me. Not a lot of guys would do that. Someday I would like to buy myself a ring that symbolizes my personal triumph, the triumph over insecurity and self-loathing. I might wear it on my left ring finger, or I might wear it on my right so there is no doubt that it is not an engagement ring. Engagement rings are beautiful but they can also be a badge of ownership, and I never want to be owned by a man again.

So while I sometimes feel like an oddball as a divorced forty-something on the Ben-Gals, for the most part I really love my teammates. The sisterhood is what makes cheerleading worth it, and it's why we put up with the unfair pay, sexual harassment, and often grimy uniforms. "I noticed your moves were really sharp on Throw," a girl will tell me. Or, "You used to have that brain fart on the second eight-count but you totally got it this time." Or, "You looked good, Laura. You were really having fun today." I compliment the other girls as much as I can. I thank them for dancing in front of me. "You were so great today," I'll say, "and I was tired. It really helped me because I fed off your energy."

We have way more fun than we should given how underpaid we are. At one practice during my third season, after the tentative corners had been set, Sarah J., who had been made captain, announced that each corner was going to come up with a name and a cheer for itself, for camaraderie and fun. We split up and sat in circles around the gym, brainstorming. My group looked around and noticed that we were all different heights, hair color and races. Someone said, "Mixed Nuts." Someone else said, "Variety Pack." No one was very enthusiastic about the names. We hadn't cracked it yet.

I suggested we do something playing off of Sarah G.'s name, since she was our corner captain that year. She said, "Sunny always calls me 'G.' It makes me feel gangsta." She put her hands into a gangsta pose, or the best approximation of a gangsta pose that a white girl from Kentucky can do.

I thought about the letter G and blurted out, "The G Spot." Everyone cracked up. We started thinking about what cheer would go with a team called The G Spot. I suggested, "Where do you go? Where do you go? Where do you go for fun? The G Spot!" We were on the floor giggling. We came up with a silly little routine where tall Sarah G. stood in the middle and when we shouted "the G spot," a petite girl named Lizzie crawled through Sarah G.'s legs like she was being born. Now every time we have a pregame conference with our corner, Sarah G. says, "Come hither. I'm going to give you some G Spot stimulation." It makes us feel unified and connected and lets us decompress before the stress of a football game.

The support the Ben-Gals give each other isn't all in the interest of having fun. When a girl is struggling with a difficult relationship, other Ben-Gals tell her she deserves to be with a guy who treats her with respect. We are elated when a girl gets a promotion or a new job or passes the bar exam. We attend weddings and engagement parties, and we give each other pointers on job interviews. Yes, there is infighting and backstabbing, but for the most part we are a sisterhood. We are a system of support for one another. We look forward to seeing one another at practice, and each of us wants the team to do well.

I work hard to be complimentary of the other girls, especially the ones who make me the most jealous. When I find myself envying a Ben-Gal who is prettier, or has longer legs, or can dance better, or has more lustrous hair, I'll say to her, "Oh my God, you look so cute today," instead of moping and feeling insecure or envious. I tell myself that she can probably use a compliment. There's likely something that makes her insecure, too. We're all different, we're born with different bodies, and we come to the team with different backgrounds. We don't all look the same and we shouldn't.

I have made many close friends through cheering and been exposed to women I would not have met otherwise. Brandy and Kimberly have become like aunts to Courtney and Marija. I never expected to have a new circle of female friends in my forties, but because of cheering I do. My friendship with the Ben-Gals will outlast my time on the team.

One of the strange consequences of having become a Ben-Gal is that after almost twenty-five years, I am back to thinking about my weight more than I should. I am proud of my body but I work nonstop for it. I wish there were a magic pill, but the only way to get in shape in your early forties is deep, ugly discipline.

There are bad things and good things about my vigilant focus on weight. It can feel tyrannical. I am extremely cautious about my food during the football season and I'm not allowed to forget about it for a week or three because then I won't cheer. I don't like the fact that I get on the scale once a day.

In the off-season I try to give myself a break. I eat what I want and don't exercise every day. Sometimes I go as long as two weeks without exercising and I usually put on six to eight pounds in the off-season. I like the break; it allows me to be a normal person again who goes out to dinner and drinks a beer or two and doesn't have to step on a scale the next day. During those months I choose to weigh myself only if I'm feeling great about my figure and want confirmation, or if I'm feeling bad because I've fallen off with my exercise and eating and need a kick in the pants. Then when April rolls around and I have to slim down for tryouts, I go back to my three-pronged approach: behavior modification, better food choices, and more exercise.

I consider myself a better dietitian to my clients than I was before I was a Ben-Gal. I care about them deeply, and because of my own personal trials I can inspire them in a way I couldn't before. They call me their cheerleader. In the two and a half years I have done weight-loss counseling, my clients' combined weight loss is sixteen hundred pounds. Most have kept it off. My mother and sister asked me for help and I put them on my program, too; they wound up losing 130 pounds combined.

While I once considered dietetics a job, I now see it as a form of healing. Sometimes, at my clients' bidding, I give bits and pieces of my own story. I counsel them on issues that are much greater than just food—behavior and relationships—because I remember what it was like to feel self-hatred. I know what it feels like to be afraid of change, to be comfortable in an unhappy present because you're fearful of the future. I know the fear of becoming someone new. I tell them that change can make them happier than they could ever imagine.

My clients struggle to believe in themselves. I tell them in their sessions what I have discovered for myself: "If you really believe you'll never get there or you're stuck the size you are and you just give up, then it's self-fulfilling. You will be stuck. But if you want to feel different, look different, and live longer, then you really can. And even if you have a bad week, you don't have to use that as an excuse to give up entirely. You can try to do better the next week."

My job as a Ben-Gal has helped me begin a long process of recovery that has allowed me to forgive myself for the mistakes I've made. The self-esteem that I get from cheerleading makes up for the low self-esteem I had during the fourteen years that I lived with Brian and the terrifying time immediately after. I envisioned myself cheering and I made it happen—Matthew be damned,

Brian be damned, everyone who said I was too old be damned. Cheering may represent the golden years of my dance career but, more important, it also represents the beginning of my living.

After my divorce, I hated myself for letting the marriage go on so long, for wasting so many years. Underneath my anger at Brian was a lot of anger at myself. He hurt me, yet I was the one who chose to marry him, who ignored the early warning signs. When I remember the woman I was for fourteen years, the lonely, depressed woman whose only joy was her children, I feel like I don't know her. But I can't undo the past. None of us can.

I understand that I stayed because I wasn't myself when I was with him. Because of that, I couldn't make sound decisions. Now that I am myself I have to try not to dwell too much on the past or the future. I'll only drive myself crazy. Instead I try to live in the moment. When I find myself ruminating obsessively about the kids, Brian's behavior, or a financial problem, I'll say, *You know*

It's all about the sisterhood.

what? I can't worry about that right now. I'll think about that when I'm running.

Being a Ben-Gal makes me feel like a person, with talent and thoughts and personality. It's strange because we are a team and dress in uniform, but within the strictures of cheerleading I have found that there is room for individuality. We are expected to conform to a rigorous set of rules but we are not expected to bury our personalities.

These days my self is still forming. I still lack the confidence of a Gisele Bündchen. It's only once in a while that I feel really good about myself—after I fit into a certain pair of jeans, after I come home from a long run, or after the new calendar comes out. Much of the time when I look in the mirror I still see short legs, a wrinkled belly, and fake boobs that I had to pay for.

My emotional baggage is like an enormous Ben-Gal wheelie suitcase, with curling irons and uniforms stuffed inside. Sometimes it catches up with me and I feel like I still have a lot of work to do on myself. The Ben-Gals tease me for being one of the sunniest people on the team. I am. I try to find the positive in every situation, not only at practice but at home. Today if I hear Marija and Courtney calling each other names like "retard" or "stupid," even as a joke, I get goose bumps, remembering the names Brian once called me. I tell them that that kind of language is inappropriate. They don't understand why I get so upset but I don't care. I want them to see that words hurt. I want to be sure that they don't grow up to be—or marry—name-callers, or worse.

Because my self-esteem was so low for so long, my spirit so depleted, it still surprises me today when I can carry on a conversation with a total stranger. I no longer lower my eyes when I walk into a room. I shake hands and give a big smile. If I hear negative voices in my head, I try not to listen to them. Instead of being my own worst judge, I try to be my own cheerleader. I hear my mother's voice singing, "Here she comes, Miss America!" I tell myself, *Come on, Laura! You can do it!* Or, *It's all right, it's okay, you're going to do great anyway!*

We are all our own best cheerleaders. The supportive people around us can help, but in the end it is up to us to be our own pep squad. We all must find the inner voice within that tells us we can, like in the children's book *The Little Red Caboose. I think I can, I think I can* soon becomes, *I know I can, I know I can.*

I try to be my own cheerleader every day, whether executing a high kick at a practice or glancing at my watch in rush hour traffic, praying I'm not late to a game. *You idiot* has been replaced by, *You're going to be fine, it'll all work out.* I don't hate myself anymore. I love myself and I make time only for people who love me, too. After twenty years, I have found my spirit again.

THE DIAMONDBACK

IN THE MIDST OF MY HECTIC THIRD-SEASON TRYOUTS I SAW THAT Mother's Day was coming up. I would have the kids that Sunday and so I called Lisa and said, "What should we do for Mother's Day?"

"Mom wants to go to Kings Island," she said. Kings Island was the amusement park where I used to go as a kid.

That Mother's Day was a gorgeous sunny day, my favorite kind of weather, Southern California weather. Lisa and her husband Jim met P.J., the girls, my mom and me there.

The Mother's Day before, the girls and I had gone together and they had ridden a new roller coaster called the Diamondback. It was the tallest roller coaster in Kings Island and went up to eighty miles per hour. They begged me to go on with them but I was still as phobic as I had been at ten years old. I waited in line with them but didn't go on.

Afterward Marija had said, "You are going on this ride next time we come. I cannot explain to you how crazy it is!"

"Oh my gosh, no, I'm not going on the Diamondback. I don't do roller coasters."

"You have to!"

"I'll go the next time I come, all right?" It seemed to assuage her, and secretly I hoped they would forget.

On Mother's Day, 2011, as soon as we got to the amusement park, the girls mentioned the Diamondback. To stall I suggested the Rugrats Runaway Reptar in the children's area. I hoped that would be enough to placate them, but after we rode it Marija said, "Let's go on the Diamondback."

"I'm not doing it."

"Well, just wait in line with us," she said. P.J. sat with my mom and I stood in line with Jim, Lisa, Marija, and Courtney for about half an hour. The Diamondback was the most popular ride in the park and everyone wanted to go on it except me. When we got to the front, they blocked me so I couldn't get off the line and before I knew it we were going up to the ride.

My heart started beating very fast. The girls were giggling at me because they knew I was afraid. Even Lisa, ever the daredevil, was grinning. I thought, *Okay, I can do this. It lasts two minutes. If the girls can, I can.*

It turned out that the cars were arranged in four-seat diamond formations. I was in the wide part of the diamond and I didn't have anyone directly next to me. More horrifying, the seat brace didn't go over the chest. On this ride it sat on the lap. This meant my entire upper body was free, as though I was riding a bicycle.

I started having a panic attack. I looked over at Marija. "I can't breathe," I said. "This isn't funny. I'm really scared. Why did you make me do this?"

"You're fine, Mom," she said, laughing, with no sympathy at all for what I was going through. I sat there and tried to compose myself. The attendant came to check my safety bar. This was happening. I wanted to be on the ground with my mom and P.J., not up here on this ride. How had I been suckered into this?

Then I tried to psych myself up. *If I can do four years of freaking Ben-Gal tryouts and make it three times, I can do this. I've been through so much and I came out better and stronger. I can do a two-minute roller coaster.* I thought about everything I had done in my years on earth. Riding that Diamondback wasn't scarier than leaving my marriage or auditioning to be a Ben-Gal or cheering on the field of an NFL stadium. Could a two-minute roller coaster be more terrifying than dancing in a miniskirt and halter top in front of sixty thousand people?

Still, I wished I had a Xanax in my purse. I took a few deep breaths. The ride operator's voice came over the loudspeaker. "Okay, everybody, are you ready for three minutes of eighty-mile-an-hour fun?"

I had thought it was two minutes. Now the man was saying it was three. The panic attack started again.

We were moving. I waited for the clicking noise on the tracks but there wasn't any. On the old style of roller coasters the clicking let you know you were on the track. The Diamondback was silent, the Prius of roller coasters. All I could feel was the wind. My body was completely free.

We came to the first hill. *Oh my God, the hill.* We raced down it so fast, I clutched my stomach in agony. *Well, that's the worst of it. Everyone knows the first hill is always the scariest.*

I was wrong. For the second hill we were out of our seats the whole time. The third was even worse. It was like going to hell three times in a row. And then, finally, the three minutes were over.

The roller coaster came to a stop. I was shaking but I was alive.

Living out my
dream

I hadn't fallen out. I hadn't thrown up. And I hadn't passed out from fear. It was awful but it had been brief. The safety bar went up and when I rose to my feet, adrenaline was coursing through me. The girls were slapping me on the back. "I knew you could do it, Mom!"

We walked down and over to P.J. and my mom. "I can't believe you did it!" my mom said. She remembered my fear of roller coasters from the times when she would sit with me while Lisa would ride The Beast.

"I know!" I cried. "Are you going to go on now?"

"No way. But I'm really proud you did it."

As we made our way around the park going on the rides that day, I realized that nothing is as scary as it seems from a distance.

It doesn't matter how old you are or how frightened or how many times you've told yourself, *I can't*. You can change. You don't have to be scared. If you have faith in yourself, you can do anything in the world you want. You can ride the highest, fastest roller coaster, even if you've always been afraid. All you have to do is sit down, hold on tight, and go.

ACKNOWLEDGMENTS

The author would like to thank and acknowledge the following individuals and institutions: Pamela Cannon, Joe Veltre, P.J. Norvell, my two amazing daughters, Linda Vikmanis, Lisa England, Charlotte Jacobs, the Cincinnati Ben-Gals (2009-2011), the Cincinnati Bengals, Deanna Hazeley, Traci Napier, Jack Brennan, Inky Moore, Bill Connolly, Brandy Sanchez, Sarah Jones, Tara Willson, Kimberly Federle, Sarah Gilliam, Whitney Tidwell, Jack Leslie and the Donners' Company, Christy Allen Varrato, Kyle Collins, Steve Nagel and Jeff Nagel, Dr. Scott Bleser, Bellbrook Medical Center, Nutrition & Wellness Specialists, Mimi Hoefflin, Chris Stock-Driggers, Elene Catinazzo, Nikki VordemEsche, Jade Stewart, Tanya Duermit, Shannon Hill and Megan Rogers of Vintage Salon, Chenese Bean of Chenese Bean Makeup Artistry, Tammy Reams, Sonya Safro, Susan Corcoran, Daniel Greenberg, Lea Coon, Lateef Oseni of Triomph Health and Wellness, Deacon Webster and Frances Webster, Ratna Kamath, Kara Burney, and Tyler Remmert. The following works were enormously useful in the writing of this book: Mary Ellen Hanson's *Go! Fight! Win! Cheerleading in American Culture* and Suzette Scholz, Stephanie Scholz, and Sheri Scholz's *Deep in the Heart of Texas: Reflections of Former Dallas Cowboys Cheerleaders.*

ACKNOWLEDGMENTS

ABOUT THE AUTHOR

LAURA VIKMANIS was born in 1968. She joined the Cincinnati Ben-Gals in 2009 and is the oldest cheerleader in the NFL. A registered dietitian and certified personal trainer, she is a graduate of California State University, Long Beach. New Line has optioned her life story for a feature film. She blogs at SkinnyMom .com and lives in Dayton, Ohio, with her two daughters.

www.CheerleaderLaura.com

ABOUT THE COLLABORATOR

AMY SOHN is the *New York Times* bestselling author of the novels *Run Catch Kiss, My Old Man,* and *Prospect Park West* (and its upcoming sequel). She has been a columnist for the *New York Post* and *New York* magazine, writing about relationships, marriage, and parenting. She lives in Brooklyn with her husband and daughter.

www.amysohn.com

ABOUT THE TYPE

This book was set in Caslon, a typeface first designed in 1722 by William Caslon. Its widespread use by most English printers in the early eighteenth century soon supplanted the Dutch typefaces that had formerly prevailed. The roman is considered a "workhorse" typeface due to its pleasant, open appearance, while the italic is exceedingly decorative.